CW00518910

Collins · *do brilliantly!*

Revision**Guide**

GCSE D&T Graphic Products

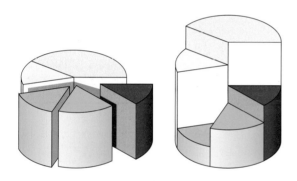

■ **John Rolfe and Ray Blockley**

■ **Series editor: Jayne de Courcy**

permanent marker

fine line marker

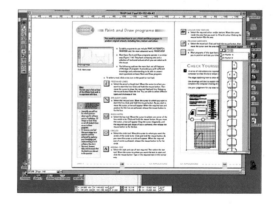

Contents and Revision Planner

KNOWLEDGE AND SKILLS SECTION

ABOUT THIS BOOK

Exams are about much more than just repeating memorised facts, so we have planned this book to make your revision as **active and effective** as possible.

How?

- by showing you exactly what examiners are looking for (Coursework Guidance)

- by breaking down the knowledge and skills into manageable chunks (Revision Sessions)

- by providing extra information to help you aim for the very top grade (A* Extras)

- by listing the most likely exam questions for each topic (Question Spotters)

- by giving you exam questions and guidance (Check Yourself – Exam Questions)

Coursework guidance

- The first section of the book **explains how to plan and carry out your coursework** effectively. It contains lots of information on what examiners are looking for in order to award high marks for a coursework project. **Examples of students' coursework** have been included to highlight what is required.

Revision Sessions

- The second section covers all the knowledge and skills that you need for your GCSE Design and Technology – Graphic Products exam. There are lots of **illustrations** to help you understand and retain the information. This section also provides you with all the necessary skills you need for carrying out your coursework successfully.

- Each area that you need to revise is divided into a number of **short revision sessions**. You should be able to read through each of these in no more than 10–15 minutes. Read through two or three of these and then take a short break.

- Ask your teacher for a copy of your own exam board's **GCSE Design and Technology – Graphic Products** specification. Tick off on the Contents list in this book each of the revision sessions that you need to cover.

■ These boxes contain some **extra information** which you need to learn if you are aiming to achieve the **very top grade**. If you have the chance to use this additional information in your exam, it could make the difference between a good answer and a very good answer.

■ It's obviously important to revise the facts, but it's also helpful to know how you might need to **use** this information in your exam.

■ The authors, who have been involved with examining for many years, know the sorts of questions that are most likely to be asked on each topic. They have put together these Question Spotter boxes so that they can help you to **focus your revision**.

CHECK YOURSELF – EXAM QUESTIONS

■ At the end of each revision session, there are some Exam Questions. By trying these questions, you will immediately find out whether you have understood and can **put into practice** what you have read in the revision session.

■ **Answers** are at the back of the book, along with **extra hints and guidance**. Note that the artwork in the questions and answers has had to be reduced from the size in the original exam papers.

■ If you manage to answer the Exam Questions for a session correctly, then you can confidently tick off this topic in the box provided in the Contents list. If not, you will need to tick the '**Revise again**' box to remind yourself to return to this topic later in your revision programme.

THREE FINAL TIPS

1 Work as consistently as you can during your Graphic Products course. Plan your coursework project carefully. Remember that it accounts for 60% of your mark.

2 Plan your revision carefully and focus on the areas you find hard.

3 Try to do some exam questions as though you were in the actual exam. Time yourself and don't cheat by looking at the answers until you've really had a good go at working out the answers.

About your GCSE Graphic Products course

GCSE specifications

- All the Graphic Products GCSE specifications are quite similar in content. The standard of work is the same because all the specifications have to meet a nationally agreed standard. This book is aimed mainly at the **AQA** and **OCR** specifications and all major differences between these boards have been highlighted.

Examinations and Coursework

- All Graphic Products GCSE specifications put greater emphasis on assessed coursework than on the terminal exam. **Coursework** is worth 60% of the overall GCSE mark whether you are doing a short-course or full-course GCSE. This means that if you get full marks for your coursework you already have 60% of your final mark before you answer any exam questions!

- You will need to produce **one** piece of high quality work for your coursework. This will consist of a design folio and a 3-dimensional prototype product. This coursework project should represent **40 hours** of supervised work.

- Your GCSE examination will consist of two papers testing your knowledge, understanding and skills.

What is assessed?

- In GCSE Graphic Products you have to develop your skills in using a variety of graphic communication techniques. You will also need to develop your investigation skills, designing and modelling skills, making skills, and testing and evaluative skills. You will be expected to produce a 3-dimensional prototype product to a high standard of quality using compliant or graphic materials. The application of ICT skills will also be assessed, such as CAD and CAM, and desktop publishing.

- In addition, there are other theory aspects which, although factual, you will learn through carrying out 'mini-projects', and investigating existing products and how they are designed and manufactured. Through this work you will gain an understanding of design issues, industrial processes and health and safety concerns.

- At least one question in the written exam will be based on a theme that is sent out to schools some time before the exam date.

Foundation and Higher tier papers

- If you decide to do the foundation examination papers rather than the higher tier examination papers, you will find the questions much easier but the maximum grade you will be able to achieve is a C grade.

- The higher tier papers are aimed at D-grade candidates and above, right up to A*. The coursework projects are identical but at foundation level you will not be expected to aim for such high marks.

- When you have completed your coursework, your teacher will be able to advise you which is the most appropriate tier for you to enter.

Higher tier							
A*	A	B	C	D	E	F	G
			Foundation tier				

COURSEWORK 1: FIRST THINGS FIRST...

SESSION 1 — What is an acceptable graphic product?

- Each exam board has a slightly different definition of what they will expect to see in your Graphic Products coursework.

- One thing that is common to all exam boards is that, whatever you choose to do and whatever you design, you *must* produce a 3-dimensional product. This means that projects that result in a 2-dimensional or 'flat' outcome, such as a poster, are not acceptable.

■ Graphic products are designed around the use of **graphic and compliant materials**.

■ A compliant material is a material that is easily **shaped, folded, cut** or **joined**.

■ The core materials for graphic products are paper, card or board, foamboard, foils and thin sheet plastics such as acetate, cellophane and high-impact polystyrene. You may use other materials, but the amount you may use and how you use them depends upon which exam board's course you are following. Check with your teacher.

■ Whichever materials you decide upon for your product, you must prepare and use them with **skill and accuracy**, and your product must be completed to a **high** level of **quality**.

The coloured panels below give an overview of what your exam board will accept as a 'graphic product'.

AQA

- You should produce a graphic product that realistically represents a 'real' artefact. It should be capable of communicating a concept to a potential user. It is likely to be a prototype.

- Your product should have the potential for commercial production.

- Your product must be capable of being evaluated and tested by the target user(s).

- Your product must be made using graphic equipment and compliant materials. You may use resistant materials for a minor part of your product or to complement it.

OCR

- You should produce a prototype graphic product that could be marketed. It must not be a non-functioning or concept model.

- Your product should be capable of being produced in quantity in your school/college, using the equipment and facilities available. Your prototype will be the first of a small batch of about 50.

- Your prototype product must be capable of being evaluated and tested by the target user(s).

- Your product must be made using graphic materials and skills. Resistant materials must only be used in a support role, for example to produce a mould for vacuum forming.

- A **prototype** is literally the 'first of its type' and should function as intended.

- A **concept** is an idea or theory.

- A **concept car** could be made out of clay, but a **prototype car** would have to be capable of being driven and moving under its own power. So a **prototype graphic product** would have to **function** just as you intend the real, manufactured, final product to function.

- **Commercial production** is the manufacture of a **marketable product** (capable of being sold) by using **industrial processes**.

- **Batch production** is an industrial process where small numbers or batches are made at a time, as opposed to **job** or **one-off** production, and **flow** or **continuous** production.

■ There may not appear to be a lot of difference between the two exam boards, but there is enough for you to lose a lot of marks if you do not follow their guidance carefully. *You have been warned!*

Front of packaging

Rear of packaging

1.1 *Nicola's self-assembly card bee and flower suitable for a child.*

Examiner's comments

- Nicola has designed and made a self-assembly card bee and flower. It is made from 280-micron board and uses traditional graphic skills as well as ICT and CAD.

- She designed the product around the industrial processes of die-cut manufacture and 4-colour process printing. Note how professional the final prototype product looks in its packaging – all made in school.

Examiner's tip:

- Always target a high-quality, professional look for your work. Make sure that your prototype product is marketable. Imagine what it would look like on display in a shop.

- One way to test this is to ask yourself: 'Would I buy this?'

- Your coursework project should represent **40 hours** of supervised work (20 hours for the Short Course), during which you will have produced your project folder and made your graphic product.

- This means that you must **plan** your time very carefully.

- It is very easy for work to build up and become a nightmare if you start to miss deadlines!

- Successful students who produce high-quality work are usually those who have planned their time with care – and stick to their deadlines.

- The marks for your coursework project are split into two groups:
  • one group for **designing skills**
  • one group for **making skills**.

AQA

AQA score coursework projects out of a maximum of **90** marks – which are split **30** marks for Designing and **60** marks for Making.

OCR

OCR score coursework projects out of a maximum of 100 marks, which are split roughly **50:50** between Designing and Making.

- Knowing which exam board you are following will enable you to **divide up your time** more accurately and profitably.

- When you know your final coursework deadline date, you can now divide up the time available to you, depending upon which exam board you are following.

- It makes sense to spend roughly the same proportion of *time* on each area as there are *marks* available for it. For example, two students following different Graphic Products courses have each been given 24 weeks in which to complete their projects:

	Student A – AQA	Student B – OCR
Designing	8 weeks	12 weeks
Making	16 weeks	12 weeks
Total	24 weeks	24 weeks

• Both students can now decide upon suitable dates by which they should have completed their design work and be ready to start making.

• But what about leaving time for testing and evaluating, carried out *after* the product has been manufactured? (See the next session.)

Time management: assessment objectives

- The next step is to break down the available time even further in order to give yourself deadlines for each section of your project, or **assessment objective**.

- This will enable you to plan your project in detail and so keep on track.

- There are assessment objectives for your coursework that you can use to help plan and target your time effectively.
  1 materials and components
  2 design and making
  3 evaluating – wider implications

- You should be able to meet all the assessment criteria with a project folder of **around 20 sheets of A3 paper**.

- This will enable you to work out **how many sheets** of paper you should be targeting to complete each assessment objective.

- Remember that the total of 20 sheets is only a recommendation. You will not lose marks if you produce a project folder with a few more or a few less sheets. *However, if you submit a folder that contains way over 25 sheets, questions are likely to be asked!*

- The following tables are rough guides:

AQA

Each assessment objective is marked with a grade of A to G.

It would make sense to vary the number of sheets of A3 paper used in each assessment objective to give you the best chance to show off your graphic skills.

As a suggestion:

1 Research	3 x A3 sheets
2 Analysis and specification	3 x A3 sheets
3 Generation of ideas	4 x A3 sheets
4 Development of solution	4 x A3 sheets
5 Planning of making	3 x A3 sheets
6 Evaluation, testing and modifications	3 x A3 sheets

OCR

Each assessment objective has a different numerical mark.

Judge the number of A3 sheets by the number of marks available in each assessment objective.

As a suggestion:

1 Identification of need / design brief (4 marks)	2 x A3 sheets
2 Research, analysis and specification (12 marks)	4 x A3 sheets
3 Generation of ideas (12 marks)	4 x A3 sheets
4 Product development (12 marks)	4 x A3 sheets
5 Product planning (12 marks)	3 x A3 sheets
6 Evaluation and testing (8 marks)	3 x A3 sheets

---

* The advice on sheet numbers will only work if you use the *whole* of each A3 sheet.

* Never forget that the key to success is high quality work.

* Your folder will be marked on its content, *not its size or weight*.

* All exam boards are now expecting to see a concise project folder where the student has edited the work that it contains.

■ You may also find it helpful to work out **how many days or weeks** you should be targeting to complete each assessment objective. This will help you set a **deadline date** for each one. (Remember that for assessment criteria 5 you need to have time for the planning *and* the making.)

■ Here is a **Gantt chart** that shows how a student has planned their coursework project:

Week number

Assessment Objective	1	2	3	4	5	6	7	8	9	10	11	12	13	14	15	16	17	18	19	20	21	22	23	24
1 Predicted	▓	▓																						
1 Actual	▓	▓	▓																					
2 Predicted		▓	▓	▓																				
2 Actual		▓	▓	▓	▓																			
3 Predicted			▓	▓	▓	▓																		
3 Actual		▓		▓	▓	▓	▓																	
4 Predicted								▓	▓	▓	▓													
4 Actual								▓	▓	▓	▓	▓	▓	▓										
5 Predicted											▓	▓	▓	▓	▓	▓	▓	▓	▓	▓				
5 Actual													▓	▓	▓	▓	▓	▓	▓	▓	▓	▓	▓	
6 Predicted																					▓	▓	▓	▓
6 Actual																			▓		▓	▓	▓	▓

■ The student has firstly predicted how long each assessment objective will take to complete (green). Then, as the project has progressed, the student has added the actual time that it had taken to complete the objective (red).

- It doesn't matter what form such a chart or table takes providing you produce it at the start of your project and, more importantly, **use it**.

- The chart on page 11 clearly shows that the student had problems and overran deadlines in assessment objectives 1, 2, 4 and 5, but was able to complete assessment objective 3 quickly, and start testing and evaluating (6) early.

- You will get **credit** for using such a chart *if* you show your **actual progress** and add notes and labels to explain **what went well**, and where you had **problems**.

- Do not be afraid to admit that you have made mistakes or that things went wrong.

Examiner's tips:

- Write notes and details on your time plan to show evidence that you have used it to record problems encountered and changes made as your project has progressed.

- Make sure you allow yourself sufficient time to test and evaluate your finished product.

Communication skills

- Before moving on to start the actual project, one thing you must think carefully about is the **quality** of your **communication skills**.

  - All exam boards have **5 extra marks** that can be awarded to your final score.

  - They are awarded when your design folder is assessed.

  - How they are awarded depends on which exam board you are following.

- **Remember:** 5 marks may not seem a lot, but don't forget that only one mark can mean the difference between a grade – *or between a pass mark or a fail...*

AQA

Quality of written communication

AQA base their mark upon the quality of your written communication.

To get all 5 marks:
- All information contained in your project must be clearly and logically presented.
- The text must be easy to read.
- You must spell, punctuate and use the rules of grammar accurately.
- The meaning of all your written work must be able to be clearly understood.

OCR

Overall presentation of the Coursework Project

OCR base their mark on the quality of the overall presentation of your finished project.

To get all 5 marks:
- You must present your work in a logical sequence.
- Your work must be concise.
- It must be clear that you have used skill to plan and edit the content of your folder.
- There must be no evidence of 'padding'.

Examiner's tips:

- Edit your project as you work. Think very carefully about what you need to include – and what can be left out. Be critical and selective. Only include relevant work. If you are not sure, ask your teacher for advice.

- Use ICT as much as you can to word process your work. Use a font that is easy to read. Use a font size no bigger than 12 pt and no smaller than 8 pt for the bulk of your work. Use the Spelling and Grammar Check facility to check your work, and *read through* what you have written before you print it.

- Ask someone to check your handwritten work for you. Use a dictionary or thesaurus.

- Consider using notes and bullet points rather than 'essay type text'.

- **Do not** waste time on borders: they will not gain you any marks. **Do not** 'shadow mount' work on coloured card. Keep your sheets full and 'busy'. Make each sheet exciting and interesting to look at through the quality of the graphic work that it contains.

- Allow yourself time at the end of your project to ensure that everything is in a logical order. Your folder should 'flow' like a story with a clear beginning, a middle and an end. Do not number sheets until all is done and you have sorted them into an easy-to-read order.

- Remember: You will not be able to talk to the examiner face-to-face. Try to make everything clear so there is no chance of any misunderstanding. You can only communicate with the examiner through the contents of your project folder.

How to find a suitable coursework task

■ Finding the **right task** for your coursework is important. It should be something that you are going to enjoy working on; remember: this work will take a number of months to complete.

■ If you choose your project well, you should end up with a theme that will both interest you and motivate you to be successful. It must be something that allows you to demonstrate your designing and making skills – **but must also meet the exam board's requirements.**

■ All exam boards produce suggestions for possible projects that have been carefully written to ensure that students are pointed in the right direction to meet the exam requirements. They are not compulsory, but should give a clear picture of what is expected. If you decide to select your own project theme, it is vital that you discuss your thoughts and ideas with your teacher.

1.2 Natasha's Panda

Examiner's tips:

• All exam boards have experienced Coursework Advisers who know precisely which project themes are most suitable *and those that are not.*

• If you decide to 'go your own way', your school should contact them to check over your ideas before you start. The service is free and contact details are available from the exam board. If in any doubt at all, contact them. They will be only too pleased to help as it can save a lot of problems later.

Examiner's comments

• Although Natasha's panda is produced from a 2-dimensional net, the product is clearly 3 dimensional.

• Projects based on the skills and techniques learnt during your Graphic Products course are usually very successful.

• The more fun and enjoyable you can make the project, the more interested in it you are likely to be.

Read and remember!

1 Your complete project should represent **40 hours work in total** (20 hours Short Course) including designing and making. Don't take on something that is clearly going to take longer than this.

2 It must have the capability for the design and production of a **3-dimensional prototype suitable for quantity manufacture**.

3 It must give you the opportunity to manufacture a **high-quality product**.

4 It must be focused around the use of **graphic and compliant materials**.

5 It must be demanding enough to **stretch your abilities** to the full. A simple project will not be awarded the same marks as a complex one, no matter how well done.

6 **Avoid multi-outcome projects** which force you to design and make a range of items. Try to stick to single-outcome projects that give you the opportunity to design and develop ideas fully and in detail.

7 Remember that you are following a *Graphic* **Products** course so your project needs to give you plenty of opportunity to show off your **graphic and modelling skills**.

8 Your project should give you the opportunity to research and explore a **range** of possible design solutions. Avoid projects that you feel have only one or two possible solutions.

9 Your project should give you the opportunity to explore and design around **industrial and commercial practices**, and **manufacturing techniques**.

10 Your project should enable you to use **ICT** and particularly **CAD** in the design work, and wherever possible **CAM** in your prototype product's manufacture. (Do not make it 100% ICT. Show your hand skills as well as your CAD skills.)

11 Your project should give you the opportunity to incorporate **new technologies** and **smart and modern materials** into your design.

CHECK YOURSELF

Have you:

- *Made sure your graphic product conforms to what your exam board expects?*
- *Planned your total project time carefully?*
- *Worked out how much time you will have for Designing and how much you will have for Making?*
- *Produced a chart with deadline dates clearly shown for each objective?*
- *Targeted the number of A3 sheets for each section of your project folder?*
- *Thought about how you will use ICT effectively?*
- *Selected the most suitable coursework project theme to stretch your ability?*

How to use ICT and CAD in design

■ You need to understand the place of ICT and CAD within design work, and the exam board's mark schemes:

• **Fact:** Using a computer **will not** make you a better designer **nor** will it improve the quality of your ideas.

• **Fact:** Using a computer **will** enable you to make changes to your designs quickly and easily, and **will** enable you to produce high-quality, realistic-looking visuals.

• **Fact:** ICT and CAD are simply tools to be used – much like you would use a pencil!

■ Remember that CAD stands for Computer *Aided* Design; the important part is the word 'aided'.

■ The examiners will be expecting to see that you have used ICT and CAD to **aid you** in your design work, and that you have used it *appropriately*. Many marks can be awarded for the appropriate use of ICT and CAD, whereas you can use lots of ICT and CAD inappropriately and not gain any extra marks at all.

■ *Don't* use ICT and CAD for the sake of it. Seek advice from your teacher if you are unsure.

1.3 *Janine's animal character designs*

Examiner's comment

• Janine has used pencil crayon to show a number of colour ways for her lettering and for her animal character designs. This is a good example of where ICT and CAD could have been used appropriately to improve the quality of the outcome and to save time.

1.4 *Saving time with ICT*

1.5 *Laura's designs and prototype 'dangly cow'*

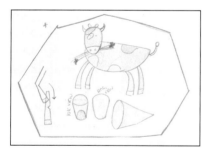 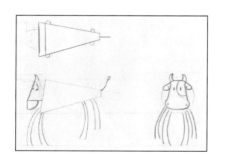 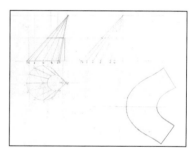

Hand-drawn sketches, orthographic views and an accurately constructed net for an oblique cone to form the body of the 'dangly cow'.

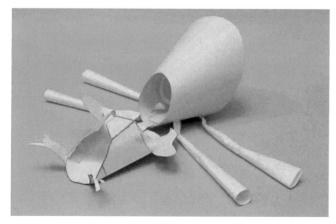 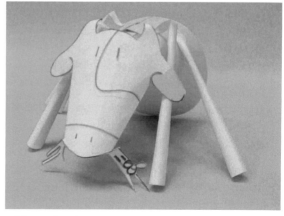

Here you can see one of the paper test models produced from the basic scanned line-drawing.

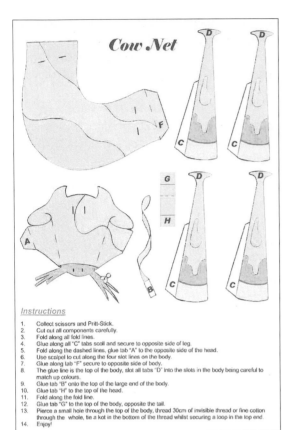

Cow Net

G
D D
A F C C
G
H
D
C C
B

Instructions

1. Collect scissors and Pritt-Stick.
2. Cut out all components carefully.
3. Fold along all fold lines.
4. Glue along all "C" tabs scoll and secure to opposite side of leg.
5. Fold along the dashed lines, glue tab "A" to the opposite side of the head.
6. Use scalpel to cut along the four slot lines on the body.
7. Glue along tab "F" secure to opposite side of body.
8. The glue line is the top of the body, slot all tabs "D" into the slots in the body being careful to match up colours.
9. Glue tab "B" onto the top of the large end of the body.
10. Glue tab "H" to the top of the head.
11. Fold along the fold line.
12. Glue tab "G" to the top of the body, opposite the tail.
13. Pierce a small hole through the top of the body, thread 30cm of invisible thread or fine cotton through the whole, tie a kot in the bottom of the thread whilst securing a loop in the top end.
14. Enjoy!

The final 2D product printed out onto 160 micron card.

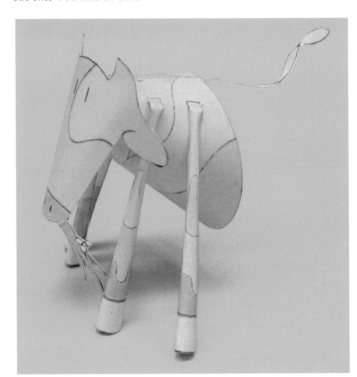

Examiner's comments

- These details taken from Laura's work show how she has used ICT and CAD to improve the quality of her final product.

- The initial work was all hand drawn to work out how the nets will fit together and then the final drawings were scanned into a PC. This produced the paper test model shown. A number of these were produced to check and adjust the fit of parts and the 'dangly-ness' of the legs, head and tail... Repeating a process is quite simple using a PC.

- Laura then used the PC to add the final details to her work before printing off and assembling the final prototype product as shown here.

- Laura was able to position the components quickly and easily using the PC, before finally adding colour, labels and instructions on-screen.

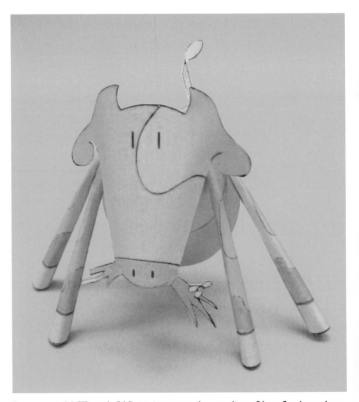

Laura used ICT and CAD to improve the quality of her final product.

Help!

- Showing evidence of how you have used ICT is straightforward if you use the Screen dump feature. On most keyboards you will find a Print Screen key, usually situated towards the top right of the keyboard. Pressing this key will place an image of the screen, along with whatever software you are using, onto the Clipboard. In effect you have stored a freeze-frame or snap-shot of your activities.

- Using the Paste command, this image of the screen can now be used in any software you wish; for example, a word processing or DTP program.

- It is a good idea to **add notes and labels** to this screen dump to explain to the examiner how you are using the software at that particular stage of your project.

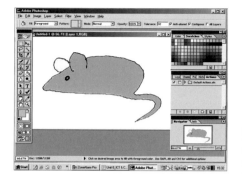

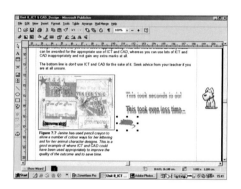

1.6 Three screendump snap-shots taken during the production of this section.

Examiner's comments

- The first two screendumps show the use of Adobe Photoshop in the production of the coloured mice, while the third shows the coloured mice being pasted into Microsoft Publisher where the rough first draft of this section of the book was produced.

- With a few labels and notes, it would be quite easy to explain, and therefore to follow, the processes involved.

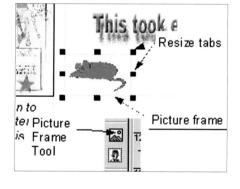

1.7 Part of the last screendump in 1.6 cropped using a paint program and then pasted into Publisher where labels and arrows have been added to show in detail the processes taking place.

Examiner's comments

- Paint and DTP programs are useful tools to help explain the ICT or CAD processes that you are using.

- There are many types of CAD software available. If you are fortunate, you may have more than one program to choose from within your school.

- A word of caution: some 3D CAD software is really intended for use by students studying 'Resistant Materials' courses. However, providing you are aware of this and work appropriately, you can achieve some high-quality results.

- One final thought: Never underestimate the power, speed and flexibility of the pencil!

COURSEWORK 2: DESIGNING

Exploring the problem and generating a design brief

■ Your chosen coursework task or project theme will form the basis of your *need for design* or **problem area**.

■ You will need to carry out some simple and brief research into your identified problem area to help you justify, generate and write a **design brief**.

■ Neatly write out your chosen problem area. See if you can find any images or photographs to help convey the theme of your chosen topic, *but use them sparingly*.

■ **Investigate** your chosen problem area *briefly*.

- Put your **thoughts** down on paper.

- Take **photographs** of the area/habitat/environment that clearly show your chosen topic.

- **Analyse** your photographs and annotate or label them.

- Check the **internet** for background information; use a **search engine.**

■ Ask **people** about your topic. Talk to those people who **will use** 'it'. Talk to those people who **may buy** 'it'.

■ Find out something about:
- their ages/age group
- their sex
- their background
- their lifestyle
- their needs/wants.

■ This will enable you to start identifying the **users** or **user group** for your design work.

■ What **problems** do any *present* users encounter? What are the **needs** of *potential* users?

Help!

- **A simple and short** questionnaire can help here. **Limit it** to 5 or 6 questions, for example:

  1 Male or Female?

  2 Age group?

  3 Do you own/use a…?

  4 Would you buy/use a…?

  5 How much would you expect to pay for a…?

Help!

- **'Present users'** are people who **currently use** an existing product (i.e. a present user of a pop-up book may be a parent teaching a child to read, or a child old enough to read).

- **'Potential users'** are people who **may buy** your intended product **if it were available** (i.e. a potential user of a pop-up book may be the parent of a very young child who intends to teach their child to read, or someone who is not satisfied with existing products).

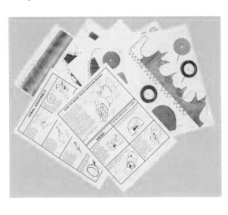 

2.1 *Martin's design for a 'Build-Your-Own Matilda Kit' based on the popular 'Robot Wars' BBC television programme. His target market is fans and collectors.*

- Try to identify the **range of users** for your product. This should enable you to describe the **situation** and why you feel there is a **need** for the product.

- Identify the **market** for your product:
  - Who is likely to buy it?
  - How many are likely to be manufactured?

- You must show that you have **considered** *from the start* how you can manufacture *more than one* **product**.
  - Try to **analyse** all the information you have uncovered.
  - Reach some **conclusions** that you can include in your design brief.

- Write a **clear and precise** design brief that includes:
  - mention of the target users
  - intended market
  - manufacture of more than one product.

- Think very carefully about how to show your findings.

- Think about how you can use: **text**; **drawings**; **graphs**; **photographs**.

- Present your work **logically**, **neatly**, **carefully** and **professionally**.

 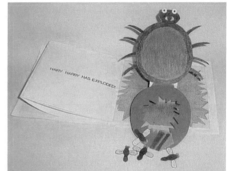

2.4 *Lydia's pop-up book*

Examiner's comments

- Lydia's pop-up book is about a greedy spider called Hairy Harry who goes for a midnight feast, eats too much and explodes.

- Lydia's design brief was quite short and simple. 'I am going to design and produce a high-quality prototype pop-up book suitable for young children who are learning to read.'

- This brief is 'open' leaving Lydia the freedom to design a fun product that features this surprise powered mechanism, where Hairy Harry's stomach pops open and spits out flies and cake!

- Gruesome, but just what a young child would find appealing! Good products come from good briefs.

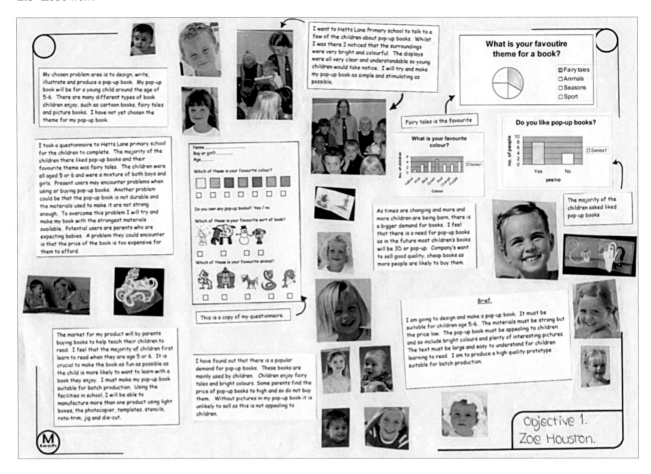

Examiner's comments

- Zoe has presented her work in a logical manner and has covered all her initial research and exploration of the problem leading to a design brief on one side of A3 paper. She has used a lot of ICT including a digital camera and spreadsheet software. The small graphs have been printed in black and white, with the important result coloured by hand.

- This is concise work that has been carefully edited before being presented. Zoe has included photographic evidence of her site visit to a primary school. The small 'cut and paste' pictures clearly convey that the focus of the activity is designing for children.

- The child-friendly questionnaire is a good idea and Zoe has made appropriate use of ICT throughout to help keep the work concise. The design brief is clear and precise.

- Zoe could have improved her work by planning the layout with greater care and in particular taking greater care over the cutting and mounting of her work. Better still, Zoe could have used a DTP package linked to an A3 printer to improve the overall quality of the sheet.

CHECK YOURSELF

Have you:

- *Investigated the range of intended users?*
- *Given examples of the intended users?*
- *Investigated and identified the target market?*
- *Shown evidence of this investigation in the form of:*
  photographs? graphs or charts? diagrams? drawings and sketches?
- *Clearly described the situation?*
- *Identified and described the need for design?*
- *Briefly analysed all your findings?*
- *Written a clear and precise design brief?*
  - *Is your design brief realistic? Will you be able to make the product?*
  - *Is your design brief 'open' to help you design?*
  - *Does your design brief enable you to design and produce a high-quality graphic product?*
  - *Does your design brief identify the intended users and the target market?*
  - *Does your design brief highlight the production of a marketable product capable of manufacture in quantity?*
- *Kept your work concise through editing and careful selection of what you include and what you leave out?*
- *Presented your work carefully and logically?*
- *Targeted your work to around two sheets of A3 paper?*

- You need to ask lots of **questions** about your project – and then find out the **answers** – and then reach some **conclusions**.

- The purpose of researching and analysing your project topic is to find **information and facts** that will **help** your design work. It should give you a clear **framework** within which to design.

- It should give you **opportunities**, as well as **constraints**, so that you can make **informed decisions** when designing.

✎ Planning your research

- The more you *plan* your research and the more *detail* you include, the *more marks* you will get.

- *Detail does not mean including lots and lots of information!* You must be selective.

Help!

- **Factual information** is information that is *real* and based on *facts*. This is called **objective** information.

- An **opinion** is what a person *feels* about something and is not based on *proof*. An opinion can be an **emotional response**. This is called **subjective** information.

- Information can be collected directly from the situation – this is called **primary research** – or it can be accessed through published material – **secondary research**.

- There are a number of **research methods** you could use to find out information:

  * **User research** – finding out relevant information about the user or user group that you have identified in your design brief. Observation is a useful form of user research.

  * **Market research** – finding out about other existing products that are available and how they meet the user's needs; interviewing consumers; identifying a target market.

  * **Site studies** – investigating the environment in which the product will be used.

  * **Expert opinions** – gathering evidence from experts or people who have detailed knowledge about your project theme.

  * **Literature search** – gathering information from books, magazines, newspaper articles etc.

  * **Internet search** – using search engines, manufacturers' sites, reviews, consumer group sites, databases etc.

  * **Email** – contacting users and user groups, manufacturers etc.

  * **Photographic evidence** – taking, analysing and annotating photographs of, for example: similar products in use, the situation, the environment, identified common faults etc.

  * **Survey or questionnaire** – using carefully worded questions to find out information from present or potential users. *Tip: Only include questions that can have a tick-box response.*

- To start with, you should produce a research plan based on:

  - **WHAT** (you need to find out)
  - **WHERE** (you will find the information)
  - **HOW** (it will help your design work).

- Make lists of questions you will need to find answers to, using the **5 Ws:**

  What...?   Why...?
  When...?   Where...?
  Who...?

- Not forgetting:

  How many...?
  How often...?
  How much...?

- You must obtain *factual* information, as well as *opinions*.

- Use as many **research methods** as you can.

✎ The design specification

- After carrying out this investigation, you should be able to reach **conclusions** from what you have discovered. In other words, you should be able to **analyse** your findings to come up with some **answers**.

- These answers will help you write your **design specification**.

✎ Questionnaire research

- Start by carrying out some primary research. Carry out full and detailed research into existing and potential users of your product.

- Produce a carefully planned and *focused* questionnaire based on what you need to find out.

  - Show your results *graphically*.

  - **Analyse** your findings – what do they tell you about your intended product?

  - How will this information help your design work?

- Have you uncovered any other areas that you now need to include in your research plan?

2.4 *Ilana's work*

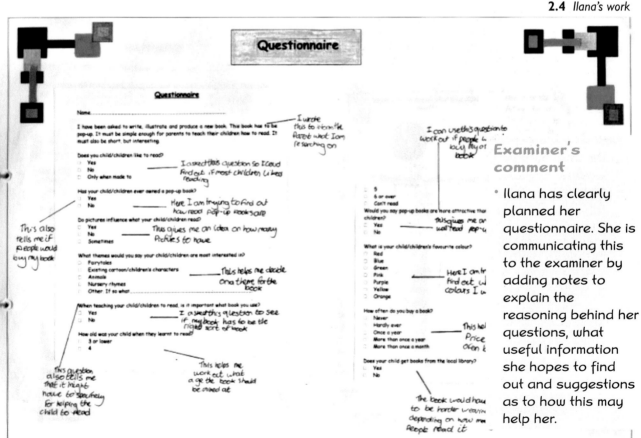

Examiner's comment

- Ilana has clearly planned her questionnaire. She is communicating this to the examiner by adding notes to explain the reasoning behind her questions, what useful information she hopes to find out and suggestions as to how this may help her.

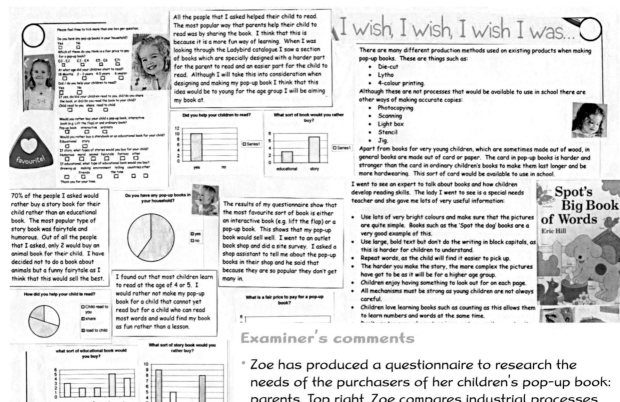

Examiner's comments

- Zoe has produced a questionnaire to research the needs of the purchasers of her children's pop-up book: parents. Top right, Zoe compares industrial processes used in the manufacture of pop-up books to those that are available in school. She then summarises an interview that she had with an expert – a Special Needs teacher who helps children with reading difficulties.

- She has used ICT to reduce the size of a copy of her questionnaire and the graphs produced from the spreadsheet. Colour has only been used to pick out the important responses to her questionnaire. Each graph has been analysed and commented on.

- This is another concise sheet that shows evidence of careful editing. The analysis of Zoe's findings from the questionnaire is good and gives her items to include in her specification, as well as pointers for her design work. Her comments on industrial processes are sufficient at this stage to help her start designing. Her interview with the 'expert' is clearly presented as a focused set of bullet points.

- *Zoe could improve her work by explaining how she is going to use the information obtained from the expert. Credit is given for demonstrating how the information gathered is going to help the design work through analysis and conclusions. Very little credit can be given for simply collecting information. The layout of this sheet is better but care is still needed.*

Examiner's tips:

- When presenting results from questionnaires, only produce those graphs which show the important and really useful information. Tally charts and tables are just as useful.

- Use ICT to help you sort the information and to keep any graphs small.

- Remember that it is the analysis of the graphs – what they tell you and how you then use that information – that will gain you marks.

- Graphs on their own are worthless, no matter how pretty!

✎ Research into existing products

■ Gather information on **existing products**. Collect examples or samples of them.

■ Take photographs of them. Disassemble them. Make clear drawings of them.
  - **Evaluate** them fully and carefully in great detail.
  - **Analyse** their good points and their bad points.
    What can you learn from them?
    How can they help your design work?

■ **Compare** what these existing products **offer** against the **needs** of the users that you have identified as part of your **intended market**.

 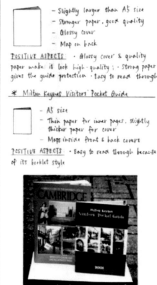

2.6 Midori's general research

Help!

- **Product analysis** is quite straightforward if you approach the task **logically**.

- Here are just a few suggestions for possible product analysis activities:

  * Start by analysing its external appearance. What clues are there to its intended purpose? Does the colour choice tell you anything? What about the font style? Is the product laminated or varnished, or is there some other surface coating?

  * Where is it intended to be used? How does it get there? Who is the target user and what is the target market? How many are likely to be manufactured? What is the scale of production?

  * Does the product fulfil its function? How does it achieve this?

  * Investigate the materials used. What materials are used to produce the product? Why have they been chosen?

  * Disassemble the product. How is it manufactured? What production processes are used? What are the stages involved in its manufacture? How is it assembled? What other materials are involved in its production?

- To score highly, do not merely describe your findings. Do not glue lots of existing products into your design folder. Take photographs and/or draw the stages of your analysis. Use ICT to help you keep your work focused and concise.

* One or two existing products, carefully analysed and evaluated in detail are sufficient to score full marks.

* *Do not describe what is obvious by looking at the product!* Examiners are looking for key words such as '...because...' and for sentences that start with key phrases such as 'This tells me that...'. Such words and phrases show that the candidate is analysing and evaluating what they see, rather than simply describing it. Use drawings and sketches to help communicate your thoughts and findings.

* Don't forget that you are carrying out product analysis to help you understand the ways that other products meet the needs of both the user and the manufacturer. This understanding needs to be clearly communicated and conclusions reached that can be used in your design specification.

2.7 Zoe's analysis

Examiner's comments

* On the left side of this sheet, Zoe has analysed and evaluated an existing product by using photographs that she has taken of a pop-up book. Note how she has used close-up detail shots to help her investigations.

* Always ensure that close-up, detail photographs are in focus. Digital cameras and ICT enable you to edit photographs so that precise details can be shown, as here.

✎ Legal aspects

■ What is the **intended use** of your project?

■ What **factors** may affect your design work?

■ Are there any **laws, regulations** or **standards** surrounding your chosen project? For example: BSI, BS-EN, DIN, ISO, e, **C€**, etc.

■ Try to contact manufacturers, retailers, wholesalers, etc. Search the internet. Track down an **expert**. Gather as much *relevant* information as you can.

Help!

- **Consumer protection** is very important in the design and manufacture of products. There are many laws and regulations in force to protect people who purchase products. Products that have met critical standards display a mark to show that they conform to these laws.

- You are likely to encounter the following **Quality Control** standards:

  * **BSI** (British Standards Institution); **BS** (British Standard)

  * **BS-EN** – a European standard adopted by the BSI

  * **DIN** (Deutsche Industrie-Norm) – a German standard similar to BSI

  * **ISO** (International Standards Organisation)

  * e – mark displayed on products that have met European Community standards

  * CE – European Community mark used to show safety for children.

- **Other consumer protection groups** that may be able to help you in your research include the Consumer's Association, RoSPA and the Trading Standards Institute.

CHECK YOURSELF

Have you:

- Planned your research?
- Identified the needs of the users?
- Identified a range of possible users?
- Carried out a range of primary and secondary research methods?
- Used ICT to find and contact other sources?
- Identified the needs of the consumer?
- Analysed and evaluated appropriate existing products?
- Briefly explored relevant manufacturing processes?
- Used ICT to help:
    - sort your data?
    - analyse your findings?
    - communicate your results?
    - keep your work concise?

✎ Materials and production methods

■ A **common trap** that many students 'fall into' at this stage is to go into very precise detail about the materials and production methods that they intend to use for their final prototype product.

  ● If you have not yet started **designing** your graphic product, how can you specify precisely which materials and production methods you are going to use?

  ● The only occasion for this to be acceptable is when projects are set around **specific manufacturing processes**; for example, lithography and die-cut.

■ In real life, designers usually **design** the product **first** – and *then* start to consider the **most suitable** materials and processes from which to manufacture it.

■ Starting off with a fixed view of the materials to be used and the manufacturing processes to be employed can seriously limit creative thinking and, therefore, the quality of designing. It is much better for you to have a rough outline of *possible* materials and production methods.

  ● **Explore** production methods used by existing products and **compare** them with the processes that you can use in school.

  ● **Investigate** the materials used in existing products. For example: measure their thickness, check their surface finish, explore how they are joined.

Examiner's tips:

* At this stage of your project, you should be aware of the manufacturing techniques and processes relevant to your chosen problem area.

* Remember that you are only looking for clues to help you in your design work.

* Do not copy out or print out lots of information from textbooks, CD-ROMs or websites. *It will not impress the examiner and will not gain you any credit.* The examiner is far more interested in your analysis of your findings, in the conclusions you draw from your investigations and how you apply your knowledge of materials and processes to the design problem.

✎ Anthropometrics and ergonomics

- All designers of products that will be used by, or come into contact with, human beings have to consider **anthropometrics** and **ergonomics**. Graphic products are no exception.

- **Anthropometrics** is the measurement of the human body. It covers everything from the average length and diameter of an adult female's index finger, through to the size of font that may be easily read in daylight from a distance of 2 metres.

- It involves measuring the **senses** and **abilities**, as well as the **physical dimensions** of **able** and **disabled** humans, of **both sexes** and of **all ages**.

- **Ergonomics** is the use of this data to help design better and safer products.

- Anthropometric data is available in many published forms, both printed and electronic, from a wide range of sources. You must ensure that you have researched and considered anthropometric and ergonomic factors if you are going to score highly.

- Remember to only include **relevant** details and factors in your project.

2.8 *Kirsty's analysis of a pop-up book*

Examiner's comments

- Kirsty has described, analysed and evaluated every detail of the book. She then summarises these findings as 'Advantages' and 'Disadvantages', justifying her reasons for each statement.

- There is sufficient evidence here to justify full marks from the in-depth analysis and evaluation of a single existing product.

- Kirsty could improve her work by investigating the materials used in greater detail. She could also highlight the points that she has discovered from analysing this product which could help her write her own design specification and also pay closer attention to the layout of the sheet.

✎ Value issues

- **Value issues** are concerns that you must think about **carefully** if you hope to design a product that meets the needs of people who live in a diverse, global society. Value issues can be difficult to research and describe accurately because of their subjective nature.

- They also include some sensitive issues and can often involve a conflict of values between the designer and the user. The designer often has to apply judgements based on **compromise**.

- However, if you manage to investigate and analyse value issues in relation to your project, and include your conclusions in your design specification, you will gain credit from the examiner.

- Value issues are also known as **SMC** (Social, Moral and Cultural) **issues**. You should also include **economic** and **environmental** issues.

- All of these value issues are closely linked. They frequently overlap and are sometimes intertwined so that they become difficult to separate and identify.

  - **Social issues** concern the need to design items that are of benefit to the community and reflect the nature of society. For example: issues surrounding a pop-up book aimed at children that shows stereotypical images of girls dressed in pink who cook and clean. *What message is this giving to young children of both sexes?*

  - **Moral issues** are concerned with the right and wrong of human behaviour. For example: the issues surrounding the design of a point-of-sale (PoS) display to be used to promote a DVD release of a film which includes scenes of excessive violence. *What images and text should be used when the PoS display may be seen by impressionable young people?*

  - **Cultural issues** are often concerned with differing cultural backgrounds, religions and lifestyles. For example: the issues surrounding the design of an item of packaging which uses a product name that causes offence to a minority religious group. *What responsibility rests with the designer to research and understand the needs of minority groups?*

  - **Economic issues** concern the cost of producing, selling and purchasing products. For example: the issues surrounding an interactive activity pack that, although designed and marketed in the UK, is to be printed and assembled in the Far East where labour and materials costs are less. *What economic effects will this have in the UK?*

  - **Environmental issues** are increasingly important as we become more aware of the finite resources of our planet. Designers have an important role in designing products that:
    - use recycled and recyclable materials
    - use a minimum of non-renewable resources
    - are efficient in their use of materials to avoid waste
    - have a long product life
    - reduce packaging requirements
    - utilise energy-efficient production techniques
    - demand low-impact manufacturing processes that minimise pollution.

* Investigating and analysing value issues is classed as a 'high order skill' by examiners due to their difficult, sensitive and subjective nature. This means that successfully researching value issues is worth a lot of credit and examiners will mark your work favourably if you include evidence of having carried this out.

* Emma has produced this sheet to bring together and analyse all the important factors that she uncovered during her research. She has grouped the points using some of the 5 Ws.

* This kind of analysis is crucial evidence if you wish to be a high-scoring candidate. It is clearly communicated and an examiner can quickly find the evidence needed to justify the marks awarded. It will help Emma to write and structure her design specification.

FINAL ANALYSIS

Page: 1

Consumer questionnaires:

WHY: I made a consumer questionnaire in order to collect information on what the general public would like to see more of, or prefer to see than what is already on the fast-food/vegetarian market. I did this so that when I design my new packaging I can maybe take what the public have said into account and include it in my final design.

WHO: I asked a variety of ages and a mixture of both vegetarians and meat-eaters to fill in my questionnaire and got some interesting results in return.

WHAT: Many interesting results were found from the questionnaires and most of them are shown on the Consumer Questionnaire results page. In brief though, all of the people asked wanted their hot take-away packaging to insulated, most people preferred paper bags for take-out meals, mainly because environmentally friendly packaging was important to them, and half of the people asked wanted new style packaging.

HOW: As I said earlier, my design process and my final design will be affected with the results of the questionnaire because I want to make all my ideas and packaging designs more appealing to the general public.

Websites:

WHY: I think that websites are extremely important in research, because examples are gained into how companies are promoted on the web, and how company websites encourage people to try their products.

WHO: I looked for Starbucks, Prêt and BB's on the web, but only two of the companies had websites.

WHAT: Starbucks and Prêt were the only two companies with websites:

* STARBUCKS' website had a lot of information on the founding of the company and the company image, but not a lot on packaging and the environment. They did have many promotional pages though.
* PRET had a lot of information on the origin of the company and the image, but also had more about the food that they provide and menu details. This site also had promotional offers pages.

HOW: I looked into websites in order to find different and interesting ways to promote the new business venture that I am designing the overall image for. My coursework will benefit greatly from the new ideas that I gained, and I will try to make my image easy to reproduce for online purposes.

Company questionnaires and letters:

WHY: I sent these letters and questionnaires to companies to gain a good idea of how the businesses that I am focussing on promote their company and to collect different examples of packaging.

WHO: I sent letters and questionnaires to four companies; Prêt a manger, V1, BB's and Starbucks. I got a reply from all four of the companies.

WHAT: These are the kind of replies that I got sent:

* PRET were very helpful. They filled in the questionnaire and sent me a whole envelope of packaging examples, order forms and other promotional information.
* V1 were also extremely helpful, they sent me packaging and also information about where their packaging come from. They also filled in the questionnaire.
* BB'S sent some promotional leaflets and also filled in my questionnaire.
* STARBUCKS only sent a letter and apologised for not being able to fill out the questionnaire, but told me to look on the website for any information that I needed.

HOW: The letters, replies and completed questionnaires will help me greatly with my project. I now know what materials are mainly used for packaging today and why, and also the general shapes and sizes of existing packaging. I also understand why certain colours and styles are used in packaging and how and why packaging is reinforced. All this will help me in my design process when choosing packaging materials and colours etc. and I have also gained some excellent promotional ideas.

Packaging Examples:

WHY: I have collected examples of packaging that are already on the market because I think that it is a good idea to examine existing packaging and try to improve it. The existing packaging is also a good example on which to base my ideas and designs.

WHO: I generally chose to collect packaging examples from McDonalds. Though the company is not vegetarian, the packaging is still extremely useful to my research, and I also chose to collect McDonalds' packaging due to the large range of packaging that they use within their company.

WHAT: I managed to get examples of many different types of packaging from McDonalds. I collected fires packaging, hot and cold packaging, packaging made from recycled materials and reinforced packaging. The examples that I collected consisted of many different colours, materials and styles. There are also many different sizes and shapes of packaging.

HOW: The packaging that I have collected for my coursework will link closely with my consumer questionnaire results. I will look at both of them and record new ideas within my designing process in order to make my new packaging more appealing, practical and environmentally friendly.

V1:

WHY: I contacted V1 mainly because it is the type of company that I am trying to create an image for and to promote. The ideas behind V1 are very relevant to my designing.

WHO: V1 is a new vegetarian/fast-food outlet that has its own style of packaging, logo and website. It also promotes itself on local radio and in local newspapers.

WHAT: I tried to gain as much information as possible from V1, this included:

* A photograph (Which I have also done a graphical drawing of)
* Website printouts.
* A menu.
* Promotional leaflets
* A Business card/map
* A wide range of their packaging examples
* And a letter/reply that was extremely informative.

HOW: All the information that I collected on V1 will be used in my design process:

* The photograph and packaging examples will help me create the overall image of my company.
* The leaflets, business card and the website printouts will help me promote my company.
* The menu will aid me in creating my own menu.
* The packaging examples, with the McDonalds packaging and the consumer questionnaire, will help me with my general packaging designs.
* And the letter reply will work with my materials page on helping me decide on what materials to produce my packaging designs out of.

Colours and Materials pages:

WHY: I looked into colours and materials to help me generally with my designing and producing. I wanted to gain some knowledge into why certain colours are used on specific packaging and why certain materials are used, how much they cost and how environmentally friendly they are.

WHO: I looked at all materials that were used in the fast-food business.

WHAT: I found examples of materials used today and analysed how they were made, how much they cost, how practical they are and how environmentally friendly they are.

HOW: All the research that I did in these two pages will help me decide on the types of materials and colours to include in my designs, to make them economical, practical and aesthetically pleasing.

2.9 *Emma's final analysis*

CHECK YOURSELF

Have you:

* *Explored production methods used by existing products and compared them with the processes you can use in school?*
* *Explored anthropometric data and ergonomic requirements?*
* *Investigated the possible impact of value issues?*
* *Investigated the materials used in existing products?*

Writing a design specification

- By this point you will probably have gathered a lot of information.

- If you've followed the advice given, you will have been selective about the information that you intend to include within your project. You will have sifted through everything and picked out that which is **useful and relevant.**

- Using all of your findings from your research you should be able to reach some **clear conclusions.**

- Use these conclusions or analysis to help you write a clear, detailed **design specification** for your product.

- Your design specification should describe the things about your chosen product that you have discovered should be **fixed** and those which you are **free to change.**

- You **must** try to identify and include the following areas:

Purpose	Function	Appearance
Aesthetics	Safety issues	Materials
Ergonomics	Product life	Making more than one
Controlling quality	Standards (BSI, etc.)	Social issues
Moral issues	Cultural issues	Environmental issues

- Exactly how you set out your design specification is up to you.

- The word 'specification' is from the words **specify** and **specific**; remember this as you write your own design specification. Do not include any vague statements.

- You may want to change your design specification as the project evolves. There is nothing wrong with this, but remember to record what has changed and why it has changed.

Help!

- **Musts** are fixed, **essential** features and cannot be changed –

  'It must be safe for children under 36 months.' or: *'It must support the weight of one DVD disc and case.'*

- **Shoulds** are **desirable** features that **might** be changed with a good reason –

  'It should be varnished.' or: *'It should be able to be produced for less than £4.00.'*

- **Mays** are **optional** suggestions that **may** be changed freely –

  'The story may contain a moral.' or: *'The product may be made from corrugated board.'*

Examiner's tips:

- Important! This design specification must be focused, not just a series of general points.

- Group your statements under headings, such as:

Must	Or perhaps...	Fixed	Or even...	Essential
Should		Might		Desirable
May		Maybe		Optional

- This will help you to prioritise your statements and, later, to evaluate and select suitable design ideas for further development.

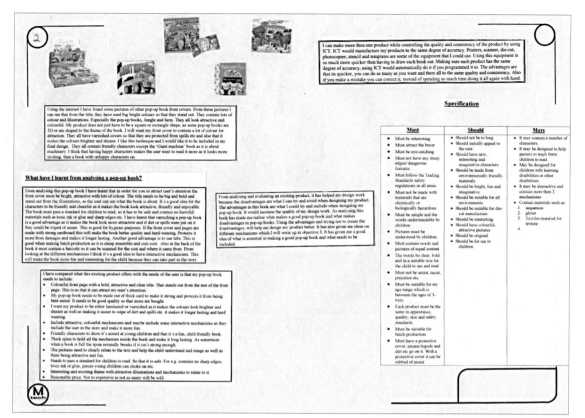

2.10 *Kirsty's analysis and specification sheet*

Examiner's comments

- By using ICT and a small font size, Kirsty has managed to fit a great deal of valuable, high-scoring information on this sheet. The separate blocks of text cover some further product analysis, evaluation of what she has learnt from her analysis of existing products and a series of conclusions of factors that she feels need to be part of her design specification. The text box top right considers how ICT can be used to control the consistency and accuracy of the manufacture of her product. In the lower right part, Kirsty presents her detailed design specification which is reproduced in figure 2.11.

- This is an excellent example of using ICT to keep work concise and focused; many candidates would have used three or four A3 sheets to communicate the same amount of information. This is very detailed work that scores very highly.

- Always remember when producing text, by hand or ICT, that you are not producing a poster; the examiner will sit at a desk to read and study your work, just as you would read a book.

- On first glance, this sheet does not look very exciting or 'graphic'. However, at this stage in the project, there are no marks for graphic skills. Kirsty has used those skills which will gain her most marks now and saved her graphic abilities for the design and development sections, where quality graphic communication skills will score highly.

- Always ensure that you know the focus of the mark scheme in the section of the project that you are working in. Exam board mark schemes are not secret documents.

- *Kirsty could have improved her work by paying greater attention to the layout of her sheet and targeting a more professional look. She could have used ICT to incorporate the images into the text blocks by working with DTP software. Using such software would also have enabled Kirsty to incorporate coloured text, text blocks and highlights which would produce a sheet with a more professional report-like appearance. Compare with Nicola's work (2.12).*

- Rough out your statements as **concise bullet points** under three separate headings.

- **Read** through them and **check** the wording carefully.

- **Sort** the bullet points into order of importance within each group.

- **Type** up your design specification using wordprocessing software on a computer.

- **Save** your work before printing it out. You will need to re-visit it as you work through your project.

- **Do not** write a large, rambling block of text!

Examiner's tips:

- Writing your design specification as a series of brief bullet points under recognisable headings will enable you to find the correct statement quickly as you assess and test your design ideas.

- Finding the appropriate statement in a large block of text is difficult and time-consuming.

- Remember that you are **not** writing an essay.

- Selection and rejection of initial design ideas will be based on the 'Must' statements. As you develop and evaluate your design proposals, you will test the designs against the 'Should' and 'May' statements. This will make your final design proposal far more successful.

- Examiners pay **very close attention** to design specifications. A bullet-point list enables them to find out quickly if you have covered the required points in detail. It shows that you are able to prioritise your findings and highlight the factors that you feel are important to your design work.

> **REMEMBER:**
> - A good design specification is **VITAL** to achieve a good grade.
> - It is the key to scoring highly in your design work and is the *only* way to achieve top marks in **all** of the other assessment objectives.

- When you have written your design specification, make sure that you **use it** and make frequent reference to it.

- Do not expect to find out absolutely everything you need for your project at this early stage. Good design projects frequently show evidence of further research all the way through the design process.

- Be prepared to carry out further investigation and research work as your project progresses.

- Record any changes that you feel you may need to make to your design specification as you progress through your design and development work. These changes will need to be made before you start to manufacture your prototype product.

Design specification for pop-up book

MUST:
- ✓ be interesting
- ✓ attract the buyer
- ✓ be eye-catching
- ✓ not have any sharp edges/dangerous features
- ✓ follow the Trading Standards safety regulations in all areas
- ✓ not be made with materials that are chemically or biologically hazardous
- ✓ be simple and the words understandable by children.
- ✓ Pictures must:
  - • be understood by children
  - • contain words and pictures of equal content.
- ✓ Words must:
  - • be clear, bold and in a suitable size for the child to see and read
  - • not be sexist, racist, prejudiced, etc.
  - • be suitable for my age range which is between the ages of 3–6 yrs.
- ✓ Each book must:
  - • be the same in appearance, quality, size and safety standards
  - • be suitable for batch production
  - • have a protective cover in case liquids, dirt, etc. go on it. With a protective cover it can be rubbed off easier.

SHOULD:
- ✓ not be too long
- ✓ initially appeal to the user
- ✓ have new, interesting and imaginative characters.
- ✓ be made from environmentally-friendly materials
- ✓ be bright, fun and imaginative
- ✓ be suitable for all environments
- ✓ be suitable for die-cut manufacture
- ✓ be interesting
- ✓ have colourful, attractive pictures
- ✓ be original
- ✓ be for use by children.

MAY:
- ✓ contain a number of characters
- ✓ be designed to help parents to teach their children to read
- ✓ be designed for children with learning disabilities or other disabilities
- ✓ be interactive and contain more than two mechanisms
- ✓ contain materials such as:
  1. Sequins
  2. Glitter
  3. Textile materials for texture.

2.11 *Kirsty's design specification for her pop-up book*

Examiner's comments

- Kirsty's design specification covers all the major points in detail and is clearly set out in appropriately headed columns.

- Simple, brief bullet points make it easier for her to refer to when evaluating and testing her designs.

- There are statements which will help Kirsty to focus on the most suitable design proposals.

- Statements regarding Value issues, Quality control and Quantity production are included.

- Kirsty could have improved her work *by sorting her bullet points into order of importance and attempting to clarify any vague statements that may exist.*

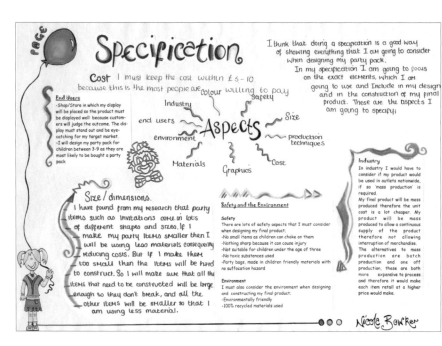

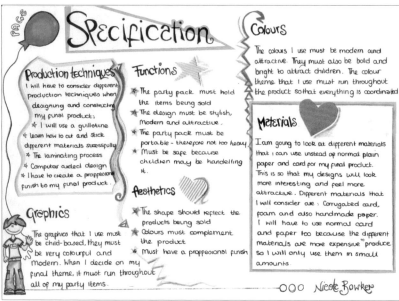

2.12 *Nicola's eye-catching design specification*

Examiner's comments

- Nicola has used headings with bullet points and statements to communicate her findings. She has used her graphic skills to produce an eye-catching design specification that covers two sides of A3 paper.

- These sheets look attractive but Nicola has also used up time in carrying out activities that are not worth any marks.

- Compare this specification with Kirsty's (2.10) – both would score a similar mark, yet Kirsty's uses a quarter of one sheet of A3 and would have taken a fraction of the time to complete.

CHECK YOURSELF

Have you:
- Carefully edited and selected the relevant information?
- Analysed and evaluated all of your findings and conclusions?
- Produced a design specification that is:
  - Focused?
  - Detailed?
  - Written as bullet points?
- Structured and prioritised?
- Checked for vague statements?
- Saved for future retrieval and use?
- Kept your work concise through editing and careful selection of what you include and what you leave out?
- Presented your work carefully and logically?
- Targeted your work to around four sheets of A3 paper?

COURSEWORK 3: GENERATING DESIGN IDEAS AND DESIGN DEVELOPMENT

Early ideas

- This assessment objective is about generating **lots** of **ideas**, **communicating** them and **developing** them towards a *realistic prototype* that answers your design brief.

- You must keep **checking** your ideas against your design specification and **evaluating** them as you go along.

- Later on you will get the chance to show the examiner all your **graphic skills** – but not yet.

  - Start by making simple, quick sketches of your first thoughts and ideas.

  - Use a pencil or something like a ballpoint pen, for speed.

  - Produce **2D** and **3D** freehand drawings.

  - Add simple notes and labels.

  - The examiner will want to know what **you** *think* about your ideas: are they good – or bad?

  - **Record** all of your thoughts using notes, sketches, and diagrams.

Examiner's tips:

- You must '**talk**' to the examiner **through** your work **throughout** the project. You will not meet him/her face to face.

- Make sure the examiner clearly understands what you are trying to achieve.

- **Don't** write an essay! Clear notes, labels and descriptions are sufficient.

- As well as drawing the whole product, draw out ideas for **parts** or **details** of your product.

- Small, quick thumbnail sketches are ideal to **communicate** ideas and concepts.

Examiner's comments

- Kirsty uses simple sketches with quick, rough colour to develop and communicate her ideas for her pop-up book.

- There is too much writing here, but the work is easy to follow and understand.

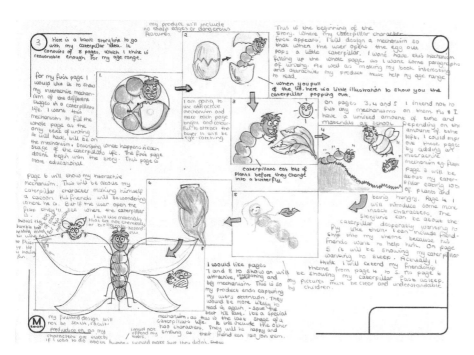

3.1 *Kirsty's early design idea page*

- Do not waste time carefully adding colour to your ideas at this early stage. Simply indicate which colours you are thinking of using. This can also be achieved by adding swatches of colour at the side of an idea to show your thoughts or you can add a small amount of colour to one section of an idea.

- Make sure you produce a **wide range** of design solutions. The more you produce the better.

3.2 *Two of Nicola's design development sheets*

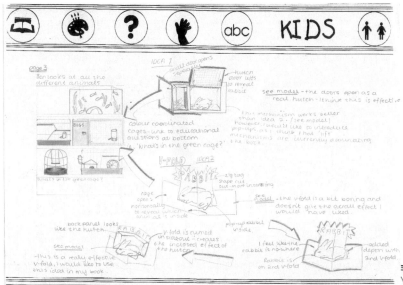

Examiner's tip:

- The examiner will expect to see a range of ideas communicated in many different ways, from freehand drawings through to ICT work using CAD.

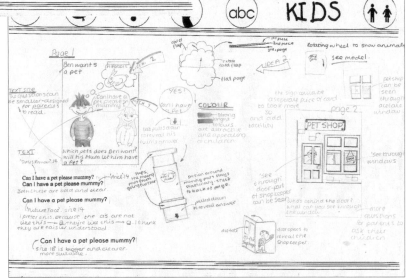

Examiner's comments

- Nicola has used simple, quick, free-flowing sketches, with little colour but lots of notes, to communicate her design work and the development of her ideas.

- This is excellent design development work. It is easy to follow Nicola's thoughts and the 3D sketches of mechanisms and notes on models prove that she is thinking about her work as a 3D functioning prototype product.

- **Think** about your ideas **very carefully**.

- At the side of each idea, list its **Advantages** *and* **Disadvantages**.

- Do your ideas **meet** the points listed in your design specification?

- List those points the idea **meets** in the specification – *and* those **it does not meet!**

- Consider carefully whether your ideas answer the **original** Problem Area and Design Brief. Write down your thoughts.

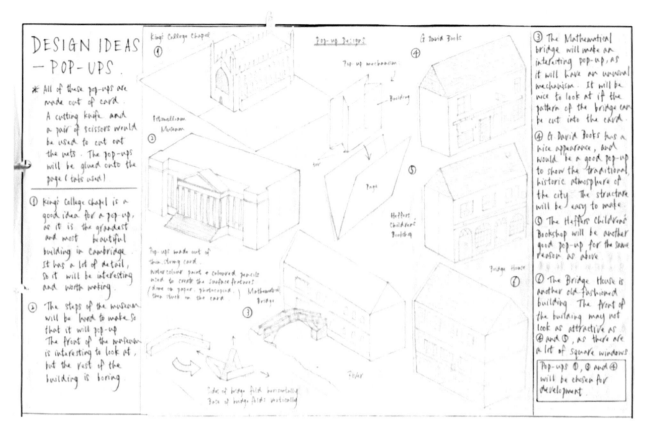

3.3 *Midori's design ideas for possible pop-up mechanisms*

Examiner's comments

• Midori has produced a range of solutions and has included details of possible pop-up mechanisms.

• She has used simple but well-drawn pencil line drawings to good effect.

CHECK YOURSELF

Have you:

• *Produced a range of rough, initial pencil-sketch ideas?*

• *Used thumbnail sketches, part-drawings and drawings of details to explore ideas?*

• *Annotated, labelled and described your ideas?*

• *Used a range of freehand graphic techniques to communicate your ideas?*

• *Briefly analysed all your findings?*

• *Used formal drawing techniques when accuracy was required?*

Developing your ideas

✎ Materials and production methods

- You should find that you have a few designs that seem to answer many of the points in your problem area, brief and design specification.

- These need to be **developed** so that they become as near to perfect solutions as you can get.

- Draw these chosen ideas out **carefully** and **accurately**. Make simple paper/card **mock-ups** to check what they will look like in **3D**, how big they need to be… *and to test whether they will work*. Any 3D test models *must* be included in your project – either the actual model or a photograph. Start to think about how you intend to make your design and from what materials.

- You will need to start discarding some of the weaker ideas, so it is important that you use your **design brief** and **specification** to help you close in on the most suitable design idea.

3.4 *Nicola's ideas for components of a party pack*

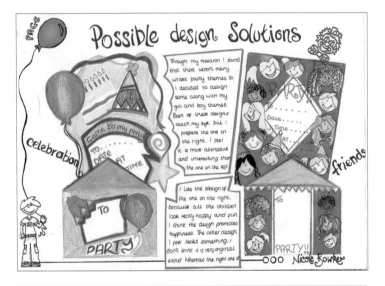

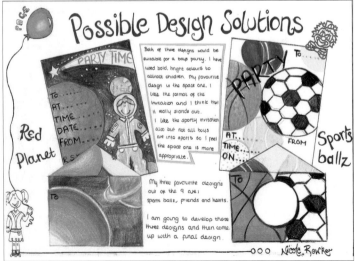

Examiner's comments

- Nicola has carefully drawn and rendered some ideas for her party pack, which have been developed from her initial ideas.

- She can clearly use colour well. These designs are exciting and vibrant – ideal for her chosen task.

- It is questionable whether Nicola needed to colour all of her designs to show her intentions to the examiner. Also, they could have been drawn to a smaller scale.

- A lot of time and space could have been saved here. The time might have put to better effect by adding more detailed and objective analysis and evaluation.

1. ADVANTAGES-
- This model would be able to have 2 moving parts so would appeal to the potential users which wanted 2 or 3 moving parts on the model.

DISADVANTAGES-
- This is not one of the potential users favourite robot.
- it would be very difficult to make this model out of card.

This idea meats the following in the specification;
- The product should look like one of the robots.
- The product may have moving parts.

This idea does not meat the following points in my specification;
- The model must not be too complex to put together.
- The product should be as original as possible.
- The product should look like one of the robots from robot wars. It should resemble either one of the following house robots from robot wars, 'Matilda' or 'Sir Killalot'

THOUGHTS;

If this design was made into a card model it would have to be simplified which I think would take away it's effect. It also would not appeal to the potential users as much as some of the other house robots as I found out in my questionnaire.

2. ADVANTAGES-
- This model would be able to have 3 moving parts so would appeal to the potential users which wanted 2 or 3 moving parts on the model.
- This is the potential users number 1 robot.

DISADVANTAGES-
- It would be very difficult to make this model out of card, so would have to be simplified which would take the effect of the robot away.

This idea meats the following in the specification;
- The product should look like one of the robots.
- The product may have moving parts.
- The product should look like one of the robots from robot wars. It should resemble either one of the following house robots from robot wars, 'Matilda' or 'Sir Killalot'

This idea does not meat the following points in my specification;
- The model must not be too complex to put together.
- The product should be as original as possible.

THOUGHTS;

If it was possible to make these intricate shapes out of card this robot would look great, but it is not possible and my specification states that the model should be kept simple. As this is the potential users number 1 robot it would be very popular and personally I like it, but overall it is just too complicated.

3. ADVANTAGES-
- This model would be able to have 2 moving parts so would appeal to the potential users which wanted 2 or 3 moving parts on the model.
- This is the potential users number 1 robot and number 2 robot.

DISADVANTAGES-
- It would be very difficult to make this model out of card, as the head is very round.
- As this is a combination it is not actually a real robot, so I do not think it would appeal to the potential users.

This idea meats the following in the specification;
- The product may have moving parts.
- The product should be as original as possible.

This idea does not meat the following points in my specification;
- The model must not be too complex to put together.
- The product should look like one of the robots.
- The product should look like one of the robots from robot wars. It should resemble either one of the following house robots from robot wars, 'Matilda' or 'Sir Killalot'

THOUGHTS;

If this was made into a card model it would be too complicated and I do not think it would appeal to the potential users plus I do not like the look of it myself.

4. ADVANTAGES-
- This model would be able to have 3 moving parts so would appeal to the potential users which wanted 2 or 3 moving parts on the model.
- This is the potential users number 2 robot.
- This model is quite simple.

DISADVANTAGES-
- There are no disadvantages for this model as of yet.

This idea meats the following in the specification;
- The product should look like one of the robots.
- The product may have moving parts.
- The product should look like one of the robots from robot wars. It should resemble either one of the following house robots from robot wars, 'Matilda' or 'Sir Killalot'
- The model must not be too complex to put together.

This idea does not meat the following points in my specification;
- The product should be as original as possible.

THOUGHTS;

I think this robot would look fantastic as a card model as nearly all of the shapes which make up this robot would be easily achieved from card. The other advantage is it would appeal to the potential users as it is there number 2 favourite robot.

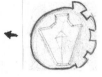

5. ADVANTAGES-
- This model is quite simple.

DISADVANTAGES-
- This model would get recognised as it is one of the robot wars contenders, but the potential users wanted the model to be one of the house robots.
- It has no moving parts.

This idea meats the following in the specification;
- The product should look like one of the robots.
- The model must not be too complex to put together.

This idea does not meat the following points in my specification;
- The product should be as original as possible.
- The product may have moving parts.
- The product should look like one of the robots from robot wars. It should resemble either one of the following house robots from robot wars, 'Matilda' or 'Sir Killalot'

THOUGHTS;

This robot would be easily made out of card but I think it is alittle too simple so would not appeal.

6. ADVANTAGES-
- This model is very simple.

DISADVANTAGES-
- This is the 'Robot Wars' logo so fans would know what it is the problem is that it is too simple and not very decorative.
- This has no moving parts.

This idea meats the following in the specification;
- The model must not be too complex to put together.

This idea does not meat the following points in my specification;
- The product should be as original as possible.
- The product may have moving parts.
- The product should look like one of the robots from robot wars. It should resemble either one of the following house robots from robot wars, 'Matilda' or 'Sir Killalot'
- The product should look like one of the robots.

THOUGHTS;

This model would not appeal as it is more like a picture than a model.

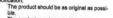

3.5 Martin's analysis and evaluation for his choice of design proposal for the 'Robot Wars' project

Examiner's comments

- Martin has used his analysis to evaluate the suitability of his ideas.

- He has listed the advantages and disadvantages of each design, followed by consideration of the points in his specification that the designs do and do not meet.

- Finally, he writes down his own thoughts.

- The red outlined block of text is Martin's final analysis and justification for his choice of design proposal.

CHECK YOURSELF

Have you:
- Evaluated your ideas objectively?
- Considered each idea's advantages and disadvantages?
- Evaluated your ideas against your design specification?
- Checked that your ideas match your design brief?

The chosen design proposal

- You need to end up with **one** really good design solution. This 'chosen design proposal' needs to be drawn out very carefully on a separate sheet of A3 paper.

- Use *all* your graphic skills to communicate this solution.

- This sheet should have a clear **title** and a **block of text** explaining *why* this is your preferred idea.

Examiner's tips:

- Elsewhere in this book you will find examples of graphic techniques suitable for this presentation drawing. This is the moment to showcase your range of graphic abilities in full and use skill and flair in producing a high-quality piece of work. Ideally, you will also use some CAD to communicate your chosen design proposal fully.

- Your range of graphical techniques may include any combination of the following:

pencil drawing	pencil crayons	marker work
pastel/chalk work	fineline or ballpoint pen	hatching and cross-hatching
thick and thin technique	airbrush work	tonal shading
white crayon and pen	coloured card and paper	grid and patterned paper
freehand	instrument work	orthographic views
perspective	isometric	planometric
exploded views	cut-away views	overlays
photocopied original work	2D and 3D CAD	etc.

This list is not exhaustive.

3.6 *Midori's presentation sheet for her final design solution*

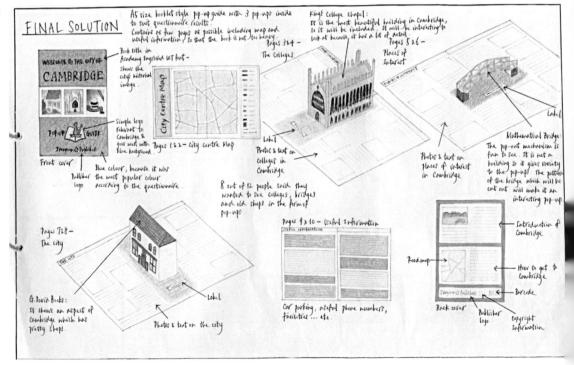

Examiner's comments

* Midori has designed a pop-up guide that features some of the landmarks in Cambridge popular with tourists. The 3D pop-ups are communicated clearly by using accurate pictorial drawings.

* The student has used a range of high-quality graphic techniques and has planned the layout and use of space on the sheet to good effect.

* Clear annotation ensures that an examiner understands what Midori is trying to achieve. This is an extremely effective sheet without having to resort to fancy, coloured borders or shadow mounting.

* Colour is used sparingly to highlight the main features of the product.

CHECK YOURSELF

Have you:

* *Made simple card and paper mock-ups to see what your ideas will look like in three dimensions?*
* *Used these models to justify decisions about size, shape and form?*
* *Photographed and recorded your models?*
* *Explored your ideas using ICT and CAD?*
* *Used CAD to communicate your ideas?*
* *Considered how the ideas could be made and from what materials?*
* *Discarded the weaker designs and selected the most promising design?*
* *Resolved any remaining detail problems?*
* *Fully justified your choice of final design proposal?*
* *Produced a high-quality presentation drawing of your chosen design proposal using a skilful combination of graphic techniques?*
* *Kept your work concise through editing and careful selection of what you include and what you leave out?*
* *Presented your work carefully and logically?*
* *Targeted your work to around four sheets of A3 paper?*

COURSEWORK 4: PRODUCT DEVELOPMENT

SESSION 1 — Test models

- This assessment objective focuses on turning your chosen design proposal into a **product**. It is concerned with **product development and not design development**.

- How are you going to turn your final, chosen idea into a **marketable product**?

- Also, how are you going to turn your final idea into a marketable product that is suitable for **manufacturing in quantity**?

- You must **justify** all your **decisions**. Give **clear reasons** for your choice. Remember: record all your thoughts as diagrams, sketches and notes.

Examiner's tips:

- You will have to make a number of **test models**, as well as **accurate models**, to identify any changes or modifications that need to be made to your design proposals and to ensure that the final product meets the design brief.

- Clear drawings and good communication techniques are vital to ensure that the examiner can follow your work and understand your intentions.

4.1 Nicola's detailed drawings and test models

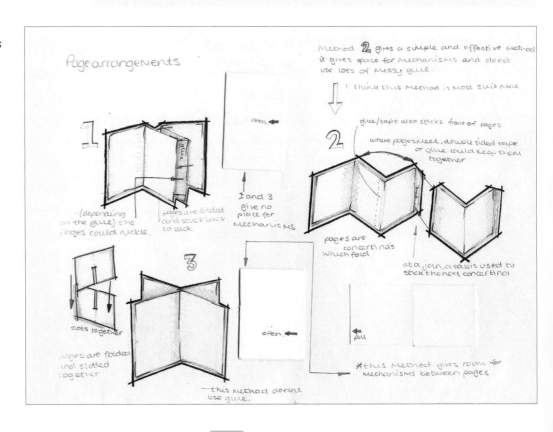

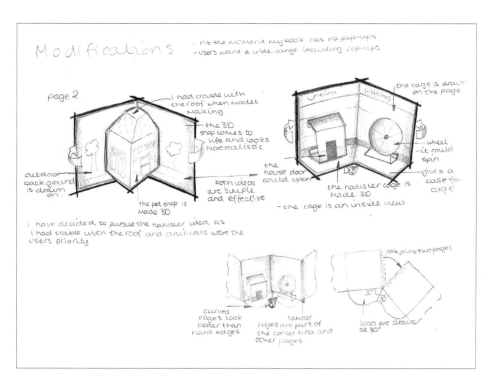

Modifications
— At the moment my book has no pop-ups
— Users want a wide range including pop-ups

page 2

- I had trouble with the roof when model making
- the 3D shop comes to life and looks more realistic

outdoor background is drawn on

the pet shop is made 3D

both ideas are simple and effective

I have decided to pursue the hamster idea as I had trouble with the roof and animals were the users priority

the cage is drawn on the page

Lydia   Writing

- wheel — it could spin

the house door could open

gives a base for cage

the hamster cage is made 3D

- the cage is an inside view

curved edges look better than hard edges

hamster pages are part of the concertina and other pages

tab joins two pages

bases are drawn at 30°

Examiner's comment

• Nicola has produced clear, detailed drawings to explore how her pop-up book is to be manufactured and assembled. It is easy to follow her thoughts.

Examiner's comments

• Investigation and research are still important in product development. Lydia has analysed existing products to work out exactly how her rubber-band-powered pop-up mechanism is to function.

4.2 *Lydia's analysis of existing products*

• Details and accurate dimensions are very important to the success of this mechanism.

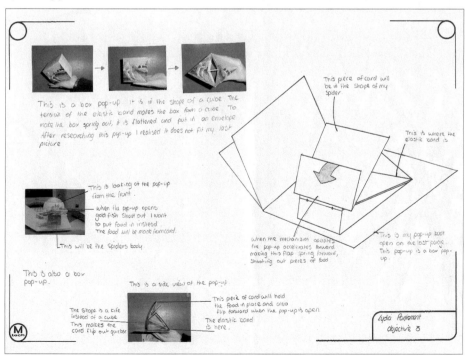

This is a box pop-up. It is in the shape of a cube. The tension of the elastic band makes the box form a cube. To make the box spring out, it is flattened and put in an envelope. After researching this pop-up I realised it does not fit my last picture.

This is looking at the pop-up from the front.
when the pop-up opens goldfish shoot out. I want to put food in instead. The food will be made from card.

This will be the spiders body

This is also a box pop-up.

This is a side view of the pop-up.

The shape is a kite instead of a cube. This makes the cord flip out quicker.

This piece of card will hold the food in place and also flip forward when the pop-up is open. The elastic band is here.

This piece of card will be in the shape of my spider.

This is where the elastic band is

when the mechanism operates the pop-up accelerates forward making this flap spring forward, shooting out pieces of food.

This is my pop-up book open on the last page. This pop-up is a box pop-up.

Lydia Parliament
Objective 3

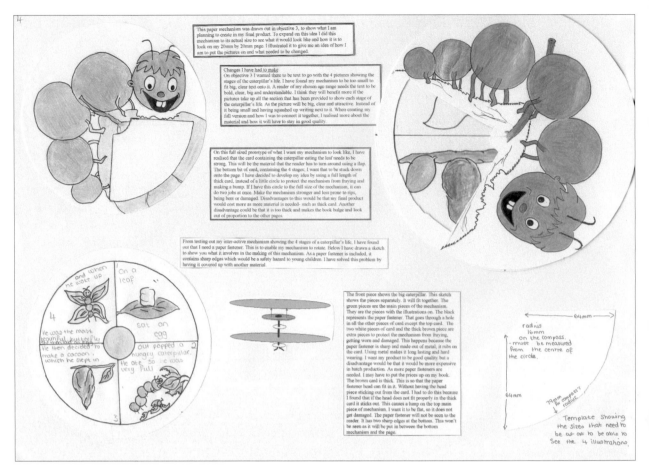

4.3 *Kirsty's working test models*

Examiner's comments

* Kirsty has made accurate working test models. She has designed and used templates to ensure that the mechanisms in her interactive book function properly.

* This work has also given Kirsty the opportunity to trial colour schemes and different graphic techniques.

CHECK YOURSELF

Have you:

* *Considered how your design proposal is to be manufactured?*
* *Considered how your design proposal is to be assembled?*
* *Produced clear drawings and notes to describe the manufacture and assembly?*
* *Produced a range of models to test your design proposal?*
* *Produced a range of part models to check and test details on your design proposal?*

- What are you going to **make** your prototype product out of?
- What are the **most suitable materials** for your prototype product?
- **How** is your prototype product going to be **made**?

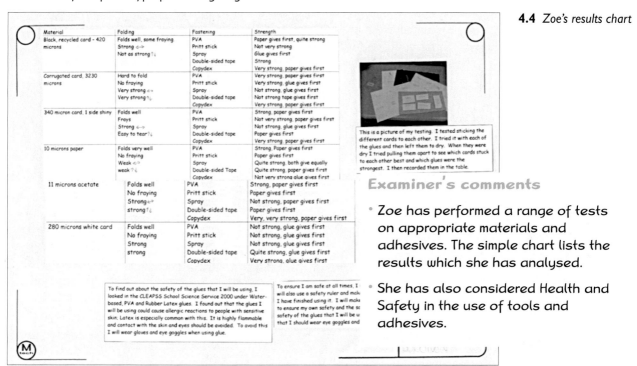

4.4 Zoe's results chart

Material	Folding	Fastening	Strength
Black, recycled card - 420 microns	Folds well, some fraying Strong ←→ Not as strong ↑↓	PVA Pritt stick Spray Double-sided tape Copydex	Paper gives first, quite strong Not very strong Glue gives first Strong Very strong, paper gives first
Corrugated card, 3230 microns	Hard to fold No fraying Very strong ←→ Very strong ↑↓	PVA Pritt stick Spray Double-sided tape Copydex	Very strong, paper gives first Very strong, glue gives first Very strong, glue gives first Not strong tape gives first Very strong, paper gives first
340 micron card, 1 side shiny	Folds well Frays Strong ←→ Easy to tear ↑↓	PVA Pritt stick Spray Double-sided tape Copydex	Strong, paper gives first Not very strong, paper gives first Not strong, glue gives first Paper gives first Very strong, paper gives first
10 microns paper	Folds very well No fraying Weak ←→ weak ↑↓	PVA Pritt stick Spray Double-sided Tape Copydex	Strong, Paper gives first Paper gives first Quite strong, both glue equally Quite strong, paper gives first Not very strong glue gives first
11 microns acetate	Folds well No fraying Strong←→ strong↑↓	PVA Pritt stick Spray Double-sided tape Copydex	Strong, paper gives first Paper gives first Not strong, paper gives first Paper gives first Very, very strong, paper gives first
280 microns white card	Folds well No fraying Strong strong	PVA Pritt stick Spray Double-sided tape Copydex	Not strong, glue gives first Not strong, glue gives first Not strong, glue gives first Quite strong, glue gives first Very strong, glue gives first

This is a picture of my testing. I tested sticking the different cards to each other. I tried it with each of the glues and then left them to dry. When they were dry I tried pulling them apart to see which cards stuck to each other best and which glues were the strongest. I then recorded them in the table.

To find out about the safety of the glues that I will be using, I looked in the CLEAPSS School Science Service 2000 under Water-based, PVA and Rubber Latex glues. I found out that the glues I will be using could cause allergic reactions to people with sensitive skin. Latex is especially common with this. It is highly flammable and contact with the skin and eyes should be avoided. To avoid this I will wear gloves and eye goggles when using glue.

To ensure I am safe at all times, I will also use a safety ruler and mak I have finished using it. I will mak to ensure my own safety and the sa safety of the glues that I will be u that I should wear eye goggles and

Examiner's comments

- Zoe has performed a range of tests on appropriate materials and adhesives. The simple chart lists the results which she has analysed.

- She has also considered Health and Safety in the use of tools and adhesives.

Examiner's comments

- Sarah has considered and tested how she is going to apply colour and texture to her design.

- She discusses industrial processes and ICT as well as hand-produced work.

- Both Zoe and Sarah have produced concise work that is clearly focused on what is appropriate for their products. Zoe (4.4) has resisted the misguided temptation to glue lots of samples of materials onto her page: one simple photograph is sufficient. Sarah (4.5) has covered a range of industrial processes without copying from a text book or adding printed materials.

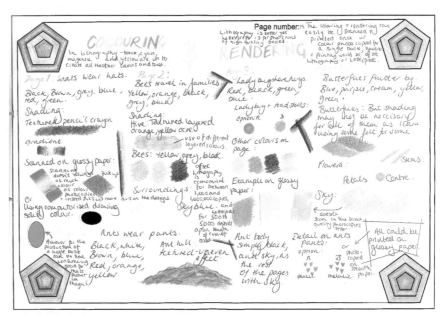

4.5 Sarah's results after testing materials

- Start by exploring what materials are **available** to you in school.
  - Which ones are **appropriate** to your product?
  - Will you have to consider **ordering specific materials** to produce your prototype product? How long will this take, and what is the likely cost?
  - Will you have to **compromise**?
- Collect samples. **Analyse** them. You will need to show that you have **tested** the materials before making a final decision about their **suitability** for your product. This could simply be a matter of making **models** to evaluate, analyse and justify which material is **right for the job.**

4.6 The results of Lydia's further investigation and analysis

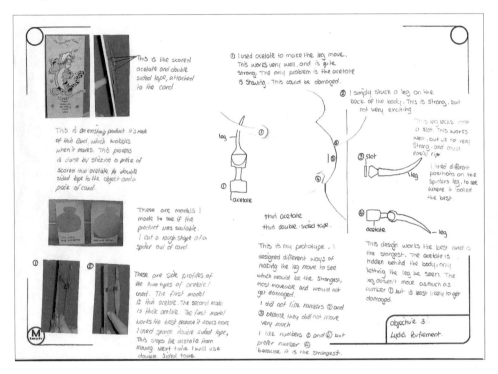

Examiner's comments

- Lydia has carried out more investigation and analysis to find out which was the best material to give her spider character 'wobbly legs'. The detail photograph shows how she incorporated card and acetate sheet in a test model to help justify her final decision.

- An examiner will want to see how you have ensured that your product will meet your design brief. Accurate, careful modelling and testing is important to ensure that you identify any changes or modifications that need to be made to your design proposal. The further research, testing and analysis shown in 4.6, along with accurate, high-quality modelling, are worth a great deal of credit.

- Ask yourself **questions** about the materials you are testing and record your answers and **decisions**. For example:
  - Does it fold/score/cut well?
  - Does the material take colour/inks/printing etc. well?
  - Which adhesive or joining method is most suitable?
- Take photographs; keep your models.
- When thinking about materials, tools, equipment and adhesives, don't forget **safety**.
  - What **tools and equipment** are you going to use?
  - What **processes** will you be using?
  - What other **resources** are available in your school? Check with your teacher.

CHECK YOURSELF

Have you:

- *Carried out further research and analysis work when required?*
- *Explored materials, tools and equipment available to you?*
- *Tested the suitability of these items for the manufacture of your prototype product?*
- *Tested the suitability of materials through modelling?*
- *Tested the suitability of adhesives and/or joining methods through modelling?*
- *Recorded the results of these tests?*
- *Justified your choice of materials, tools and equipment?*
- *Considered and analysed how your product could be manufactured in quantity?*
- *Designed and produced any templates, jigs or moulds required?*
- *Tested, evaluated and modified any template, jig or mould produced?*
- *Highlighted and overcome any Health and Safety concerns?*

SESSION 3 — Selecting an appropriate production method

Examiner's tips:

- Many candidates overlook the fact that as part of your product development you will need to test and evaluate the most suitable production methods for the manufacture of your prototype product. This will involve finding out about tools, equipment and processes.

- You will have to simulate, as closely as possible, industrial production processes and show evidence that you understand what effect this could have on your prototype product.

- This will also mean that you have to understand and use quality assurance and quality control.

Help!

- You will **not** be expected to **make** your prototype product using industrial processes — you are very lucky if your school has the facilities to do this! However, you must be able to **understand and apply** industrial and commercial production techniques to the development of your product. The only way this can be achieved in most schools is to simulate industrial production processes. How this is achieved depends very much on which exam board's course you are following (see below).

- **Quality assurance** is about making sure that mistakes will be avoided and that processes will perform as intended. Quality assurance uses control systems that are active before making takes place. **Quality control** is using some form of system to check the quality and accuracy of the product **during production**, at key stages in the manufacturing process known as **critical control points**.

AQA

- You will need to show that you understand and can apply a wide variety of industrial and commercial techniques and processes to the development and manufacture of your prototype product.

- You must show that you have considered which industrial production processes would be most suitable for your product if your prototype were to go into quantity manufacture.

- You will need to show evidence of having a thorough understanding of the range of manufacturing processes available and justify why you feel that the one you have chosen is most appropriate.

OCR

- You will need to show how a small batch of your product would be made using school based technologies, while simulating an industrial process.

- How can you make more than one product while controlling the quality and consistency of the product? In other words, how can you ensure that the products are all manufactured to the *same degree of accuracy*?

- You must show that you have carefully designed and made any templates, jigs or moulds that you intend to use.

- You do not have to manufacture the whole of your product using your control system; one component made this way is sufficient for you to gain high marks.

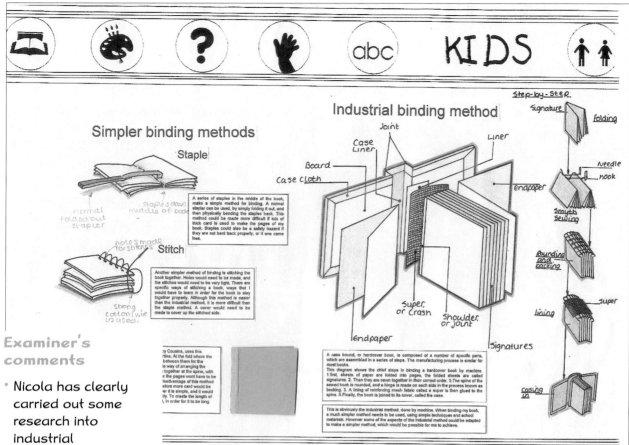

Simpler binding methods

Staple

normal foldabout stapler

staples down middle of book

A series of staples in the middle of the book make a simple method for binding. A normal stapler can be used, by simply folding it out, and then physically bending the staples back. This method could be made more difficult if lots of thick card is used to make the pages of any book. Staples could also be a safety hazard if they are not bent back properly, or if one came lose.

Stitch

holes made for stitches

strong cotton / wire is used.

Another simpler method of binding is stitching the book together. Holes would need to be made, and the stitches would need to be very tight. There are specific ways of stitching a book, ways that I would have to learn in order for the book to stay together properly. Although this method is easier than the industrial method, it is more difficult than the staple method. A cover would need to be made to cover up the stitched side.

Industrial binding method

Joint, Case Liner, Board, Case Cloth, Super or Crash, Shoulder or joint, Endpaper, Liner, Endpaper, Signatures

Step-by-step: Signature, folding, Needle, hook, Smyth Sewing, Rounding and backing, Super, lining, casing in

A case bound, or hardcover book, is composed of a number of specific parts, which are assembled in a series of steps. The manufacturing process is similar for most books.
This diagram shows the chief steps in binding a hardcover book by machine. 1.first, sheets of paper are folded into pages, the folded sheets are called signatures. 2. Then they are sewn together in their correct order. 3.The spine of the sewed book is rounded, and a hinge is made on each side in the process known as backing. 3. A lining of reinforcing mesh fabric called a super is then glued to the spine. 5.Finally, the book is joined to its cover, called the case.

This is obviously the industrial method, done by machine. When binding my book, a much simpler method needs to be used, using simple techniques and school materials. However some of the aspects of the industrial method could be adapted to make a simpler method, which would be possible for me to achieve.

4.6 *Nicola's research into industrial bookbinding processes*

Examiner's comments

- Nicola has clearly carried out some research into industrial bookbinding processes. She uses high-quality drawings and notes to communicate her findings. She has simulated the industrial process using a small model to test how this can be achieved in school (orange card).

- This high-quality graphic work shows a good understanding of the link between industrial processes and how they can be simulated in school with the technologies available.

- Will your product need any **manufactured items** in its construction? Where will you get these from? What is their cost? You will need to show that you have tested and analysed these items and give **clear reasons** justifying your decisions.

- Plan and produce a **flow chart** to show the stages of production for your product. Try to include **sub-assemblies** where appropriate. You must include **quality control** stages and **feedback loops**.

- Clearly show and state **all modifications** that you make to your design proposal throughout this assessment objective. Then, together with the information that you have uncovered and the final decisions you have made, write a final **product specification** of your prototype product.

- Produce clear and accurate **dimensioned drawings**, by hand or using CAD, of your final prototype product.

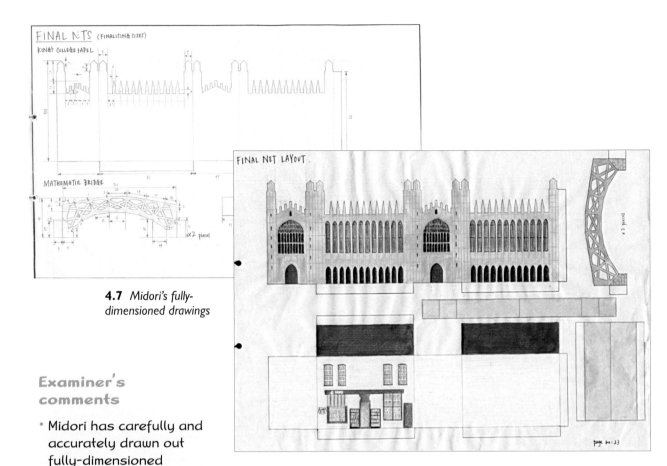

4.7 *Midori's fully-dimensioned drawings*

Examiner's comments

- Midori has carefully and accurately drawn out fully-dimensioned drawings for the nets that form part of the mechanisms for her pop-up visitor's guide.

- Accurate drawings **must** form part of your work at the end of this assessment objective. They can provide a 'blueprint' for making your product.

- This is a further example of excellent graphic abilities being demonstrated through the rendering of details on the final coloured nets for Midori's guide book. Examiners will expect to see graphic skills learnt during the course used throughout the project.

CHECK YOURSELF

Have you:

- *Produced a flowchart with sub-assemblies and feedback loops to control the manufacture of your product?*
- *Considered quality assurance and quality control?*
- *Used ICT and CAD to test, model and communicate your design proposal?*
- *Checked your design proposal against the design brief and design specification, and recorded any modifications made?*
- *Produced a set of final, accurate, fully-dimensioned drawings?*
- *Considered the consequences of high-volume production on your product?*
- *Reviewed all your work and considered the accuracy of your original design specification?*
- *Produced a final product specification to incorporate any changes?*
- *Kept your work concise through editing and careful selection of what you include and what you leave out?*
- *Presented your work carefully and logically?*
- *Targeted your work around four sheets of A3 paper?*

COURSEWORK 5: PLANNING AND MAKING

- The key to scoring highly in this assessment objective ultimately relies on two aspects:
  - thorough planning
  - high quality making.

SESSION 1 — Planning

Examiner's tips:

- Remember that your focus is on planning the making of a high-quality prototype graphic product suitable for presenting to a client for testing and evaluating.

- Make sure that you produce your planning work before you start making!

- Use a range of appropriate methods to show how you have planned each stage of the production of your prototype.

- Careful, detailed planning is more likely to produce a high-quality graphic product.

- Start by making a **plan of action** based upon **time deadlines**. Think carefully how you can best divide up your time to gain the highest possible score. Check out the **Gantt chart** that is shown on page 11; Gantt charts are very useful for planning efficient use of time.

  - Make a thorough and detailed list of all the **materials** you will need. Make sure that you include all dimensions, in particular: **length x width x thickness.**

  - List all **manufactured items** that you may be using. Give all the relevant details.

  - List all the **equipment**, **tools** and **machines** that you will be using. Make sure you find out the correct names for these items.

  - List and **explain** all of the **processes** that you will be using to manufacture your prototype.

  - Explain **how and where** tools and processes are to be used.

  - Don't forget to include the use of **CAM** wherever possible.

  - Carry out a **risk assessment** to identify all the possible **safety hazards** that you may encounter.

  - Give complete details of how you will **overcome** all Health and Safety issues.

- Now you must put all the points that you have identified above into an **order of work**.

- This must be a **logical sequence** of stages that you will follow to make your prototype product.

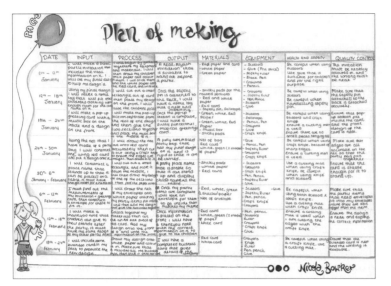

5.1 Nicola's planning

- Nicola has divided up her time into weekly slots and then produced a chart that clearly sets out the activities planned for each week.

- Each column identifies a particular set of activities, the final column being Quality Control.

- It is a good idea to leave sufficient space within the plan to be able to add notes and comments as you progress. An annotated plan that you have clearly used is far more interesting to an examiner.

- Some form of **block process diagram** is useful to help plot out each stage of your manufacturing process.

- Flowcharts are not really suitable for this work as they cannot contain sufficient detail.

5.2 Zoe's plan of action

Examiner's comments

- Zoe has produced a block flow diagram to provide an overview of the manufacture of her product. Each stage is quite clearly described as part of a logical sequence.

- She has included the use of her control system within the appropriate stages, as well as the use of ICT to aid manufacture.

- Using ICT to produce a plan of action enables you to structure the statements, as well as add details and correct errors quickly and easily.

- Logical sequences can also be communicated concisely and clearly through the use of **annotated storyboards**.

- It is another way that you can show off your **graphic skills** to the examiner. Annotated storyboards allow you to **explain** each stage quickly without using lots of text – brief notes, labels and bullet points are sufficient.

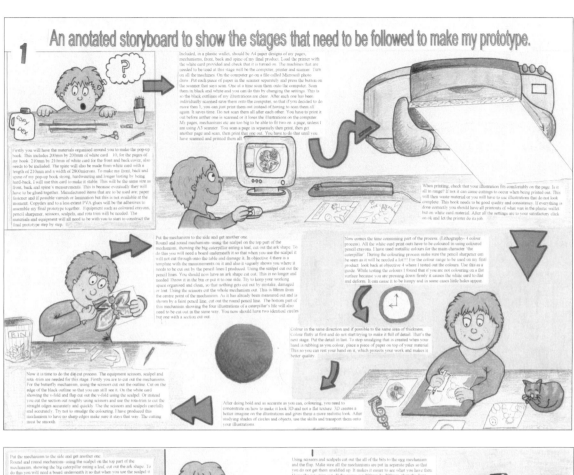

- As well as a plan of action with time deadlines, Kirsty also produced this illustrated and very detailed storyboard to communicate the stages in the production of her prototype.
  It covers every aspect of planning, marking out, making and assembling her product.

- Although this is excellent work, simple but clear line-drawings could have been used to communicate the stages and processes just as well – and would have been worth a similar mark.

■ However you plan the manufacture of your product, you must try to cover **every point**.

■ A good check is to imagine giving your planning work plus a pile of materials to a complete stranger. Would they be able to manufacture **your product** following your planning work only?

CHECK YOURSELF

Have you:
- *Produced a time plan that includes deadlines?*
- *Annotated and **used** your time plan?*
- *Listed all the materials you will need with full dimensions?*
- *Listed all manufactured items that you will need?*
- *Listed all the equipment, tools and machines that you will be using?*
- *Listed and explained the processes you will be using?*
- *Explained how and where tools and processes are to be used?*
- *Planned how you can use CAM to manufacture part of your product?*
- *Carried out a risk assessment of all your planned processes?*
- *Identified and overcome all safety hazards?*
- *Produced an order of work that is in a logical sequence?*
- *Used block flow or process diagrams with sub-assemblies identified?*
- *Produced a clear storyboard to guide manufacture?*

Examiner's tips:

- Your priority is to make a high-quality product.
- You must show that you can work with skill and care to a high standard.
- You must use tools and equipment accurately and safely.

- You will need to prove to the examiner that you have:
  - been resourceful and adaptable
  - worked independently and safely.
- You will need to keep an illustrated record of your making that you can use as evidence. This record will also help you to evaluate your product.

5.4 *Kirsty's final prototype product*

Examiner's comments

- Kirsty's final prototype product is a high-quality, fully functioning pop-up book based on the lifecycle of a caterpillar. All of the mechanisms function as intended and the product is now ready for testing and evaluation.

- Careful, detailed planning enabled this to be a successful project.

- Your first task is to mark out and prepare your materials **economically**. This is an environmental consideration to avoid waste. You will need to show evidence of how you have carried this out.

- Keep an **illustrated production diary** as you make your product. Nothing fancy, just something where you can jot down **what** you did and **when**; somewhere you can add **photographs and sketches** as you go along to help record your making.

- Use the diary to note any **problems** that you may have with your 'making'. **Be honest.** Show how you **overcame** these problems, perhaps how you **adapted** your plan of action and order of work. **Record** all **changes** that you may have to make. Ensure that you **refer** to them in your evaluation.

- Your production diary should prove that you are **resourceful and adaptable**. Use it to show that you can work **independently** and **safely**.

- Include this production diary in your project folio for assessment. *It is worth a lot of marks!*

- **Don't** write it up neatly! Examiners will expect to see **working documents** with rough notes and thumbnail sketches. They will be **suspicious** of 'squeaky-clean', beautifully presented diaries.

SUCCESSFUL GRAPHIC PRODUCTS 3D WORK

These projects were produced by GCSE Graphic Products students. All of these prototypes were assessed as being high-quality products.

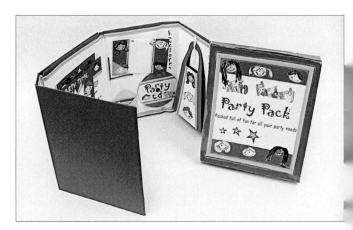

Charlotte's range of products for a vegetarian fast-food outlet

Nicola's exciting and vibrant activity-filled party pack suitable for young children

Rachel's rubber-band-powered pop-up point-of-sale display stand for cosmetics, to be distributed as a flat-pack

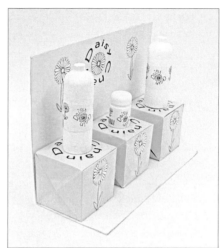

Ryan's packaging and model for an MP3 player. Note how he has simulated embossed lettering with letters cut out from self-adhesive vinyl using CAM and then coating with spray paint.

Detail from Zoe's pop-up book that shows the mechanism she adapted and modified to make the two figures appear to dance when the tab is pulled. She had to combine a number of materials to achieve this.

CHECK YOURSELF

Have you:

- *Economically marked out and prepared your materials?*
- *Kept an illustrated production diary?*
- *Recorded your progress and included photographs and sketches?*
- *Noted any problems encountered and how you overcame them?*
- *Noted any modifications made to the plan of action and order of work?*
- *Provided evidence that you have been resourceful and adaptable?*
- *Provided evidence that you can work independently and safely?*
- *Worked to the best of your ability?*
- *Demonstrated creativity and flair?*
- *Demonstrated skill and attention to detail?*
- *Demonstrated that you have pride in your work?*
- *Produced a high-quality graphic product?*
- *Presented your work carefully and logically?*
- *Targeted your folder work to around three sheets of A3 paper?*

Examiner's tips:

* Leave yourself sufficient time to carry this out properly. Tests take time to plan and design, as well as the time they take to carry out and evaluate.

* Remember that you are testing and evaluating your prototype product – *not reviewing or evaluating your project*.

* If you have kept a detailed production diary while manufacturing your prototype product, you will find this section much easier to complete.

---

* The emphasis in this final assessment objective is on testing your **final product.**
* Does it do what you intended it to do?
* Does it answer the design brief and the final product specification?

■ Start off by checking your prototype product against your brief and final product specification. Write out your specification again (easy if you used ICT and saved it) and answer each point in turn.

■ Clearly note **any changes** that you have had to make – and **give reasons**.

■ Be critical. Give praise where it is due. But above all, be **honest**.

■ Examiners like to see a **balanced** evaluation.

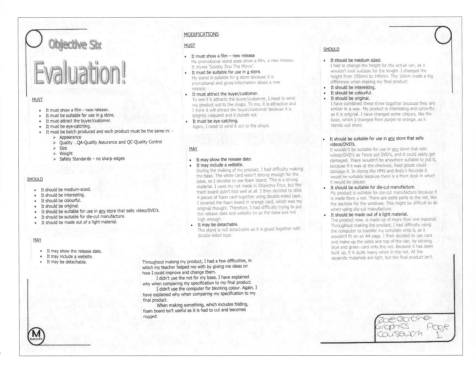

6.1 *Zoe's evaluation*

Examiner's comments

* Zoe has reprinted the whole of her specification before selecting those points where she has a comment to make. Here she has highlighted her comments by using blue ink – simple, but clear and effective.

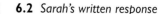

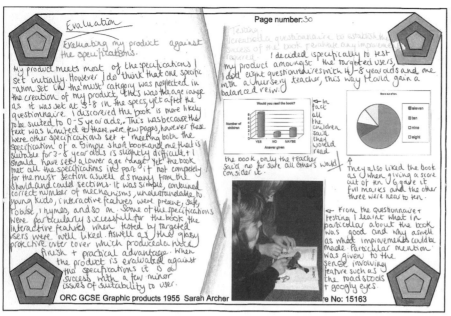

ORC GCSE Graphic products 1955 Sarah Archer

Examiner's comments

* Sarah has written her response to her specification as part of a block of text down the left half of the sheet. It is not so easy to pick out the points she is trying to make.

* Note the small graphs from a questionnaire and the photograph of users with her product.

■ How well did you use the **resources** available to you when manufacturing your product? Did you use them **appropriately**?

■ You should include some **statements** about the following resources:
  • time
  • materials
  • tools
  • equipment
  • processes
  • production methods.

■ You must show **clear evidence** that you have carried out **detailed testing** of your prototype product. These tests must be **planned carefully** because your target is to arrive at some **meaningful conclusions** about your product.

■ These conclusions should include possible **modifications or improvements** to your product – or highlight a need for **further development**.

■ **Evidence of testing** may be in the form of photographs, questionnaires, charts and tables, written statements from users, experts or other professionals, and so on.

Examiner's tips:

* **Don't** use your friends or family when testing your product. You must have an *objective response* to help you in your analysis and evaluation if you are to score highly. Use a real client, if possible – and let them evaluate the project.

* Try to ensure that any testing has *depth* and is not superficial. Try to be *professional* when planning and carrying out your testing.

When making my product, there were areas that I thought went well, and areas that could be improved in some way. Below, are areas, which went well and some, which need improvement:

> **Time:** I didn't use my time wisely, apart from at the beginning of the course. As it was something new, it was interesting and different, although I have enjoyed doing the project. Now, I regret not using my time properly as there was a lot of work involved in the making and planning. If I did the project again, I would split up each objective and set myself deadlines.

> **Materials:** I think I used the materials well, as I drew everything out as near to the edge as possible. By doing this, I would be saving the materials, which could be used again. For most of the project, I needed the spare material, so instead of getting a new sheet, I used what was left.
I don't think I used the foam board well, as I didn't test it out before making the product. Therefore, I wasted a bit of the material, as I didn't know the properties of it before hand.

> **Equipment:** I used the equipment well and I was safe when using it. When using a scalpel, I pointed it downwards when moving around the room, and I always used a safety mat and ruler.
I cut the materials on the guillotine from right to left to avoid my work being ripped.
I also walked around with scissors pointing downwards to avoid being harming others.

> **Production Methods:** Throughout making my product, I think it went quite well. In areas, I think I hurried to try and finish it. I realised I would make a mess of it if I didn't take my time and look at what I was doing. Luckily, I noticed this at the beginning of the making process.

> **Extra Help:** During the making, I required help off my teacher, because I didn't understand parts or I needed help. For the majority of the time, I worked independently, to show I can work on my own and that I will try and found out information for myself.

Testing out my product

When I completed my product, I did a detailed test, to see if I could see any problems.

While looking at my product I found out that:

> There were gaps where the tabs were. To control this next time, I would make the tabs bigger so it is easier to stick together. Trying to stick it together while the tabs were small was difficult, and I required help off a friend.
> The parts stuck down on the net (sides and top) were beginning to come apart when I put it together as it curved. To make it look more presentable, I used double-sided tape to stick down the parts that weren't.

The two problems above were the only main problems that I found on my final product.

Before making my product, I made a template to ensure the sides of the van were equal. The template was originally made to transfer the shape onto the computer. I thought using the computer would be easy to do for transferring it but I soon realised that the shape didn't fit onto A4. As I had difficulties transferring the shape onto the computer, it was used to get the right shapes for the blue and green card. If I could of used the computer, it would have been a lot easier, but because I did it by hand, it was difficult to get the shapes correct. If I could improve in this area, I would make sure the sides fir onto A4 so it could be done on a computer. By doing this, the quality of my product would increase by a large amount.

Throughout doing this project, I have enjoyed it a lot. It has given me the chance to try something new, and use materials and equipment I have never used before.
If I did the project again, I would try something new, so I can learn a wider range of skills.

Above, is the van in which I did on the computer. As you can see, it didn't work, as the van wouldn't fit onto A4, even when the print options were changed.

Tabs need to be bigger, too small for constructing product.

Zoe Gardine
Graphics   Page
Coursework   2

To see what others thought of my product, I have made a questionnaire to see if it is suitable to be used in a store. I have included photographs when sending to a store.
My results are shown by pie charts.

The questions I will use in my questionnaire are:

> Looking at my product for the first time, what do you initially think of my product?
> Looking at my product carefully, what would you give it out of 10 (1 = poor, 10=excellent)?
> How much would you pay for the stand?
> Would you buy the stand for yourself/the store?
> To you, is the stand of (a high quality ----> poor quality)?
> If you could change the stand to how you would like it, how many areas would you change?

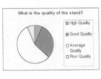

Zoe Gardine
Graphics   Page
Coursework   3

6.3 *Zoe has used ICT to produce her evaluation*

- Make sure that you produce **sketches** and **accurate detailed drawings** to communicate your proposals for modifying your product after you have completed your testing. Don't just write about them. Use ICT and CAD to help you.

- You must show that you have thought about and evaluated your chosen **system** to control manufacture. For example: did you use a template, jig or mould? How did it **perform**? Did it do what you **expected** it to? Was it **easy to use**? What **problems** did you encounter/overcome?

- Could you **improve** this control system? Or **develop or modify** it to make it **easier** to use? Or to improve the **quality** of your product?

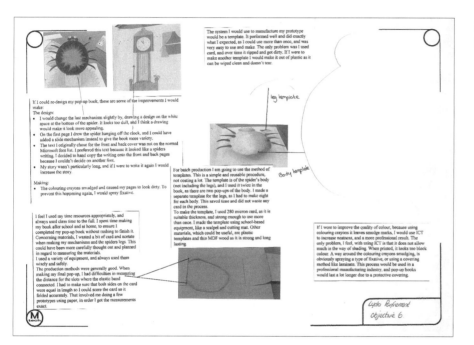

6.4 Lydia's detailed evidence of testing and evaluation

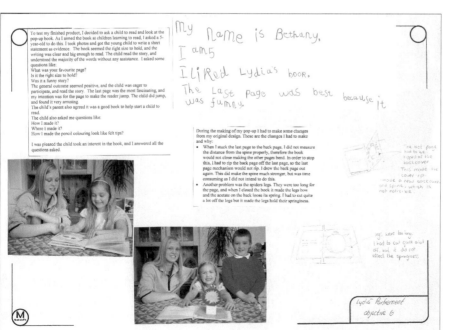

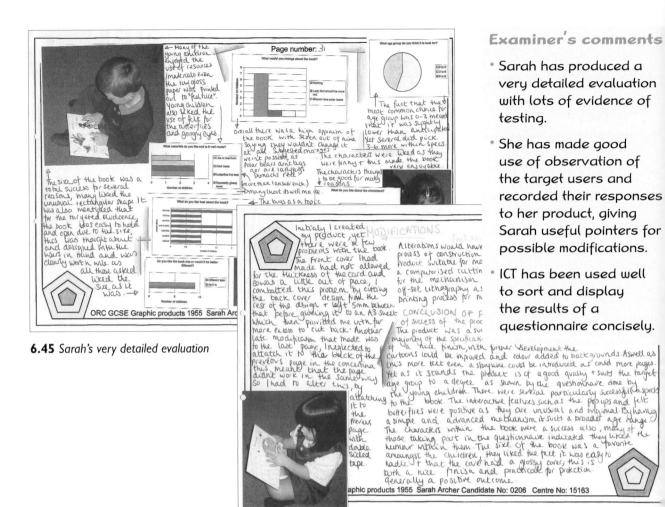

6.45 *Sarah's very detailed evaluation*

• Sarah has produced a very detailed evaluation with lots of evidence of testing.

• She has made good use of observation of the target users and recorded their responses to her product, giving Sarah useful pointers for possible modifications.

• ICT has been used well to sort and display the results of a questionnaire concisely.

CHECK YOURSELF

Have you:

• Compared your final prototype product with your final product specification?

• Compared your product point by point and analysed how well it answers the design brief and the specification?

• Reviewed your production diary and recorded and evaluated any changes made?

• Reviewed your use of resources?

• Carefully planned a range of tests for your product?

• Tested your product with the target user(s)/user group(s)?

• Observed your target users using your product?

• Interviewed your target users?

• Produced photographic evidence of testing?

• Annotated this photographic evidence?

• Produced carefully planned questionnaires?

• Carefully analysed the results of these questionnaires?

• Reviewed your system to control production?

• Analysed the effectiveness of this system?

• Suggested how this system could be improved?

• Produced annotated sketches and detailed drawings to show suggestions for further development of your prototype product?

• Kept your work concise through editing and careful selection of what you include and what you leave out?

• Presented your work carefully and logically?

• Targeted your work to around three sheets of A3 paper?

UNIT 1: TOOLS AND EQUIPMENT

REVISION SESSION 1 — ■ Using drawing equipment ■

You will need to be familiar with using the following range of drawing equipment in order to produce accurate drawings and illustrations. Reference will be made to the specific use of drawing equipment at various points throughout this revision guide.

1.1 Drawing equipment

✎ A3 drawing board and T-square

■ You can fix paper to the board using masking tape or clips. You can then draw horizontal parallel lines by moving the T-square up and down the board.

✎ Set squares

■ You should use these in conjunction with a drawing board and T-square to draw accurate specific angles. The two most common forms are:
- 90 degree–45 degree–45 degree set square
- 90 degree–60 degree–30 degree set square.

✎ Protractor

■ Angles can be measured and drawn to an accuracy of 1 degree using a protractor.

✎ Pair of compasses

■ You need to use these to draw accurate circles and arcs. A pair of compasses that holds a pencil are adequate for most purposes, but the type with its own lead is generally more accurate.

✎ 300 mm rule

■ Try to use this length of rule rather than the shorter versions which are available. Measurements to an accuracy of 1 millimetre can be made using a good-quality rule. In exams, it is common to allow a small tolerance on lengths and angles that you are required to measure or draw.

✎ Pencils

■ You can use a 2B pencil for shading and toning a drawing, while a 2H pencil is better for construction and fine detail lines. A compromise would be to use a sharp HB pencil for both purposes.

> **⚡ A* EXTRA**
>
> You should have your own drawing equipment. Check with your teacher exactly what equipment you will need. **Do not** rely on only using a rule and pencil. Make sure that you know what equipment to use in a given situation. Where accurate drawings are required, make sure that you fix the question paper down using clips or tape.

> **💡 QUESTION SPOTTER**
>
> ▶ Make sure you read the questions carefully, as not all of them will require you to use drawing instruments.
> ▶ If only the word 'draw' is used, this means you are required to use appropriate drawing equipment.
> ▶ If the question says 'draw freehand' or 'sketch', then the answer can be done without using drawing instruments.

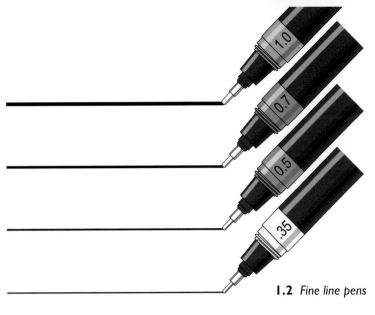

Fine line pens

- You can use these for sketching, outlining and enhancing drawings. It is useful to have a range of nib thickness (e.g. 0.35, 0.5 and 0.7 – see Figure 1.2). Try to have at least one 'thick' (0.7) and one 'thin' (0.3) pen which you keep just for your graphics work.

Eraser

- A good quality soft white pencil eraser will help you to correct errors quickly.

1.2 *Fine line pens*

CHECK YOURSELF – EXAM QUESTION

1 The freehand sketch below shows a route plan for a train journey between Aberdeen and London Kings Cross.

On leaving Aberdeen the train passes through Dundee, Edinburgh, Newcastle, Durham, Darlington, York, Doncaster, Newark, Peterborough and Stevenage before arriving at London Kings Cross.

(a) Using instruments, draw the route plan. The small dots can be drawn freehand. *(4 marks)*

(b) Add the names of **four** of the places that the train passes through. Marks will be awarded for careful printing. *(4 marks)*

■ Using drafting aids ■

If you use appropriate drafting aids you can often speed up the production of a drawing and improve its accuracy.

✎ Circle template

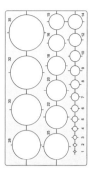

■ This is particularly useful when drawing small circles or where only part of a circle (an arc) is needed (e.g. when rounding the corners of a shape). A template with circle diameters from 3 mm up to 30 mm (Figure 1.3) is adequate as larger sizes can be easily drawn with a pair of compasses.

1.3 *Circle template*

✎ Ellipse template

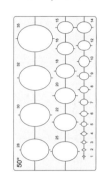

■ Using this type of template can make the drawing of circles on an **isometric view** straight forward. A template with sizes between 2 mm and 50 mm (Figure 1.4) would be the most useful. These sizes relate to the diameter of a circle which becomes an ellipse when drawn on an isometric view.

1.4 *Ellipse template*

✎ Flexi curve

■ This consists of a plastic strip with a lead and steel core (Figure 1.5). It can be bent to form awkward curves. It is useful, for example, for joining the plotted points when drawing a large ellipse.

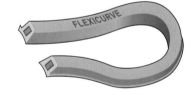

✎ French curves

■ These are made from rigid plastic and enable a range of curves to be drawn (Figure 1.6). They can be useful when drawing ellipses and curves which otherwise might have to be drawn freehand.

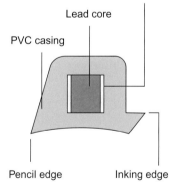

Steel springs

Lead core

PVC casing

Pencil edge   Inking edge

1.5 *Flexi curve*

1.6 *French curves*

2   Use the information given in the freehand sketch below to draw the information sign.

The sign should be drawn full size, using instruments.

Centres for the arcs must be shown clearly.   *(9 marks)*

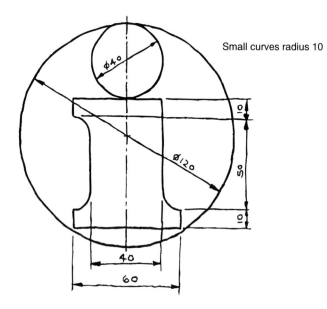

Small curves radius 10

Hints:
It would be useful to have a circle template to use when drawing the three radius 10 curves. Grids are often printed on the papers as an aid to candidates.

Using colouring media

Colour is an essential factor in the successful design of graphic products. You must to able to use colouring media to enhance drawings.

✎ Coloured pencils

- These offer one of the cheapest and easiest ways of applying colour to your work. In general, you will find the most useful range of colours to have is red, yellow, blue (the primary colours), green, orange, purple (the secondary colours), black and white.

- You can easily get different **tones** (light and dark) using pencils. Not pressing very hard on the pencil gives a light tone, while a darker tone can be obtained by applying more pressure.

✎ Marker pens

- Coloured felt markers come in two main forms: water based and spirit based. While the water-based type are cheaper, spirit markers generally give the best results (Figure 1.7). These markers require a lot of practice to achieve high quality results.

- Almost all of the colour work that you will be required to do in the timed exam can be carried out using pencils.

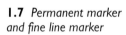

1.7 *Permanent marker and fine line marker*

CHECK YOURSELF – EXAM QUESTION

3 The specification for a logo, to be used by a holiday company called Sun Tours, is given below.

SPECIFICATION

The logo should:
(1) include the name Sun Tours
(2) include the symbol shown right (size may vary from that given)
(3) use **two** colours to suggest heat and sunshine.

Draw good quality sketches of two possible logo designs.

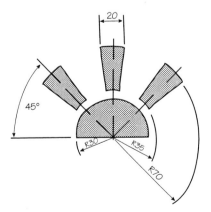

(10 marks)

Using tools and equipment for model making

You will need to be familiar with using the following tools and equipment to make two-dimensional (2D) and three-dimensional (3D) models and products.

✎ Scissors

■ There are two main types: double point scissors and round tip safety scissors. Both types are suitable for cutting paper and thin card.

✎ Craft knives

■ You should use these (Figure 1.8) in conjunction with a safety rule and cutting mat. In general, a craft knife will give a more accurate cut than scissors but is more dangerous to use. In addition to paper and thin card, a craft knife will also cut thick card and boards, including **foamboard**. On thicker materials, make several strokes with the knife rather than trying to cut through in one go.

1.8 *Craft knives*

✎ Safety rule

■ This type of rule (Figure 1.9) enables straight lines to be cut safely using a craft knife. The top of the rule helps you to hold it firmly while keeping your fingers away from the blade of the knife.

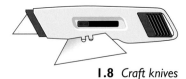

1.9 *Safety rule*

✎ Cutting mat

■ These non-slip mats (Figure 1.10) provide a good surface for all cutting work using a craft knife or circle cutter. The surface literally heals itself when cut.

1.10 *Cutting mats are made of alternate layers of soft and hard PVC*

✎ Circle cutter

■ You should use one of these (Figure 1.11) to cut precise circles in paper, thin card and foamboard. It is used in the same way as a pair of compasses.

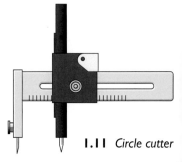

1.11 *Circle cutter*

✎ Perforation cutter

- You should use this (Figure 1.12) to create a perforated line. Perforating involves making a series of small cuts along a fold line to release tension in the paper or card. This allows it to fold and flex more easily.

1.12 *Perforation cutter*

CHECK YOURSELF – EXAM QUESTION

4 A school is to hold a fund-raising day.

It will take place on the school field where six stalls and an events area will be set up.

Each person working on the refreshment stall is to wear a T-shirt with either a DRINK logo or a FOOD logo on it.

The logo designs are to be applied to the T-shirts with the aid of stencils.

(a) State the name of a suitable material for the stencil and explain your choice. *(2 marks)*

(b) In order to make the stencil:

Hint: As the stencil needs to be used at least 20 times, paper or card would not be suitable.

    (i) list the tools and equipment required *(2 marks)*

    (ii) use sketches and notes to explain the processes used. *(6 marks)*

(c) In order to locate the stencil on the T-shirt and apply the design:

    (i) list the tools and equipment required *(2 marks)*

    (ii) use sketches and notes to explain the processes used. *(6 marks)*

Final T-shirt design

Using printing equipment

You should be able to use the following printing equipment to develop:
(a) good presentation and communication techniques
(b) good–quality graphic products.

✎ Photocopying

■ Photocopying (sometimes referred to as **dry printing**) is a quick, easy and economical way of producing black and white copies. You can use this method to print on plain or coloured paper and thin card, as well as clear acetate sheets. It is easy to reduce or enlarge original copies.

■ This method of printing is particularly useful when you want to combine several images from different sources and give the appearance of them being printed on to one sheet. This technique is often referred to as **'cut and paste'**.

■ An example of the technique is shown in Figure 1.13. Four separate pieces have been stuck on (left) and photocopied in order to give the appearance of them all having been printed on the same surface. It is better to 'tear' the pieces out rather than cut them out as this helps to avoid a shadow when the work is photocopied (right).

1.13 *Photocopying*

Four separate pieces stuck on

Photocopied version

1.14 *Photocopier*

■ By photocopying on to clear acetate sheets it is possible to 'overlay' several images before making the final copy.

■ In this form of printing, the ink (or **toner** as it is more often called) has a negative charge which makes it attractive to the positively-charged printing area. The ink is held in position until it is fixed by heat.

■ Perhaps the easiest and cheapest way of reproducing drawings and illustrations in school is by using a photocopier (Figure 1.14). Photocopying is particularly useful where many repeat copies of an original piece of work are required. It is a simple method of 'batch production'.

✎ Screen printing

■ **Screen printing** is a versatile printing technique. It is used widely by businesses and industry, as well as by artists. It is a low-cost printing method which is best suited to short runs (up to a few hundred) and in situations where fine detail is not required.

■ You can use screen printing to print on to any material with a flat surface. Posters, T-shirts, shop display boards, fabrics and wallpapers are frequently produced using screen printing. The process uses a **screen** and **stencil**. The holes in the stencil correspond to the image to be printed. It is one of the few commercial methods of printing which can be used easily in a school situation.

■ The basic process of screen printing is outlined below.

1.15 *The screen printing process*

Stage 1: *Make a frame from four strips of wood and cover it with a piece of fine nylon netting. This can be fixed in place using a staple gun.*

Stage 2: *Cut four strips of gum paper and use them to mask the inside edges of the screen. This will stop the ink from spreading and act as a reservoir for the ink before it is pulled across the screen.*

Stage 3: *Cut a paper stencil. Remember the cut-out parts will form the final printed design.*

Stage 4: *Position the paper stencil on the surface to be printed and place the screen over the stencil.*

Stage 5: *Put some printing ink on the gum paper reservoir at the side of the screen.*

Stage 6: *Using a squeegee (a car window wiper will work well) pull the ink across the screen towards you.*

Stage 7: *Lift the screen and place the print on a flat surface to dry.*

Stage 8: *Clean all of the equipment.*

■ This design in Figure 1.16 is ideal for making a screen printing stencil. Notice how a square grid has been used to help in the drawing of the stencil. The toned areas are the pieces to be cut out.

1.16

CHECK YOURSELF – EXAM QUESTION

5 Four school friends are in a band called 'The Illusions'. They have written and recorded ten songs which they intend to release on a cassette tape entitled 'WILDER'.

Fifty copies of the cassette are to be produced.

The paper inserts to go into the plastic cassette boxes are to be designed on a computer and printed using a photocopier.

Two possible design ideas are shown below.

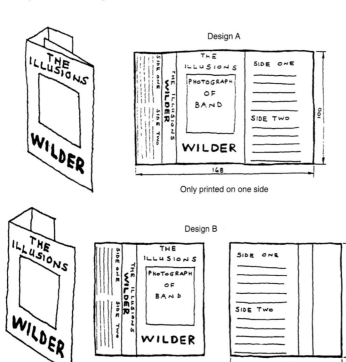

(a) Explain, with reasons, which of the two designs would be easier to produce.

(2 marks)

(b) Name a piece of equipment that could be used to input a photograph of the band into a computer system.

(1 mark)

◼ Using photographic equipment

You should be able to describe how photographic equipment can be used in the process of designing and making graphic products.

1.17 *35mm compact camera*

✎Conventional still camera

◼ You should be familiar with how a camera can be used to record research and the stages of your design-and-make activities (Figure 1.17).

✎Digital camera

◼ You can use this type of camera (Figure 1.18) for the same purposes as a conventional camera, but the images are stored on a computer disc or memory card rather than a film. It has numerous advantages. For example, you can see the pictures you have taken instantly and delete any that you are not satisfied with.

◼ The pictures can be transferred to a computer. This process is called uploading or importing. Once the images have been uploaded to the computer they can be saved as files. These files can be opened, closed, printed and e-mailed. It is possible to send the images anywhere in the world almost instantly. The images can be modified by loading them into appropriate design software.

1.18 *Digital camera*

CHECK YOURSELF – EXAM QUESTION

6   In Computer Aided Design, photographs from film and digital cameras are a valuable resource for the graphic designer.

Explain briefly the stages involved when images are imported in to a computer system from **either** a film camera **or** a digital camera.

(4 marks)

💡 QUESTION SPOTTER

▷ You will not require specific knowledge about particular makes or models of camera, but you will need an understanding as to how they can be used as an aid to the design and manufacture of graphic products.

▷ Questions will be based around how a camera can be used to record, store and print images.

UNIT 2: DRAWING SYSTEMS

Third angle orthographic projection

Designers normally work as part of a team, and not as individuals. In order to communicate with other members of the design team there has to be a common drawing language that every member understands. Just as you use the spoken and written word to communicate with your friends, design teams have to communicate with each other through the use of common drawing systems.

Plan

End view   Front view

2.1 *Third angle orthographic projection drawings of a shampoo bottle*

✎ Two-dimensional drawings

- **Orthographic projection** uses two-dimensional drawings which show at least two, and usually three, separate views (or elevations) of a three-dimensional object. The three views most commonly used are called the **front view**, the **end** (or side) **view** and the **plan**.

  - The front view is the one which generally shows the most detail about the object.

  - The plan view is always drawn directly above the front view.

  - An end view looking at the right of the object should be drawn to the right of the front view.

  - A view looking at the left side of the object should be drawn to the left of the front view.

- The plan and front view *must* be directly in line with each other. This is illustrated in the third angle orthographic drawing of a shampoo container shown in Figure 2.1. Notice how construction lines are projected to help draw the other two views and to make sure that details are in the correct position.

- The symbol shown at the bottom of Figure 2.1 is used to indicate that third angle orthographic projection has been used to draw the object.

- Third angle orthographic projection drawing is particularly useful when accurate details about the shape and size of a product are required. For example, when designing a piece of packaging, an orthographic drawing of the product to be packaged would be helpful.

✎ Hidden detail

- Parts of an object which cannot be directly seen on an orthographic view can be indicated using hidden detail lines. These consist of thin, short dashes - - - - - - - - - - - - .

- An example of how hidden detail lines can be used is shown in Figure 2.2. By adding hidden detail to the front view, information about the inside shape of the mug can be given.

2.2 *Outlines for a souvenir mug*

✎ Dimensioning

- **Working drawings** need to be dimensioned so that the person who is designing and making the product knows what size it is in real life, regardless of the size that it has been drawn.

- Basic points that should be remembered are:

  - All **measurements** should be read from the bottom right-hand side of the paper.

  - Limit lines should be drawn out from the object and numbers written above a dimension line stretching between the limit lines.

  - Smaller measurements should be placed closer to the drawing.

  - All measurements should be the real life (full size) of the object and are usually given in millimetres (mm) – but there is no need to write 'mm' on your drawing.

- The drawing in Figure 2.3 illustrates how these points are applied.

- In Figure 2.4 you can find out about the methods used to dimension circles, radius curves, angles and small sizes.

Drawings that will easily fit on to the paper can be produced full size. The drawing of a stamp shown here is the exact size of the actual stamp. It has been drawn to a **scale** of 1:1.

If an object is too small for the detail to be seen clearly you need to draw it larger, using a recommended **enlargement scale** (2:1, 5:1, 10:1 or 20:1). This drawing of the stamp has been enlarged to twice its original size (that is, 2:1).

If an object is too large to fit on to the paper, you will need to draw it smaller than its real size, using a **reduction scale** (1:2), 1:5, 1:10, 1:20, 1:50 or 1:100). For example, an object drawn half its actual size is drawn to a scale of 1:2.

2.3 *Dimensions added to the souvenir mug outline*

Dimension line

50

95

ø70

Full height of mug given in millimetres

This symbol indicates the diameter of a circle

Limit line

2.4

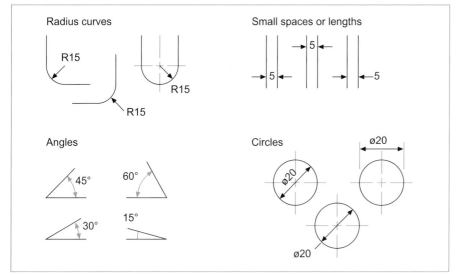

Radius curves

R15

R15

R15

Small spaces or lengths

5

5

5

Angles

45°

60°

30°

15°

Circles

ø20

ø20

ø20

ø20

2.5 *Cross-sections through different chocolate bars*

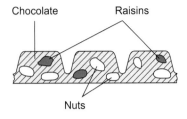

Chocolate   Raisins

Nuts

Section through a fruit-and-nut chocolate bar

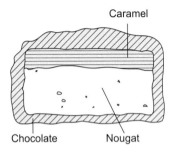

Caramel

Chocolate   Nougat

Section through a caramel bar

2.6 *Drawings for a display stand made from two pieces of foamboard*

✎ Sectional views

- Cut-away sections are one of the best ways of showing the construction and internal details of an object. A good way of explaining what a **sectional view** is like is to think of a bar of fruit-and-nut chocolate or a caramel bar. By taking a cross-section (or slice) through the bar it is possible to show the ingredients inside (Figure 2.5).

- The key points to remember when producing a sectional view are:
  - Cross-hatch the cut surface. This involves drawing **parallel lines** at 45 degrees across the area.
  - Cross-hatch different parts in different ways.
  - Show where the section has been taken.
  - Label the section.

- Figure 2.6 shows the drawing of a display stand. It illustrates how the points above can be applied.

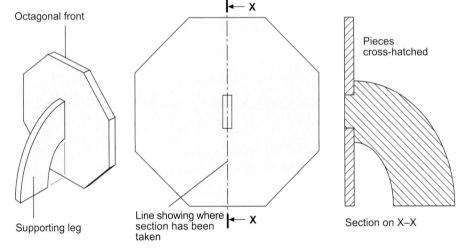

Octagonal front

Supporting leg

Line showing where section has been taken

Pieces cross-hatched

Section on X–X

CHECK YOURSELF – EXAM QUESTION

I   An activity pack is to contain a series of illustrations showing various vehicles used at the airport. The pictorial drawing shows a service vehicle used to tow aircraft.

Draw full size, in third angle orthographic projection:

(a) a side view of the service vehicle looking in the direction of arrow **A**;

(b) an end view of the service vehicle looking in the direction of arrow **B**.

(18 marks)

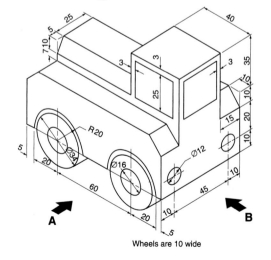

Wheels are 10 wide

▬ Isometric drawing ▬

Designers use three-dimensional drawings (sometimes called pictorial drawings) to get a better idea of what the product they are designing will look like and to communicate their proposals to a client. Three-dimensional drawing methods show three sides of a product on a single view.

- You will need to be familiar with producing and using the following types of three-dimensional drawings:
  - Isometric (see below)
  - Planometric (see Revision Session 3)
  - One point perspective (see Revision Session 4)
  - Two point perspective (see Revision Session 4).

✎ Making an isometric drawing

- To make an isometric drawing you need a 30 degree–60 degree set square and a T-square. You always start by drawing the corner of the object which is nearest to you and extending these lines to draw a box (or crate) into which the object will just fit. To do this you need to know the overall height, width and length of the object. In isometric drawing, vertical lines remain vertical and horizontal lines are drawn at **30 degrees** (Figure 2.7).

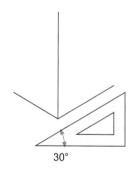

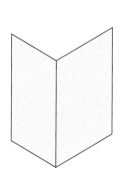
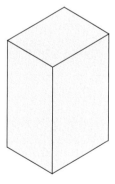

Stage 1   Stage 2   Stage 3

2.7 *Stages in isometric drawing*

✎ Isometric grid paper

- Isometric grid paper helps you to do isometric sketches and drawings quickly. As the grid is in 5mm sections, drawings can often be done without measuring yet keep them in the right proportion. Grid paper can be used under plain paper and the drawing traced through (Figure 2.8). The techniques for producing an isometric view using grid paper are the same as you would use with a set square and T-square.

> ☼ **QUESTION SPOTTER**
>
> ▸ Some questions will ask you to produce a 'pictorial' view. (Pictorial means 3D.) In this case, you would have a choice of which type of drawing to use. Select the one that you feel is the most suitable for the given situation or the one that you feel most confident about drawing.
> ▸ Other questions will ask for a specific type of drawing. In this situation it is important that you use the correct method as you can sometimes lose marks if you don't.

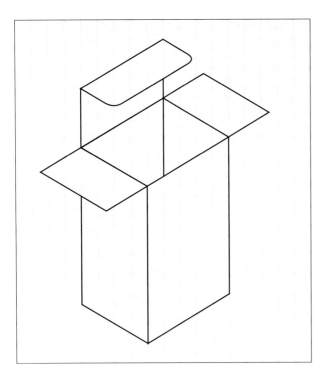

2.8 *Examples of how an isometric grid can be used to produce isometric drawings*

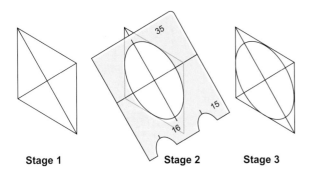

Stage 1   Stage 2   Stage 3

2.9 *The stages in drawing an isometric view of a circle*

✎ Drawing circles on an isometric view

- There are no true shapes on an isometric view, so circles become distorted and appear as **ellipses**. You will find an **isometric ellipse template** (Figure 2.9) particularly useful when drawing small circles on an isometric view.

- **Stage 1:** you need to draw an isometric view of a square into which the circle would just fit.

- **Stage 2:** draw the diagonals on the isometric square. To position the ellipse accurately align the marks on the template with the diagonal lines.

- **Stage 3:** Draw round the inside of the isometric ellipse template to complete the circle.

- When drawing larger isometric circles, use compasses to draw four arcs to form the ellipse. This technique is shown in Figure 2.10.

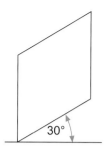

1 Draw an isometric square

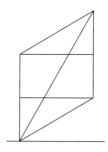

2 Draw two horizontal lines and one diagonal line

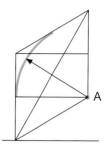

3 Place your compass point on A and draw an arc as shown

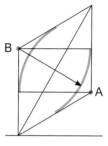

4 Place your compass point on point B and draw another arc

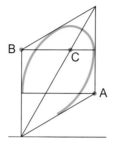

5 Place your compass point on C and draw an arc to blend in with the other two arcs

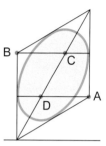

6 Draw another arc, placing the compass point on D to complete the isometric drawing

2.10 *How to construct an isometric circle*

Card lid

Card tray

Vacuum formed plastic insert to hold CD Rom and instruction booklet

2.11 *Packaging for a computer game*

✎ Exploded views

- You can use this type of drawing to show how the separate parts of a product fit together. When an object is 'exploded' you must draw the parts in relation to each other and in the same order in which they fit together. The example in Figure 2.11 shows the packaging for a computer game. The plastic insert goes into the tray and the lid fits over the top. Notice how the three views all line up.

- 2D and 3D **exploded views** can be drawn using any appropriate drawing system, but isometric views are normally used.

QUESTION SPOTTER

▸ Not all questions will require you to use drawing instruments.
▸ Check the question carefully before you start. Where an answer has been started for you, make sure that you line your work up with the 'starter lines'.

⚡ A* EXTRA

Make sure that you start your answer by drawing a box – called a 'crate' – into which the object being drawn would just fit. Use an ellipse template to draw any small isometric circles. Make sure you know how to use the template – it can save you a lot of time.

2 The orthographic drawing gives details of an ice lolly.

Complete the advertisement shown by adding a full-size isometric drawing of the ice lolly.

The position of corner A is given.

(9 marks)

3 Shown below is a design for a mobile which is to be used as part of an advertising campaign for a CD called 'HITS 99'.

The mobile is to be made from foamboard.

Draw an exploded pictorial sketch to show how two pieces of foamboard would need to be cut and joined to make the cross part of the mobile.

(3 marks)

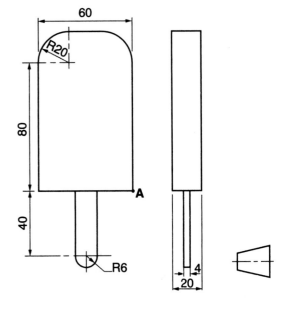

Cool down with a lolly!

▬ Planometric drawing ▬

This drawing system is sometimes called axonometric. Planometric views are produced using a 45 degree–45 degree set square and T-square.

■ Start by drawing a true plan of the object but inclined at an angle of 45 degrees (see Figure 2.12, Stage 1). Project the vertical faces from the plan view (Stage 2) and add the top using a 45-degree set square (Stage 3).

2.12 *Creating a planometric drawing of a rectangular box*

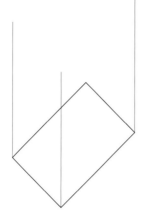
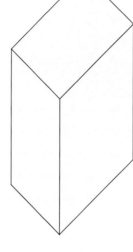

| Stage 1 | Stage 2 | Stage 3 |

■ When you draw a **cylinder** the plan view will be a circle. Start by drawing the circle (Figure 2.13, Stage 1). Project the centre of the circle vertically and measure the height of the cylinder. Draw a second circle to make the top (Stage 2) and complete the drawing by joining the two circles (Stage 3).

■ **Planometric drawing** is particularly useful when the plan view of the object involves a lot of circles and semi-circles. The bottle for after shave in Figure 2.14 is a good example of this type of product.

2.13 *Planometric drawing of a cylinder*

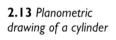
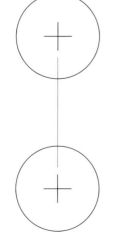

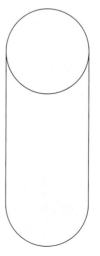

| Stage 1 | Stage 2 | Stage 3 |

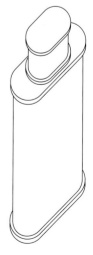

2.14 *After shave bottle*

4 Details of a recycling survey carried out at a supermarket are given in the table below.

Materials recycled	Bottles	Cans	Paper	Clothes
No. of items	250	200	500	50

This information is to be displayed by dividing up the height on a 3D drawing of a metal drinks can.

The first division has been drawn and labelled for you.

Complete the drawing by:

(i) adding the other three divisions

(6 marks)

(ii) labelling them

(2 marks)

(iii) adding shading to improve the 3D effect of the cylindrical can.

(2 marks)

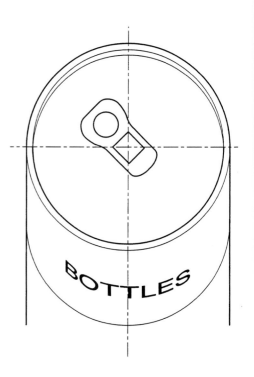

■ Perspective drawing ■

The most realistic three-dimensional drawings are produced using perspective drawing techniques. We naturally see things in perspective, so drawings done in this way can appear very lifelike. Unlike other forms of three-dimensional drawing, perspective views give the impression of depth and distance by taking into account the fact that horizontal lines appear to meet at a point in the distance. This point is referred to as the vanishing point (VP).

■ You will need to be familiar with two types of perspective drawing:

   • One point perspective

   • Two point perspective.

✎ One point perspective

■ In **one point perspective**, one side of the product is drawn as if you are looking straight at it. Start by drawing this side. Next you need to select a VP. This goes above the first rectangle if you want to see the top of the object, or below it if you want to see the underneath. Lines are now drawn from each of the front corners to the vanishing point (see Figure 2.15).

■ Depth is added by drawing lines parallel to the front surface. You can now use these techniques to draw the additional detail required to complete the perspective view.

2.15 *One point perspective*

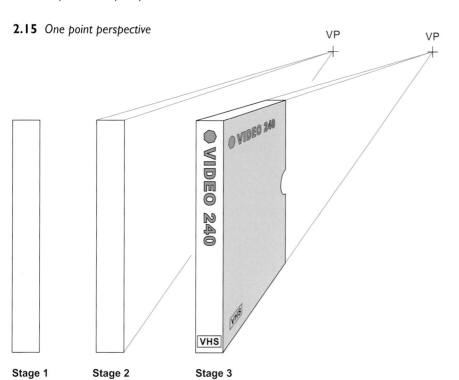

Stage 1   Stage 2   Stage 3

QUESTION SPOTTER

▶ You will often be given the position of the vanishing points. When this is not the case, extend the given perspective lines until they meet. This will give you the position of a VP.

▶ Make sure that all the 'depth' lines go back to vanishing points.

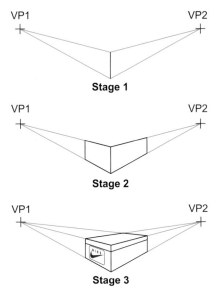

Stage 1

Stage 2

Stage 3

2.16 *Box for a pair of trainers*

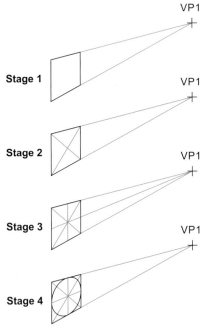

Stage 1

Stage 2

Stage 3

Stage 4

2.17 *Drawing a circle in perspective*

✎ Two point perspective

- **Two point perspective** enables you to draw objects at an angle to the view. It therefore gives a more realistic view than one point perspective.

- Start by drawing the corner of the object which is nearest to you. Select **two** vanishing points (VP1 and VP2 – see Figure 2.16). The criteria for positioning these is the same as one point perspective – it depends if you want to look down on the object or up at it. Both vanishing points must be on the same horizontal line.

- Draw lines from the front corner back to the two vanishing points. Estimate the length and width required and draw two vertical lines.

- Now draw lines from the top corners to the vanishing points.

✎ Circles in perspective

- To draw a **circle in perspective** start by drawing the square into which it will fit (Figure 2.17, **Stage 1**).

- **Stage 2:** Draw the diagonal lines on the 'square' to enable you to find the centre.

- **Stage 3:** Draw lines through the centre. In this case, one will be vertical and one goes back to the vanishing point.

- **Stage 4:** You now need to draw a curve through the four points where these lines touch the 'square'.

✎ Estimating depths in perspective

- This simple construction will enable you to **estimate depths in perspective**.

  - Start by drawing the box into which the object will fit (Figure 2.18).

  - The next step is to draw the diagonal across the length of the object.

  - Divide the front corner into the number of parts you require the length to be split into, in this case 3.

  - Take these divisions back to the vanishing point. Where these lines cut the diagonal, draw vertical lines and you will have your three divisions. Notice how each division is slightly smaller than the previous one.

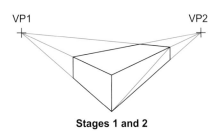

Stages 1 and 2

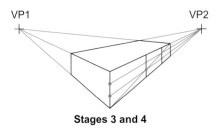

Stages 3 and 4

2.18 *Estimating depths in perspective*

- This technique has been used to produce the lettering shown in Figure 2.19.

2.19

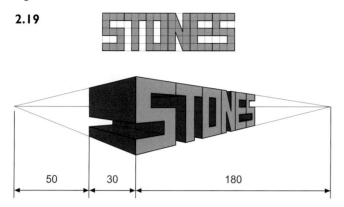

| 50 | 30 | 180 |

CHECK YOURSELF – EXAM QUESTION

5   An isometric view of a promotional product called a 'Tumble Cube' is shown below. The 'Tumble Cube' is made up of four card boxes each 60 mm x 120 mm long. The four boxes are hinged to allow the shape to be altered so that all four boxes can be in line.

The isometric view shows how the top two boxes are able to move.

(a) Complete the isometric view by drawing a second letter L on the top surfaces of the 'Tumble Cube'. Both letters should be the same size. Corner A of the letters is given.

(3 marks)

(b) The 'Tumble Cube' is arranged in its tumbled position with all four boxes in line.

Complete an estimated two point perspective view of the 'Tumble Cube' it its 'tumbled' position with all four boxes in line.

(4 marks)

(c) Add the parts of the letter L which will be visible.

(3 marks)

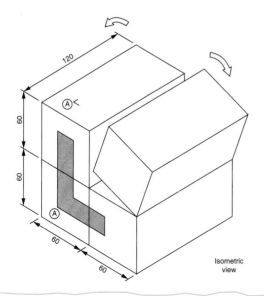

Isometric view

Assembly drawings

Some graphic products are made up of several separate parts (sometimes called components). These separate parts need to be assembled in the correct manner in order to produce the final product.

2.20 *Exploded view of packaging to hold chocolates*

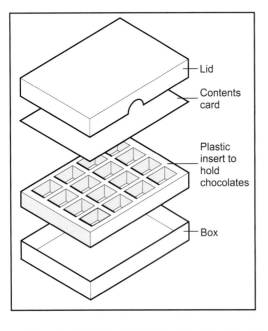

Lid

Contents card

Plastic insert to hold chocolates

Box

- Look at the packaging for chocolates shown in Figure 2.20. It consists of four parts:
  - a box
  - a contents card
  - a plastic insert to hold the chocolates
  - a lid.

- Information about the parts to be assembled is generally given in the form of an **exploded view** or a series of **orthographic views**.

- When confronted with this information about the separate parts, it can appear a difficult task to produce one drawing of the assembled parts. With the chocolate box it is obvious how the parts fit together because we are familiar with this type of product. When faced with unfamiliar products, you need to look for sizes that will enable one part to fit into or onto another part.

CHECK YOURSELF – EXAM QUESTION

6 Read the instructions below for a card model of a Jumbo Jet. Then make a full-size freehand pictorial sketch, in isometric form, showing the assembled card model. Include detail and colour.

(16 marks)

1 Cut out the pieces.
2 Glue together both sides of the fuselage, wings and tailplane.
3 Cut out the slots for the wing and tailplane.
4 Curve each engine into a cylinder and glue along the shaded area.
5 Slot in the wing and tailplane and attach the engines with glue in the positions indicated.

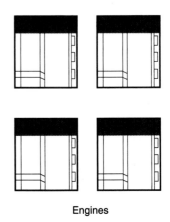

Engines

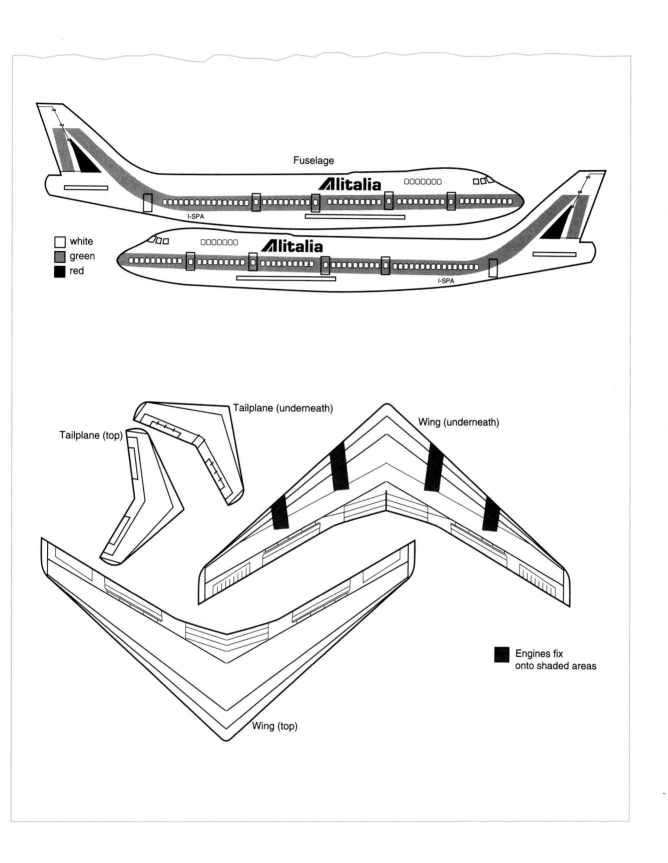

Fuselage

Alitalia

I-SPA

white
green
red

Alitalia

I-SPA

Tailplane (underneath)

Wing (underneath)

Tailplane (top)

Engines fix
onto shaded areas

Wing (top)

Pictograms

Pictograms use symbols or simplified pictures to represent information. They eliminate the need for people to read a particular language in order to understand the information presented. Pictograms are commonly used on packaging and in public buildings such as airports, as shown in Figures 2.21 and 2.22.

2.21 *Examples of pictograms used on packaging*

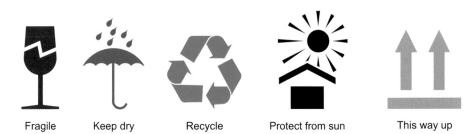

| Fragile | Keep dry | Recycle | Protect from sun | This way up |

2.22 *Examples of pictograms used in public places*

Toilets   Restaurant   Telephone   Escalator

A* EXTRA

When designing a pictogram you need to remember that it must relate to a specific object or activity – be simple, clear and easy to understand and remember.

QUESTION SPOTTER

▸ You could be asked to design a pictogram in the same style as a given example (e.g. 2D, block colouring, 'wordless').

- In an exam situation, you will generally not require much prior knowledge about **specific** pictograms. You will sometimes be asked what facility or activity a design indicates and to analyse existing designs. This will often include suggesting how and where they could be used.

- You will be required to design pictograms for specific situations, as well as making modifications and improvements to existing designs.

CHECK YOURSELF – EXAM QUESTION

7   Direction signs are needed to guide people around the Museum.

The drawings (i) – (iv) below shows four possible designs for directions signs.
From these, the Museum chose (iv).

(a) State which you think is the best design and why you prefer it.   *(1 mark)*

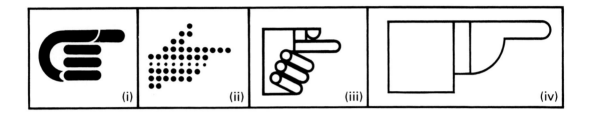

(b) Use instruments to make a full-size drawing of the direction sign shown
in drawing (iv).   *(5 marks)*

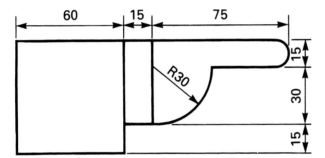

UNIT 3: BASIC GRAPHIC SHAPES

REVISION SESSION 1 ━━━ **Triangles**

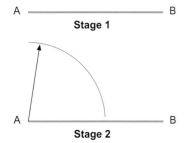

Stage 1

Stage 2

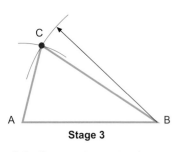

Stage 3

3.1 *Constructing a triangle*

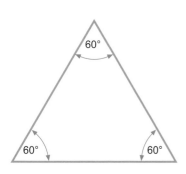

3.2 *Equilateral triangles*

3.3 *Examples of road signs using equilateral triangles*

Being able to construct geometrical shapes accurately is an important skill. These shapes form the basis for many graphic products such as logos and nets (developments) for packaging.

✎ Basic triangles

- You need to be able to recognise and draw these types of triangle:
  - Equilateral
  - Isosceles
  - Right angle
  - Scalene.

- You can use a pair of compasses to draw any triangle if you know the length of each of the three sides. Start by drawing the base AB (Figure 3.1, Stage 1).

- Set the compasses to the length of side AC and make an arc with centre at A (Stage 2).

- Set the compasses to the length of side BC and make an arc with centre at B. The two arcs cross at C. You can now draw the other two sides of the triangle (Stage 3).

✎ Equilateral triangle

- All the sides of an **equilateral triangle** are the same length and the internal angles are all 60 degrees (Figure 3.2).

- An equilateral triangle can easily be drawn using a 60-degree set square.

- Equilateral triangles appear on many road signs (Figure 3.3).

✎ Isosceles triangle

- An **isosceles triangle** has two sides and two angles the same (Figure 3.4).

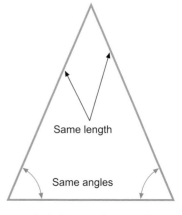

Same length

Same angles

3.4 *An isosceles triangle*

✎ Right angle triangle

■ As its name suggests this type of triangle has one right angle (90 degrees). A set square is a good example of a **right angle triangle** (Figure 3.5).

✎ Scalene triangle

■ None of the sides or angles are the same in a **scalene triangle**.

■ Isosceles, right angle and scalene triangles can all be drawn using a protractor to measure the angles and a pair of compasses to strike off the length of the sides.

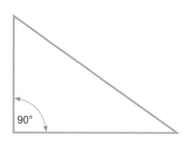

3.5 *Right angle triangle (also a scalene triangle)*

CHECK YOURSELF – EXAM QUESTIONS

1   A freehand drawing of part of the Anglia Television logo is shown below.

(a) Add the names of the shapes that form the logo.   *(1 mark)*

The Anglia Television logo is made up of:

eleven small _____

one _____

(b) Use instruments to make a drawing of the Anglia Television logo.
Sizes are given on the freehand drawing.
(4 marks)

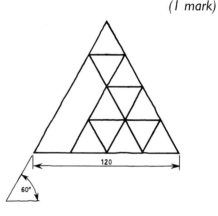

2   A drawing of a logo for a television programme called 'Sixty Minutes' is shown below.

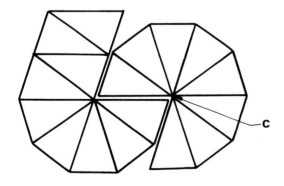

(a) Name the **type** of triangle that has been used to form the number.

(1 mark)

(b) Using the information given in the small drawing above, complete the drawing of the logo.

(5 marks)

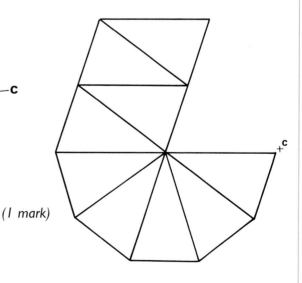

Quadrilaterals

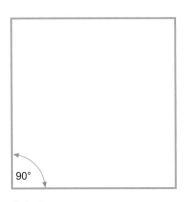

3.6 *Square*

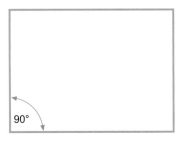

3.7 *Rectangle*

This group of shapes all have four sides. You need to be able to recognise and draw the following types of quadrilateral:
- Square
- Rectangle
- Rhombus
- Parallelogram.

Square

- A **square** is a very familiar shape. All the sides are the same length and all the angles are 90 degrees (Figure 3.6).
- It is very easy to draw using a T-square and the 90-degree angle on a set square.

Rectangle

- The shape of a **rectangle** is sometimes referred to as an **oblong**. As with the square, it is a very familiar shape. Opposite sides are the same length and all the angles are 90 degrees (Figure 3.7). It is drawn in the same way as a square.

Rhombus

- The best way to describe a **rhombus** is that it looks like a square that has been 'pushed sideways' (Figure 3.8).
- All the sides are the same length and the opposite sides are parallel.
- It can be drawn using a T-square for the horizontal lines and a protractor to measure the angles.

Parallelogram

- A **parallelogram** is a rectangle that has been 'pushed sideways'.
- Opposite sides are parallel and the same length (Figure 3.9). It can be drawn in the same way as a rhombus.

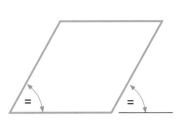

3.8 *Rhombus*

3.9 *Parallelogram*

Polygons

A polygon is a shape that has five or more sides. You need to be able to recognise and draw the following types of polygon:
• Pentagon
• Hexagon
• Octagon.

■ You can use a pair of compasses and a protractor to draw any polygon if you know the length of one side or the size of a circle that the polygon will just fit into.

Drawing a polygon when you know the length of one side

■ The external angle equals 360 degrees divided by the number of sides (n). In the case of the pentagon shown in Figure 3.10 this will be 360 divided by 5, giving an angle of 72 degrees.

■ Start by drawing side AB and then follow the sequence of instructions.

Drawing a polygon in a circle

■ The angle at the centre equals 360 degrees divided by the number of sides (n). In the case of the hexagon shown in Figure 3.11 this will be 360 divided by 6, giving an angle of 60 degrees.

■ Start by drawing the circle and then measure the angles from the centre.

✎ Hexagons

■ A **hexagon** has **six** sides. You need to know how to draw a hexagon when you are given the length of one side or the distance across the flats. (This is sometimes shown as **A/F.**)

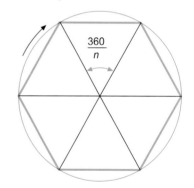

3.10 *A polygon drawn from the length of one side*

3.11 *A polygon drawn in a circle*

3.12 *Drawing a hexagon*

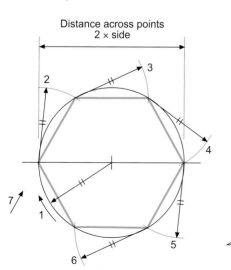

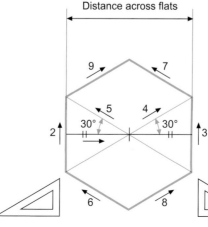

▸ Geometrical shapes
are frequently used
as background shapes
for logos and signs.
▸ Questions involving
these shapes are
common on many
exam papers.
▸ Try to remember their
names and how to draw
them by linking each
one to a particular logo
or sign. For example,
the background shape
of the MG badge is an
octagon (see Figure
3.13).

■ When you know the length of one side of a hexagon, you can use this
distance as the radius of a circle. The radius is then marked off around
the circle as shown in Figure 3.12 (left).

■ The sequence of instructions for drawing a hexagon when you are given
the distance across the flats is shown in Figure 3.12 (right).

✎ Octagons

■ An **octagon** has **eight** sides. You need to know how to draw an octagon
when you are given the length of one side or the distance across the
flats (this is the same as being told the size of a square that the
octagon will fit into).

■ The sequence of instructions for drawing an octagon when you are
given the length of one side (AB) is shown in Figure 3.13 on the left.

■ To draw an octagon in a square (one side of the square equals the
distance across the flats) you need to follow the sequence of
instructions given on the right in Figure 3.13.

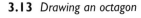
3.13 *Drawing an octagon*

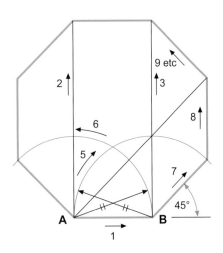

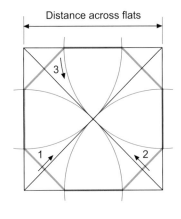

⚡ A* EXTRA

▸ Practise with your drawing
instruments so that you
are confident about
drawing the required
range of basic graphic
shapes. This will avoid you
wasting time in an exam
thinking about how to
draw them.
▸ Remember that you can
use 'any appropriate
accurate method'. Study
the examples given in this
guide and decide which
methods you will use.

✎ Pentagons

■ A **pentagon** has **five** sides. Generally you will be given the length of one
side. You can draw the required pentagon using a protractor to measure
the external angle as described at the start of this section on polygons.
Remember that for a pentagon each angle is 72 degrees.

3 The Octagon Leisure Centre requires a sign. The freehand drawing below shows the letter designs to be used for the word Octagon.

Using instruments, complete the drawing of the sign.

(9 marks)

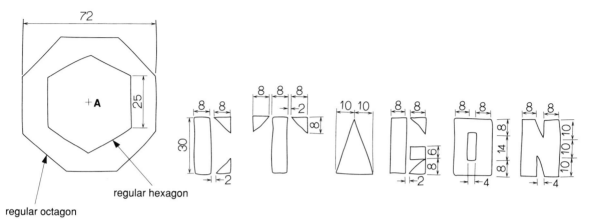

regular hexagon

regular octagon

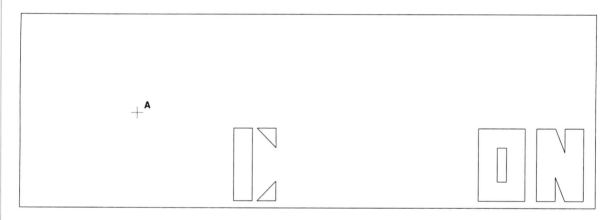

4 Each of the drawings (i) to (v) shows a road sign. State the name of the shape that has been used for the background of the road sign.

(9 marks)

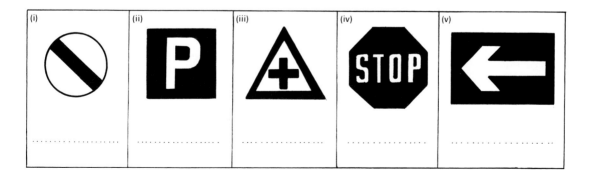

The ellipse

The ellipse is another important geometrical shape which is commonly used in the design of logos. Unfortunately, there is no instrument which will draw any size of ellipse. Templates may help with smaller ellipses, but you need to know how to draw any size of ellipse.

- The two most common ways of drawing an ellipse are **The Trammel Method** and **The Concentric Circle Method**. You only need to be able to do one method.

- Usually you will be told the lengths of the major and minor axes of the ellipse. In Figure 3.14, **M** equals the length of the major axis and **m** equals the length of the minor axis.

- The **trammel method** uses a strip of paper with distances marked off, as shown in Figure 3.15. One point (A) stays on the minor axis, one (B) on the major axis and the third (C) is plotted as a point on the ellipse. The trammel is moved to allow further points to be plotted.

- As its name suggests, the **concentric circle method** is based on two concentric circles (circles with the same centre). The sequence of instructions is as shown in Figure 3.16.

- Both methods enable a series of points to be plotted which are then joined by a curve. This can be drawn freehand or with the aid of a flexi curve or french curve (see page 69).

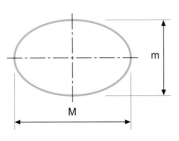

3.14 *Ellipse*

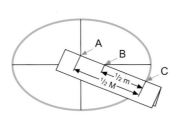

3.15 *Trammel method*

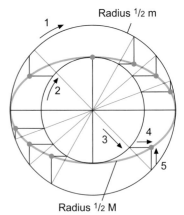

Radius ½ m

Radius ½ M

3.16 *Concentric circle method*

CHECK YOURSELF – EXAM QUESTION

5 The opening titles for a film called 'The Eye' are to include an animated sequence of an eye closing. In planning this sequence a series of three drawings is required: the first showing the eye fully open, the second showing the eye half closed and the third showing the eye fully closed.

The first and third drawings are shown completed. Complete the second drawing by adding:

(a) an ellipse, major axis 110 millimetres and minor axis 30 millimetres. *(5 marks)*

(b) the parts of the circles that can still be seen. *(2 marks)*

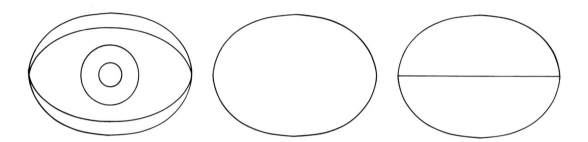

Shapes formed from combination of circles, tangents and tangential arcs

A tangent is a straight line that just touches a circle or curve.
A tangential arc is a curve which touches another curve.

3.17 *Tangents and tangential arcs*

■ Figure 3.17 shows examples of how these lines and curves can be drawn.

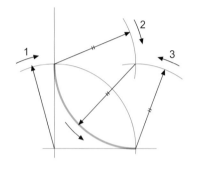

To draw an arc tangential to two lines at right angles

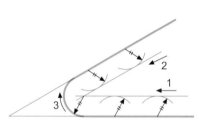

To draw an arc tangential to two lines making an acute angle

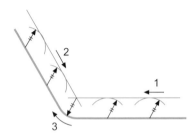

To draw an arc tangential to two lines making an obtuse angle

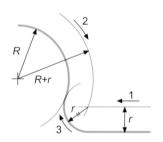

To draw circle of radius r tangential to a line and circle of radius R externally

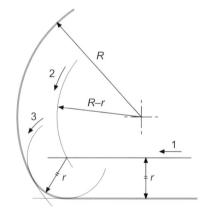

To draw circle of radius r tangential to a line and circle of radius R internally

■ All of the examples in Figure 3.17 are concerned with rounding corners. A much easier way of doing this would be to use a **circle template**. This is perfectly acceptable in an exam situation.

■ The examples in Figure 3.18 show the more complex use of tangential arcs. Questions involving their use occur rarely on exam papers. The curves involved can not generally be drawn with templates because they are too big.

■ Notice how sizes are worked out by adding and subtracting radii.

3.18 *More complex tangential arc*

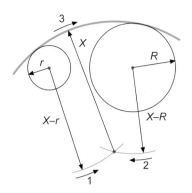

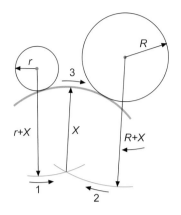

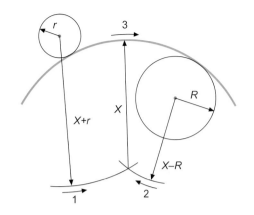

To draw circle of radius r touching two circles (of radii R and r) and including both

To draw circle of radius x touching two circles (of radii R and r) excluding both

To draw circle of radius x touching two circles (of radii R and r) to include one only

CHECK YOURSELF – EXAM QUESTION

6

As part of a special promotion a restaurant is to give away hats made from thin card.

A sketch of the outline of the net (development) is given below.

Use instruments to draw the net (development) of the hat to a scale of 1:2 on the given centre line.

Centres for all the arcs must be shown clearly.

(11 marks)

Hint: You should start a question of this type by drawing the centre lines. Then mark in the positions of the centres that you are given sizes for and draw the curves (e.g. the radius 120 curves). You can work out the positions for the other centres using the techniques explained above.

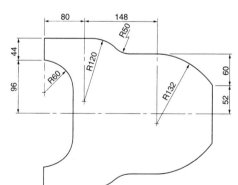

UNIT 4: ENHANCEMENT TECHNIQUES

Use of tone

4.1

4.3 Highlighting

The addition of tone by shading can enhance the three-dimensional appearance of a drawing.

- As a general rule for objects having vertical and horizontal surfaces shading falls into three **tones** – light, medium and dark areas. The lighter surfaces face towards the light and the darker surfaces are turned away from the light (Figure 4.1).

- Variations in tone can also be achieved using lines and dots. The closer together the lines or dots are placed the darker the tone (Figure 4.2).

Graduated tone using lines

Graduated tone using dots

4.2 *Graduated tones*

- On a curved surface, such as the top of a perfume bottle, the amount of light that is reflected gradually gets less as the surface turns away from the light (Figure 4.3). You need to include a 'highlight'. This is a very light, almost white, area which is closest to the direction from which the light is coming.

Thick and thin lines

- Thick and thin lines can be used to create impact on a drawing and to make an object look more solid.

- They help your eyes and brain to understand the form of an object better.

- Lines are used to show where two surfaces meet. As a general rule, you use a thick line where you can see only one of these surfaces and a thin line when you can see both (Figure 4.4).

- You can apply the rule to both flat and curved surfaces.

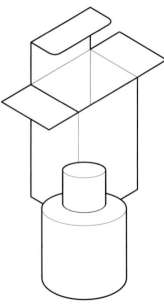

4.4 *Thick and thin lines*

✎ Texture

- Lines and dots can be used to enhance the form of an object and help to show what materials it is made from.

- You will need to use textural representation to illustrate the following range of materials:
  - wood
  - plastics and glass
  - metal (matt and chrome)
  - concrete.

✎ Wood

- For **wood** you can use lines that correspond to the grain structure (see Figure 4.5).

- For the purposes of illustration there are three types of grain pattern that are used:
  - **end grain** showing the growth rings
  - **side grain** – this tends to be rather fine
  - **facing grain**, which is broad and wavy.

✎ Chrome and polished metals

- This type of material can be represented by the use of heavy black lines that reduce in width as the surface turns towards the light. The shading follows the outline of the form (Figure 4.6).

✎ Matt or dull metal

- A series of evenly spaced lines are drawn which follow the form of the object (see the bottle top in Figure 4.7).

✎ Clear plastic and glass

- Transparent materials can be difficult to render because they have no natural colour of their own. An effective method is to use light blue to shade the surface and then to rub out areas to represent the reflections. Use feint broken lines to show details that can be seen through the glass or plastic (Figure 4.7).

✎ Opaque plastic

- This material can be shown as a solid colour except for white bands which indicate reflections (see Figure 4.8, top).

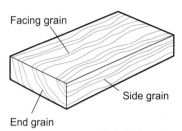

Facing grain
Side grain
End grain

4.5 *Enhancing wood*

4.6 *Enhancing metals*

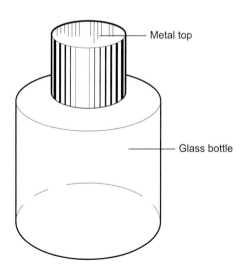

Metal top

Glass bottle

4.7 *Enhancing transparent materials*

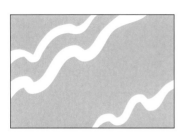

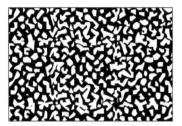

4.8 *Enhancing plastics*

✎ Textured plastic

■ This type of plastic is best represented by the use of small irregular shapes over the whole surface (Figure 4.8, lower).

✎ Concrete

■ Concrete contains larger stones as well as the basic sand and cement mix. The sand and cement can be represented by light stippling (a series of dots) while the stones are shown as small irregular shapes (Figure 4.9).

✎ Dry transfer tone

■ A large number of dry transfer tones are available, but they tend to be rather expensive. There are two main types: one can be applied by rubbing the transfer on to the drawing in the same way as instant lettering (Figure 4.10). The other type has a self-adhesive backing. The required shape is cut out and stuck over the drawing (Figure 4.11).

4.9 *Poster showing a concrete bin*

4.10 *Rub down transfer*

4.11 *Self-adhesive tone*

CHECK YOURSELF – EXAM QUESTIONS

1 On the right is a drawing of a menu holder.

Add appropriate colour, shading and texture to the wood and clear plastic on the drawing. *(6 marks)*

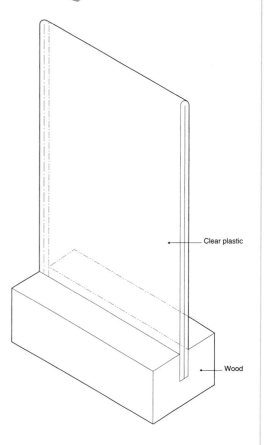

Clear plastic

Wood

2 Details are given about one of the counters to be used in a game.

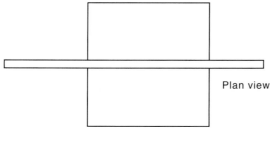

Plan view

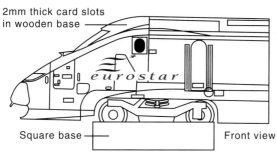

2mm thick card slots in wooden base

eurostar

Square base

Front view

Add pencil shading and texture to the pictorial drawing of the base to:

(i)   enhance the 3D appearance;   *(1 mark)*

(ii) show that the base is made from wood.   *(1 mark)*

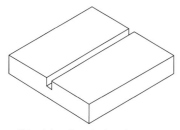

Pictoral view of wooden base for counter

UNIT 5: DATA PRESENTATION

Data is information collected by people who carry out research. You will need to be able to translate or transpose written data into the following visual forms covered in Revision Sessions 1–5.

Tables

- If you carry out a questionnaire or survey, you will need to collate (or put together) all of the information obtained to make any use of it. A table is a good way to show the answers graphically to each of the questions in a questionnaire or the information obtained from a survey.

- An example of an unfinished table is shown below. It is going to be used to show the results of a survey to find the information displayed on various products and/or their packaging. A series of ticks would be placed in the boxes and this would then allow the information displayed on each of the items to be compared quickly and easily.

5.1 *Unfinished table*

Information	Bar code	Product name	Manufacturer	Contact details	List of contents (ingredients)	Best before	Safety warning	Price	Weight or volume
Product Shampoo									
Spray deodorant									
Talcum powder									
Shower gel									
Deodorant stick									
After shave									
Perfume									

CHECK YOURSELF – EXAM QUESTION

1 A sketch map of Allerton Road is given.

Complete the table, showing the number and name of each type of property.   *(2 marks)*

Type	Clothes		Pubs	Hair-dressers		TV	Others	Empty	Video
Number		2			1			1	

CLOTHES | NO 287 EMPTY | CAFE | VIDEO | PUB   PUB | HAIR | TV | OTHER | OTHER | OTHER | HAIR | TV | CLOTHES

ALLERTON ROAD

VIDEO | HAIR | TV | OTHER | OTHER | OTHER | OTHER | CLOTHES | HAIR | PUB   PUB | SHOE | OTHER | HAIR | VIDEO | CAFE

REVISION SESSION 2 ▰ Line graphs ▰

Line graphs are useful for showing changes over a period of time. They are used to show the relationship between two factors, such as time and distance in Figure 5.2.

⚡ A* EXTRA

Both axes must be labelled and a title given to the line graph. Where several lines are plotted on the same graph, different colours or types of line should be used.

■ The line graph in Figure 5.2 plots the position of a song in the top twenty during the month of June. Notice how the numbering on the vertical axis has been reversed (normally it would be 1–20 or 0–20) in order to make the graph easier to understand.

■ To draw a line graph, a series of points are plotted and joined together by straight lines.

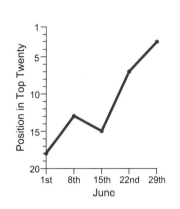

5.2 *Line graph to show chart position of a song during June*

CHECK YOURSELF – EXAM QUESTION

2   A race for four cars was four laps long. At the end of lap one, car number 4 was in first place, car number 1 in second place, car number 3 was third and car number 2 was in last place.

After two laps, car number 4 was still in the lead, car 3 was in second place, car 1 was third and car 2 was still last.

At the end of the third lap, car 1 had moved up to first place, car 2 was in second place, car 4 was third and car 3 was in last place.

Car 2 finally won the race, car 4 was second, third was car 1 and car 3 was last.

Draw a graph or chart to illustrate this information.   *(6 marks)*

Bar charts

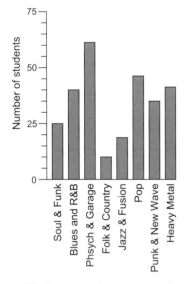

5.3 *Bar chart showing musical tastes of Year 11 students*

In a **bar chart** the information is shown as a series of bars each of the same width with a gap left between each bar (Figure 5.3). The bars can be drawn horizontally or vertically.

■ Single bars are sometimes used as a **proportionate chart**. The bar represents the whole and the parts of it proportions or percentages of the whole (Figure 5.4). Between 1988 and the end of 2001, Kylie Minogue had 34 hit singles. The proportionate chart shown in Figure 5.4 illustrates how these singles were spread out over the 14-year period.

5.4 *Kylie Minogue's hit singles, 1988–2001*

■ **Histograms** are similar to bar charts. They still have two axes but the bars do not have a gap between them.

5.5 *3D bar charts*

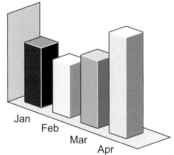

3D bar charts

■ **Three-dimensional charts** are visually more interesting than 2D ones. They allow the illustrator to use a variety of presentation techniques in order to create visually interesting effects such as those shown in Figure 5.5 (e.g. different shades and colours to enhance the 3D effect).

CHECK YOURSELF – EXAM QUESTION

3 An American football game is made up of four quarters each lasting 15 minutes.

In the first quarter of a game between the Broncos and the Giants, Broncos had possession for 8 minutes and the Giants for 7 minutes.

In the second quarter Broncos had possession for 6 minutes and Giants for 9 minutes.

In the third quarter Broncos had possession for $7\frac{1}{2}$ minutes and Giants for $7\frac{1}{2}$ minutes.

In the final quarter Broncos had possession for $2\frac{1}{2}$ minutes and Giants for $12\frac{1}{2}$ minutes.

Draw a graph or chart to illustrate this information.

Marks will be awarded for the effective use of colour and a suitable key. *(8 marks)*

Pie charts

A pie chart is a diagram which uses a circle which represents the whole (Figure 5.6). The circle is cut into sectors to represent information as a proportion or percentage of the whole.

- To draw a pie chart you need to convert percentages into degrees. For example, 40% would be converted as follows $\frac{40 \times 360}{100} = 144$ degrees.

- A protractor is used to divide the pie chart into sectors. Each sector must be accurately measured and labelled.

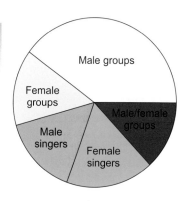

5.6 *Make up of Top Twenty chart*

✎ 3D pie charts

- Greater interest can be created by adding colour and by the use of a third dimension. Showing a sector partly removed can add to the visual impact of the pie chart (Figure 5.7).

5.7 *3D pie charts*

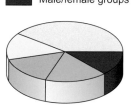

☐	Male groups
☐	Female groups
▨	Male singers
▨	Female singers
■	Male/female groups

- Isometric and planometric are the best forms of 3D drawing to use for this type of presentation.

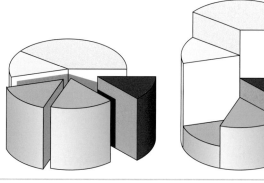

CHECK YOURSELF – EXAM QUESTION

4 The table below shows details of a survey to find the popular colours for watches.

Colour	Blue	Red	Black	White	Yellow
No. of people	180	90	150	120	180

(a) Complete the given outline of a pie chart to illustrate these figures. *(2 marks)*

(b) Convert the pie chart to isometric form and add it to the given drawing of a watch. *(4 marks)*

PIE CHART

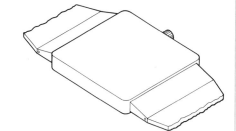

Pictographs

A pictograph uses the principle of a bar chart but pictorial symbols help to explain the statistical data. As well as creating visual impact, this type of graph can be easier to understand (Figure 5.8).

5.8 *Pictograph showing daily attendance figures at an international exhibition*

Monday		1000
Tuesday		3000
Wednesday		4000

- The symbols used must relate to a specific object. They must be simple, clear and easy to understand (Figure 5.9).

5.9 *Types of symbols that would be suitable for use on a pictograph*

CHECK YOURSELF – EXAM QUESTION

5

(a) Part of a chart showing daily attendance figures at an international exhibition is shown below. Each symbol on the chart represents 1,000 people.

Monday		
Tuesday		
Wednesday		
Thursday		2,500

Complete the chart for Thursday, to show an attendance of 2,500 people *(3 marks)*

(b) Why would it be hard to show an attendance of less than 500 people using this type of chart? *(1 mark)*

(c) State why it is quicker to produce this type of chart using a computer. *(2 marks)*

(d) Change the outline given below to produce a new symbol
to represent 1,000 child visitors.

(3 marks)

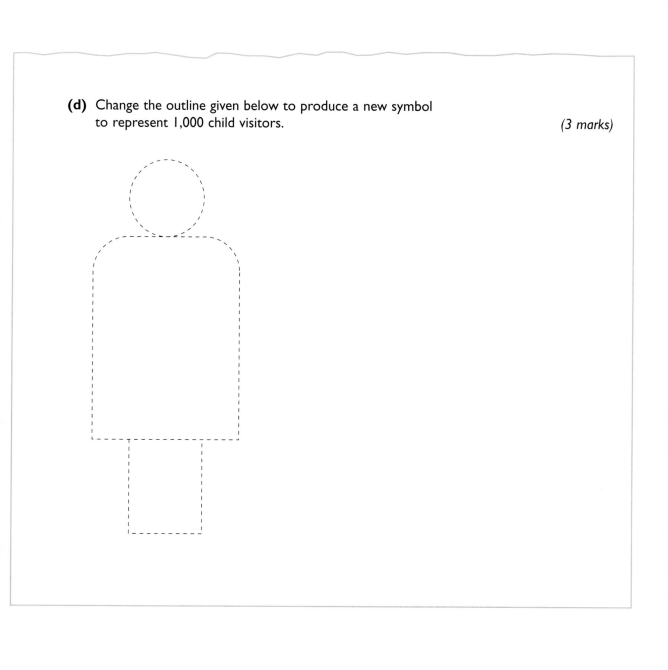

UNIT 6: MODEL MAKING AND PRODUCT MANUFACTURE

REVISION SESSION 1 ▸▸ **Nets: cubes and prisms** ◂◂

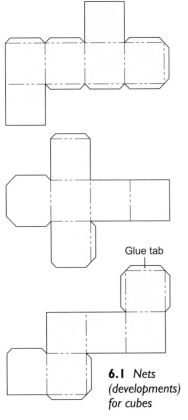

6.1 *Nets (developments) for cubes*

A *net* (sometimes called a surface development) is the flat shape of paper, card, sheet plastic or other thin material that is designed to be cut out and folded up to make cartons, boxes, display stands etc.

- Before a development can be drawn, you need to know the shape of each of the sides of the object that you want to make.

- You will need to know how to design and make products from appropriate materials based on the developments of the following shapes:
  - Cubes
  - Prisms
  - Cylinders
  - Pyramids.

CUBE

- A **cube** has six square surfaces. It can be made in a number of ways. The nets shown in Figure 6.1 are all different but will produce exactly the same cube. Glue tabs must be included so that the development can be stuck together.

- A dotted line is often used to show a fold line but the correct method is a longer dash followed by two short ones.

  . . . . dotted line

  ——— -- ——— -- ——— -- fold line

- Any rectangular box can be made from six sides but obviously they would not all be equal in size.

- Most items of packaging will include the features shown on the net (development) in Figure 6.2.

- What would the net for the boxes shown in Figure 6.3 be like?

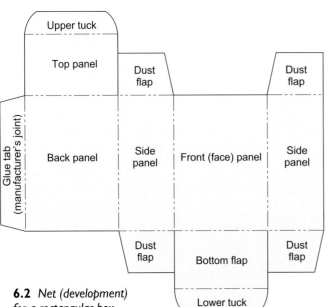

6.2 *Net (development) for a rectangular box*

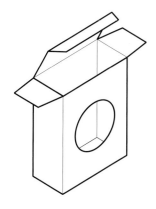

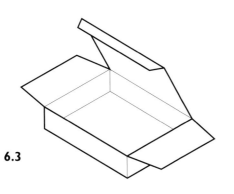

6.3

⚡ **A* EXTRA**

Make sure that you always choose the development which fits your material best and creates the least waste.

6.4 *Examples of prisms*

PRISMS

- Both ends of a **prism** are the same regular shape. The prism is named after the end shape, as shown in Figure 6.4.

- The technique used to draw the net for any type of prism is basically the same (Figure 6.5).

- Draw the plan and front view of the prism (Stage 1).

- Project across the height of the prism and mark off the length of the sides. Numbering the corners of the shape will help you to do this (Stage 2).

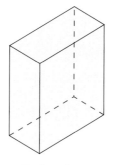
Rectangular prism

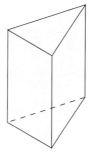
Triangular prism

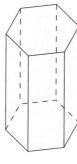
Hexagonal prism

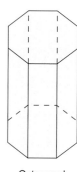
Octagonal prism

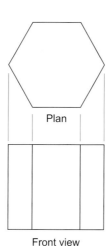

Plan

Front view

6.5 *Technique for drawing a prism*

Stage 1

💡 **QUESTION SPOTTER**

▸ Make sure that you know how to draw the nets of various types of prism, as they form the basis for the design of many items of packaging.

Stage 2

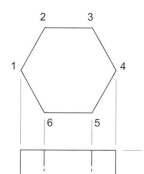

Net (development)

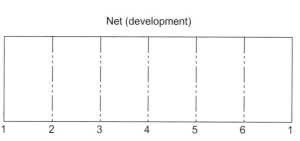

- Add the two ends (the glue tabs), fold in flaps and fold lines (Stage 3). This net will produce a hexagonal box with a fixed base and opening top.

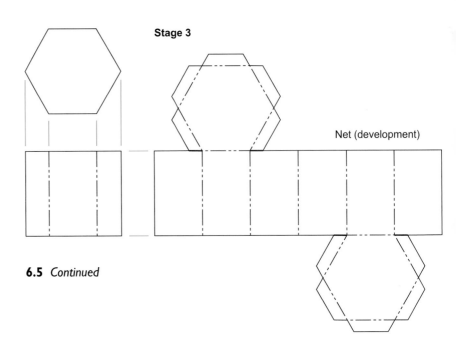

Stage 3

Net (development)

6.5 *Continued*

CHECK YOURSELF – EXAM QUESTION

1 As part of an advertising campaign a company called Universal Packaging are giving away small globes of the world packaged in a box – a pictorial view of which is shown below.

(a) Complete the net (development) of the box which has been started by adding all necessary flaps and glue tabs. You must be able to open and close the top of the box.

(b) Draw, to a suitable size, the letters U and P on to the development so that when the box is folded the letters will appear in the positions shown in the pictorial view.

(8 marks)

Nets: cylinders, pyramids, cones and truncated shapes

CYLINDER

- A **cylinder** is made from a rectangular piece of card. It is easy to find the height of the card, and the length is equal to the circumference of the cylinder. This is best found by measuring the distance across one 30 degree sector and stepping this off 12 times, as shown in Figure 6.6.

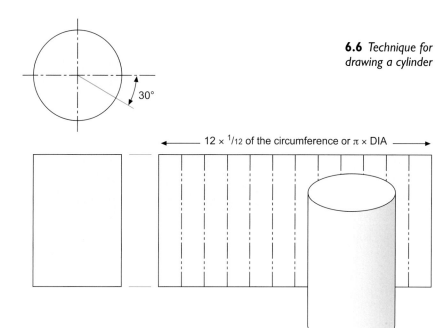

6.6 *Technique for drawing a cylinder*

30°

12 × ¹/₁₂ of the circumference or π × DIA

PYRAMID

- The base of a **pyramid** is a regular shape. Sloping edges go from the corners of the base to meet at the top, or apex, of the pyramid. The pyramid is named after the shape of the base, as shown in Figure 6.7.

- The technique used to draw the development for any type of pyramid is basically the same (Figure 6.8).

6.7 *Pyramids*

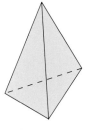
Triangular pyramid

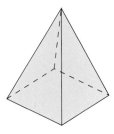
Rectangular pyramid

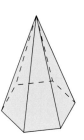
Hexagonal pyramid

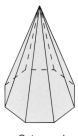
Octagonal pyramid

- **Stage 1:** Draw the plan and front view of the pyramid. You must make sure that the plan is arranged so that one of the sloping sides is horizontal.

- **Stage 2:** Set a pair of compasses to the length of the sloping side on the front view and draw an arc with its centre at A. Step off the length of each side of the base on this arc.

- **Stage 3:** The base, fold lines, glue tabs etc. can be added as required.

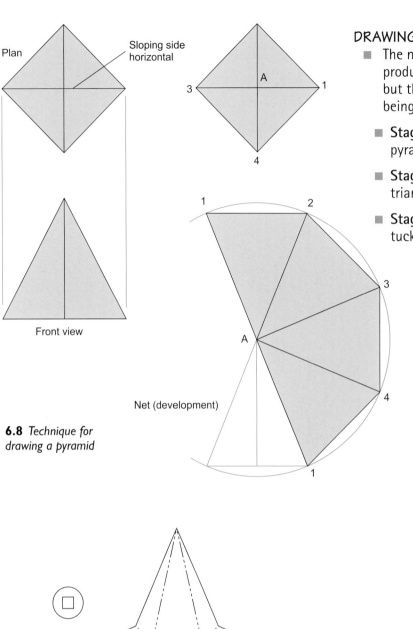

Plan

Sloping side horizontal

A

3 —— 1

4

Front view

6.8 *Technique for drawing a pyramid*

Net (development)

A

1 2 3 4

1

DRAWING A 'STAR' NET

- The net for a pyramid can also be produced as a 'star' shape (Figure 6.9), but this can result in material being wasted.

  - **Stage 1:** Draw the base of the pyramid.

  - **Stage 2:** Draw the correct size triangle on each side of the base.

  - **Stage 3:** Add glue tabs and/or tuck-in flaps.

CONE

- To draw a **cone**, start by drawing the plan and front view (Figure 6.10).

- Set a pair of compasses to the length of the sloping side on the front view and draw an arc with its centre at A.

- You now need to measure the circumference of the base of the cone along this arc. This is best done by measuring the distance across one 30-degree sector and stepping this off 12 times, as shown in Figure 6.10.

6.9 *Technique for drawing a 'star' net*

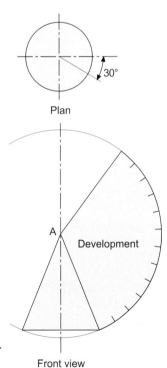

30°

Plan

A

Development

Front view

6.10 *Technique for drawing a cone*

TRUNCATED SHAPES

■ The word 'truncated' means that part of the top of the shape has been cut off, perhaps to form a lid. Two examples of simple truncations are shown in Figure 6.11. Each box is in the form of a rectangular prism with the top cut to form a 'flip up' lid.

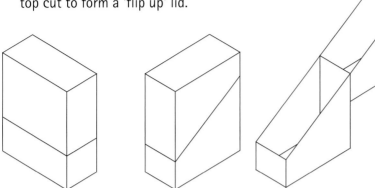

6.11 *Truncated shapes*

■ The net (development) is drawn in a similar way as for a complete prism. The process is shown in Figure 6.12.

- Start by drawing the plan and front view.

- Lines are then projected across from the front view and the length of each side of the prism marked off.

- Lines are projected from where the prism is cut and the shape marked on the development.

- The numbers on each corner make it easy to follow a line down from the plan to the front view and across to the development.

6.12 *Technique for drawing a truncated shape*

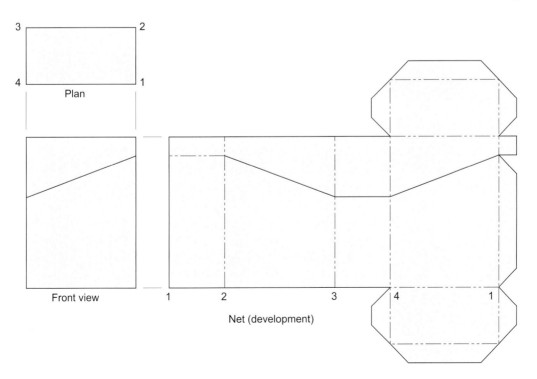

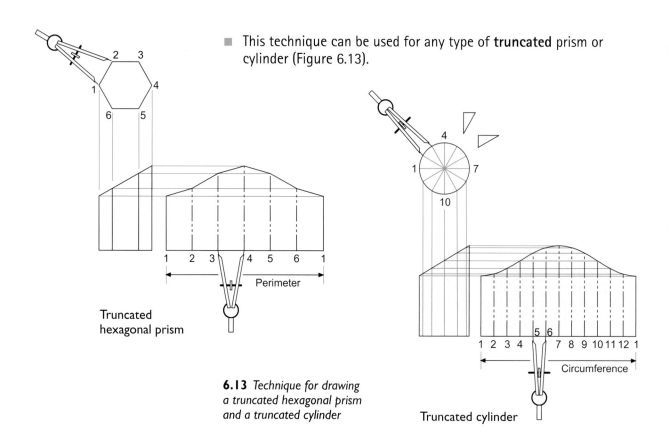

■ This technique can be used for any type of **truncated** prism or cylinder (Figure 6.13).

Truncated hexagonal prism

6.13 *Technique for drawing a truncated hexagonal prism and a truncated cylinder*

Truncated cylinder

QUESTION SPOTTER

▸ Exam questions based on truncated pyramids and cones are rare.

■ The technique involved in drawing the development of a truncated pyramid or cone is similar to that used for a complete shape. The process is explained in Figure 6.14. Once again, by numbering the corners on the plan and net it is fairly straightforward to follow a line from the plan down to the front view and round onto the development.

6.14 *Technique for drawing a truncated pyramid and a truncated cone*

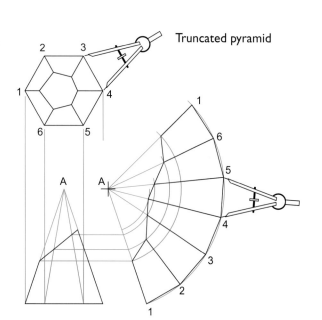

Truncated pyramid

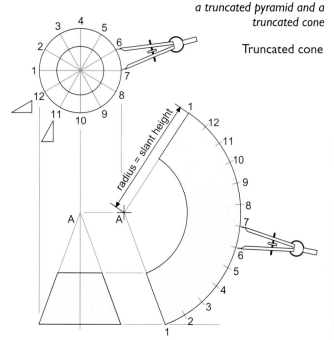

Truncated cone

2 An exploded view of a card and foamboard model rocket is shown. Three templates are required to help children make the rocket.

(a) Use instruments to draw full size:

– a template for the base

(2 marks)

– a template for the fins (construction for the quarter ellipse must be clearly shown)

(3 marks)

– a template for the nose cone.

(2 marks)

(b) (i) Use drawings and notes to show the most economical way that the three fins and the base could be marked out on a single piece of foamboard.

(2 marks)

(ii) Add dimensions to the drawing showing the size of foamboard required. *(1 marks)*

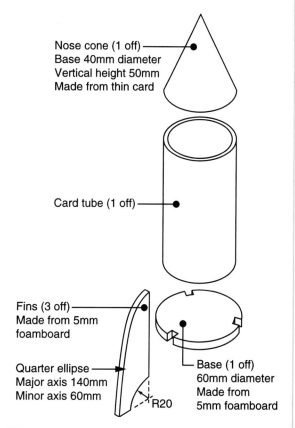

Nose cone (1 off) —
Base 40mm diameter
Vertical height 50mm
Made from thin card

Card tube (1 off) —

Fins (3 off) —
Made from 5mm
foamboard

Quarter ellipse —
Major axis 140mm
Minor axis 60mm

R20

Base (1 off)
60mm diameter
Made from
5mm foamboard

3 The drawing shows a plastic case to hold two CDs. The plastic case is to be packaged in a card box with a lift-off lid.

Specification for the packaging:

– it must have a separate lift-off lid

– the box must be made from a single piece of card

– the lid must be made from a single piece of card

– it must be very easy to remove the plastic case from the packaging.

(a) Use sketches and notes to develop a design for the box and lid. These should show that each of the requirements of the specification has been carefully considered and fulfilled.

(3 marks)

(b) Draw, to a scale of 1:2, the developments (nets) required to make the card box and lid.

(7 marks)

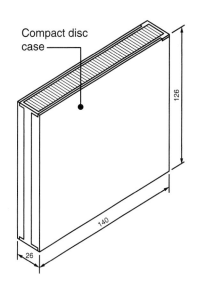

Compact disc case

126

140

26

Nets: slot and tab fixings

Many nets are glued together, but some graphic products are joined using slots and tabs. This method of fixing is commonly used when products are transported in a 'flat pack' form, to be assembled later. For example, a point-of-sale display stand would be sent to shops flat packed as it is cheaper and easier to transport.

■ The more common types of slot and tab fixings are shown in Figure 6.15.

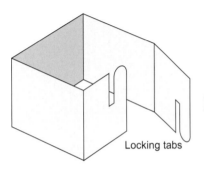

Locking tabs

6.15 *Types of tabs*

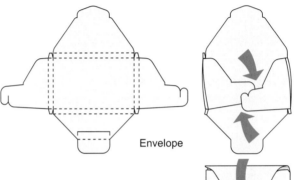

Envelope

Fold side flaps inwards and lock by hooking together the locking tabs.

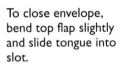

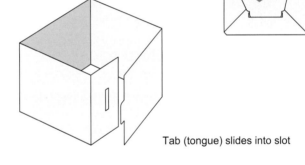

Tab (tongue) slides into slot

To close envelope, bend top flap slightly and slide tongue into slot.

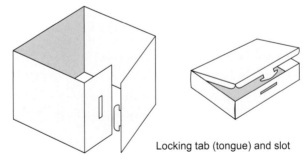

Locking tab (tongue) and slot

■ The leaflet dispenser shown in Figure 6.16 is an example of a product where the net is made from one piece of card and where the assembly requires no gluing.

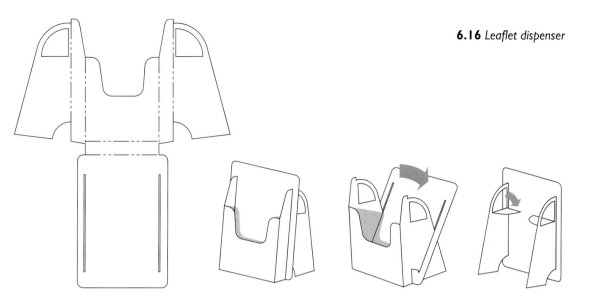

CHECK YOURSELF – EXAM QUESTION

4   Pictorial views of a folder to hold activity sheets and games for a trip to Paris are shown.

The folder is made from one piece of card with the front corners glued together.

(a) A modification is required which will allow the folder to be assembled without the use of glue and yet keep it fastened together securely.

Use notes and sketches to show this modification to the corner A of the folder.

(4 marks)

(b) The drawing below shows a handle which is to be attached to the top of the folder. The handle is made from thin polystyrene sheet. It is to be securely attached to the folder but in such a way that it can be removed easily.

Use notes and sketches to show an appropriate method of attaching the handle to the folder.

(3 marks)

Not to scale

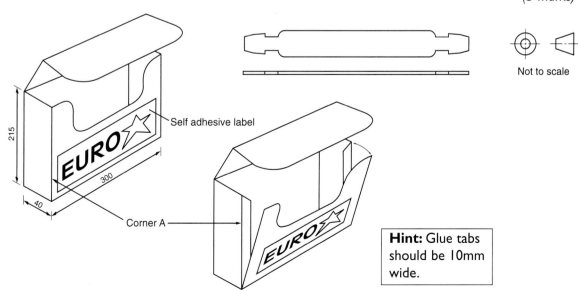

215
300
40
Self adhesive label
EURO
Corner A

Hint: Glue tabs should be 10mm wide.

Fabrication

When individual pieces are cut out and joined together it is called fabrication. You will need to know how part or all of a graphic product can be fabricated from thick card, foamboard or thin plastic sheet (Figure 6.17).

- **Foamboard** is an extremely good material from which to fabricate products. It is stable, lightweight and can easily be cut with a **sharp** craft knife. Figure 6.18 shows some examples of the things that you can do with foamboard.

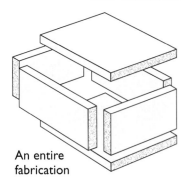

6.17 Fabrications

An entire fabrication

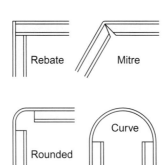

Rebate   Mitre

Curve

Rounded

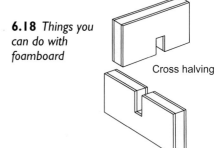

6.18 Things you can do with foamboard

Cross halving

- **Thick card** and **plastic sheet** can be fabricated using butt joints which are glued together. Interlocking pieces can also be made by cutting slots in the material to make a cross-halving joint. The slots must be the same width as the thickness of the material that is going to go in them.

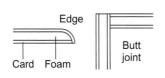

Edge

Butt joint

Card Foam

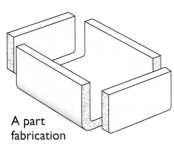

A part fabrication

CHECK YOURSELF – EXAM QUESTION

5 The illustration shows a tray made from card. Students are to use these trays to sell packets of sweets at a fund-raising day.

To make it easier to see the different types of sweets, the inside of the tray is to be divided into six pieces using strips of foamboard 60 mm wide and 4 mm thick.

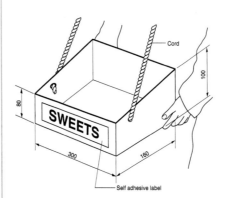

Use sketches and notes to show how the strips of foamboard could be cut and slotted together to make the divisions between the six spaces.

(4 marks)

■ Forming ■

You will need to know how to make part of a product from thin plastic sheet by line bending and/or vacuum forming.

✎ Vacuum forming

■ This is a good way of producing simple shapes from thin plastic sheets. **Vacuum forming** is used in the manufacture of items such as blister packs and inserts to go inside packaging to hold products in place – see Figure 6.19.

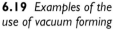

Blister pack

6.19 *Examples of the use of vacuum forming*

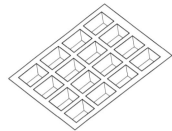

Insert tray for a box of chocolates

MAKING THE MOULD

■ Wood is generally used to make the mould. All sides of the mould must slope, otherwise it is difficult to remove the formed plastic from the mould (see Figure 6.20).

■ The corners of the mould should be slightly rounded to avoid the possibility of them puncturing the thin plastic sheet as it is being formed.

THE PROCESS OF VACUUM FORMING

■ **Thermoplastics**, such as high impact polystyrene (HIP), are used for vacuum forming.

  • **Stage 1:** The mould is placed in the vacuum forming machine and a sheet of polystyrene is clamped above it (Figure 6.21).

  • **Stage 2:** The plastic is heated until it becomes very flexible. First it sags, then it goes flat. At this stage it is ready to vacuum form.

  • **Stage 3:** The mould is raised and the vacuum pump turned on. This sucks out the air between the mould and the plastic, and pulls the plastic tightly over the mould. When cool, the plastic can be removed and cut to the required shape.

6.20 *Making the mould for vacuum forming*

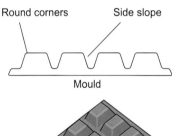

Round corners   Side slope

Mould

Stage 1	Stage 2	Stage 3

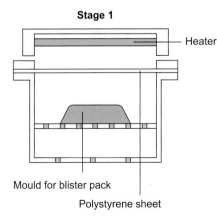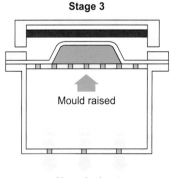

Heater

Mould for blister pack

Polystyrene sheet

6.21 *Stages in the vacuum forming process*

Mould raised

Air sucked out

✎ Line bending

■ **Line bending** is one of the easiest ways to shape sheet polystyrene. Many simple bent shapes can be made in this way.

6.22 *A strip heater*

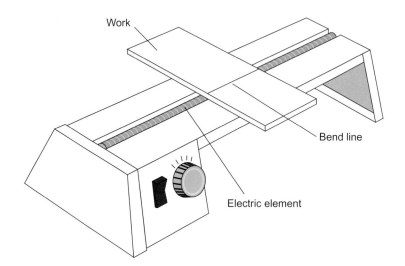

Work

Bend line

Electric element

- **Stage 1:** Mark the position of the bend (Figure 6.22).

- **Stage 2:** Switch on the **strip heater** (sometimes called a **line bender**). This has an electric element mounted under a narrow opening.

- **Stage 3:** Place the bend line over the heat. When the work is soft place it in some sort of former and hold it there until it cools. A simple former for creating a right angle is shown in Figure 6.23.

■ Simple shapes can be made by line bending (Figure 6.24). It is designed to hook over the top of a display stand and is intended to hold a mobile phone.

6.23 *A simple former for creating a right angle bend*

6.24 *A simple shape made by line bending*

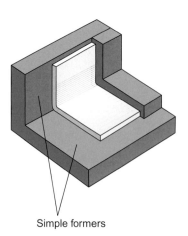

Simple formers

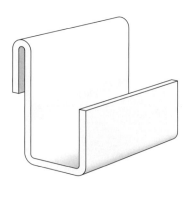

CHECK YOURSELF – EXAM QUESTION

6 **(a)** Name a plastic that is suitable for vacuum forming. *(1 mark)*

(b) Batteries are often sold in blister packs like the one shown below. The plastic blister is made using the vacuum forming process.

Draw, full size, three orthographic views of a design for a former to be used in the production of a blister pack to hold four batteries of the size and type shown.

(5 marks)

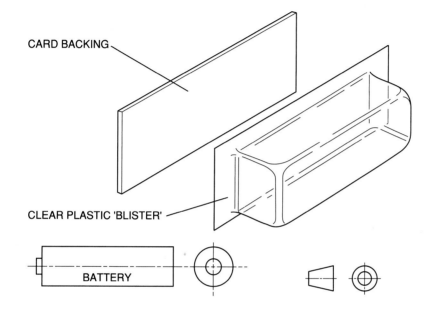

CARD BACKING

CLEAR PLASTIC 'BLISTER'

BATTERY

Typography and layout

The art of lettering style and design is called typography. Each lettering style generally consists of capital letters (upper case) and small letters (lower case).

- When designing and making graphic products you need to select suitable type (text) styles and appropriate point sizes. You should be able to use correct layout techniques, such as text justification (see page 130).

- Ergonomic considerations must be taken into account when selecting **text style**, **text size** and **colour combinations**.

✎ Type style

- Typography is not just about neat lettering. As a designer, you will need to select and use lettering styles very carefully.

- When designing a graphic product it is generally best to use no more than two main lettering styles. A range of sizes of the two lettering styles can, however, be used. This rule can be broken in order to create special effects providing the words can still be read easily.

- Generally, type styles fall into one of four main groups:

  - sans serif
  - serif
  - script
  - decorative or freehand.

6.25 *A CD cover using a sans serif text*

6.26 *A CD cover using a serif text*

SANS SERIF
- These type styles have a strong, bold and clear appearance. They can be modern looking and are often used for titles and headings (Figure 6.25).

SERIF
- Serif texts are easy to read. They have a traditional and reassuring appearance (Figure 6.26).

> ⚡ **A* EXTRA**
>
> A typeface should be chosen based on the effect, meaning or impact required.

SCRIPT
- These look more personal but are sometimes difficult to read (Figure 6.27).

DECORATIVE OR FREEHAND
- Decorative/freehand texts are useful when you want to attract attention such as for a main title or product name (Figure 6.28). They can give a word a particular feel or association, but can be difficult to read.

6.27 *A CD cover using a script text*

6.28 *A CD cover using a decorative text*

QUESTION SPOTTER
- Some exam papers may ask you to design letter styles by <u>hand</u> and apply them to drawings.
- You also need to be aware of DTP programs, and have used them.

Point size

- Type is measured in **points**. One point is approximately 0.25 mm. Therefore a 10 point typeface would be 2.5 mm high.

- Printed text in books, magazines, newspapers etc. is generally no smaller than 10 points (pt), as smaller sizes become difficult to read.

- Main page titles or headlines are sometimes between 24 and 36 points.

- For sub-headings a size between 14 and 16 points is suitable.

10 points 14 points 16 points

24 points 36 pt

6.29 *Front page of daily tabloid newspaper*

✎ Text layout

■ Text can be arranged in various ways to produce different effects and to suit a range of situations. The most common types of layout are:

Centre justification

This means that each line of text is 'centred' on the page. Its uses include headings and titles.

Left justification

This means that the text is aligned to the left. It is generally used to line up text on the left of a page or the left-hand side of an illustration.

Right justification

This means that the text is aligned to the right of the page or illustration.

Fully justified

This means that the text lines up with both the left and right margins. It is generally used in books and newspapers. The spaces between letters and words have to be adjusted in order to achieve this type of layout.

■ The word **justified** refers to the way text is aligned.

CHECK YOURSELF – EXAM QUESTION

7 Complete the block diagram to show **three** selections that would need to be made, from a computer program menu, in order to make the changes between the first and final format.

(3 marks)

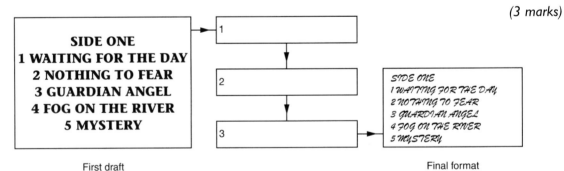

SIDE ONE
1 WAITING FOR THE DAY
2 NOTHING TO FEAR
3 GUARDIAN ANGEL
4 FOG ON THE RIVER
5 MYSTERY

First draft

SIDE ONE
1 WAITING FOR THE DAY
2 NOTHING TO FEAR
3 GUARDIAN ANGEL
4 FOG ON THE RIVER
5 MYSTERY

Final format

The way that colour is used can affect how easy it is to read text. Effective designs often use contrasting colours for the background and the lettering.

Easy to read	Hard to read

✎ Ergonomic considerations

- Ergonomics is concerned with making things easier for people to use. **It is important that all lettering is easy to read.** Typeface style, size, the space between letters and words, the colours used for both the letters and the background all contribute to the readability of any piece of lettering.

- Creating new styles for letters and numbers can be quite a challenge. One approach is to adapt and modify existing designs that you have seen, perhaps by changing one or two letters to provide something more distinctive.

- It is easy to design and draw large-scale bold lettering using grids. Start by using a square grid, as shown in Figure 6.30. Look carefully at letter shapes. Some will require more sections than others, but most will fit a space of five squares high and three squares wide.

- When you have practised using a square grid, move on to try sloping, isometric and perspective grids.

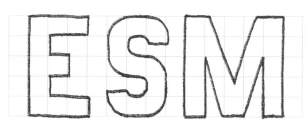

6.30

CHECK YOURSELF – EXAM QUESTION

8 The drawing below shows the side view of a lorry used by a sports car racing team called FAST WHEELS.

(a) Develop a design for the word FAST. The lettering used should be the same height and style as that used for the given word WHEELS. *(2 marks)*

(b) Using instruments, add a drawing of your design for the word FAST to the side view of the lorry.

(5 marks)

Colour theory

Primary

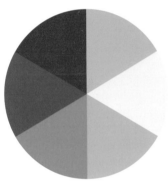

Primary and secondary

6.31 *Colour wheels*

6.32 *Yellow blending into red*

You need to be able to select and justify your choice of colour based on aesthetic considerations and an understanding of the colour wheel.

Colour wheels

- Red, blue and yellow are the **primary colours** (Figure 6.31, top). These colours cannot be made by mixing any other colours together.

- The **secondary colours** – green, orange and purple – are produced by mixing the primary colours together. For example, green can be obtained by mixing blue and yellow (Figure 6.31, lower).

- **Complimentary colours** are those that are opposite each other on the colour wheel, for example red and green. These colours create contrast.

- Colours which are close to each other on the colour wheel – such as yellow and orange – are referred to as **harmonising colours**. They do not create any real contrast. For example, if you were selecting a colour to go on an orange coloured piece of packaging and you wanted it to stand out and be easily read you should use a contrasting colour such as blue rather than a harmonising one such as yellow.

- Harmonising colours are better used if you want to blend two colours together, as shown in Figure 6.32.

HUE AND TONE

- The actual colour (e.g. red) is called the **hue**. White is added to lighten the tone and black is added to darken it (Figure 6.33).

- This tonal effect can be created by pressing harder or softer with a pencil.

6.33 *Hue and tone*

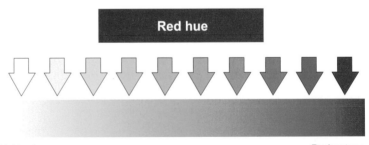

Red hue

Lighter tone   Darker tone

Aesthetics

- Aesthetics is concerned with the visual appearance of a product and what makes it appealing to potential customers.

- Colour:

  - is an essential factor in the success of a product and is often the first thing that draws a person's attention towards it;

  - communicates meanings and associations;

  - helps to define moods;

  - affects the way we feel about products.

COLOUR ASSOCIATIONS

- Colours are connected with feelings.

  - Red is the colour of fire and is therefore considered a 'hot' colour. We often associate red with such things as love and danger. Red signs with a white background are **do not** signs (Figure 6.34).

6.34 *Colour associations used in signs*

  - Green is symbolic of the natural world and is considered a 'calm' colour. It is used to indicate first aid and safety. Green signs displaying information in white are **safety** signs.

  - Yellow reminds us of the sun and is considered a 'stimulating' colour. Yellow and black provide the greatest contrast and are often used together to indicate **hazards**.

  - Blue is the colour of the sea and sky. It is considered to be a 'cool and calming' colour. Blue is used to identify electrical equipment. Blue signs with a white background are **must do** signs.

  - Orange is associated with sunsets and the autumn. It is considered an 'intense' colour and is best used sparingly. Orange is used to indicate **hazards**.

  - Purple is a very 'rich' colour, suggesting **wealth and extravagance**.

  - **Black** is traditionally the colour of **death**. It is, however, frequently used to suggest quality and hi-tech products.

  - White is the colour of snow. It suggests **purity and innocence**. It is a colour associated with products such as detergents and kitchen appliances.

QUESTION SPOTTER

▸ You will be asked to select colours based on aesthetic considerations and your understanding of the colour wheel.

▸ You should use colour associations both in your own design work and in the analysis of existing designs.

A* EXTRA

To gain full marks, you should always try to explain and justify the use of a specific colour in a particular situation (e.g. why red is one of the main colours used in the design of Valentine cards).

CHECK YOURSELF – EXAM QUESTION

9   Study the company symbols on the right and answer these questions.

(a) Which of the two designs do you think is easier to identify and remember, and why? Think about its shape, colour and style of lettering.

(4 marks)

Colour is an important element in the design of symbols and logos.

(b) Name the four primary colours and the three secondary colours.

(5 marks)

(c) Suggest a suitable colour for a symbol for each of the following:

– a fast-food chain

– a health drink

– an environmentally-friendly product.

Give a clear reason for each of your choices.

(5 marks)

UNIT 7: ICT APPLICATIONS

CAD/CAM

You need to understand how CAD/CAM is used both in school and in industry when designing and making graphic products.

✎ CAD

- **Computer aided design (CAD)** is about using ICT (information and communication technology) to assist a designer when designing a product and producing working drawings.

- You can use CAD to assist you as a designer in a number of ways:

  - Drawings can be generated faster than producing them by hand.

  - The quality and accuracy of the work produced is much higher.

  - Drawings can be stretched, rotated, duplicated and flipped over (Figure 7.1). This enables, for example, the product that has been drawn to be viewed from a variety of different positions.

  - Libraries of standard features and components can be accessed and used in the work without any drawing having to take place.

  - Existing drawings can be modified and added to very easily. Different surface colours and textures can be tested.

  - It is easier and quicker to visualise design concepts and outcomes.

  - Part and whole products can be modelled and animated to see that moving parts work in the way intended (Figure 7.2).

  - Computer simulation allows analytical tests to be carried out on products subject to stress and fatigue.

  - Designs can be shared electronically via e-mail, the Internet and video conferencing using a web camera.

  - Nets (developments) can be created for packaging.

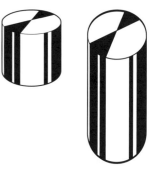

7.1 *Drawings can be stretched, rotated, duplicated and flipped over*

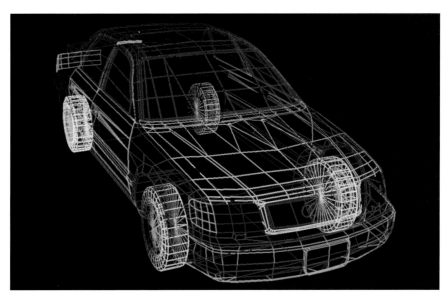

7.2 *Computer-animated drawing showing how moving parts work*

7.3 *Robots used to undertake tasks*

✎CAM

■ **Computer aided manufacture (CAM)** means any aspect of manufacturing that uses a computer system to assist in the process.

■ You can use a computer to generate, process and store the number systems that are required to control machinery and equipment.

■ All computer-controlled machines are, in fact, CNC (computer numerical control) machines because all control is numerical. CNC simply means control by numbers.

■ CAD benefits the manufacture in a number of ways:

  • If they are programmed correctly, computer-controlled machines make fewer mistakes than humans.

  • They can increase productivity as they can operate continuously for 24 hours a day.

  • Labour costs are reduced because fewer human operators are required.

  • The standard of manufacture is very accurate, reliable and consistent.

  • Robots can undertake tasks which would be considered unsafe for humans.

CHECK YOURSELF – EXAM QUESTION

1 A drawing of a logo design is shown.

The logo has been designed in the USA. The printing will be done in the UK.

State how ICT has helped the designers to communicate the designs to the printing company.

(3 marks)

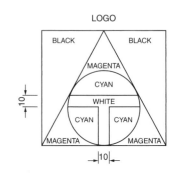

Self-adhesive signs

You need to understand how CAD/CAM is used in the manufacture of self-adhesive vinyl signs. The following case study outlines how this process would be carried out in a commercial context.

RESEARCH

- The first stage in the production process is when a customer expresses an interest in having a product made.

- Once this happens, a researcher from the manufacturer has a meeting with the customer. Together they talk through exactly what is required and produce a detailed written outline of what they visualise the end-product to be like (Figure 7.4). This becomes the specification for the product.

7.4 *Preparing the specification*

DESIGN

- Once the specification is complete, it is given to the designer. The designer creates a sheet on the computer of about four designs, matching what the customer has specified. The design sheet is printed and sent to the customer (Figure 7.5).

- The customer is given time to make comments. When a final decision has been made on what they require, the project returns to the design company with the go-ahead for production to start.

'a' raised and inset

La Strada

Logo in neon lettering, characters close, but not linked

Italian flag

Pizza - Pasta in chrome lettering

Pizza - Pasta

Three stylised, very simple brush strokes with the colours of the Italian flag

7.5 *Rough designs*

7.6 *The final company logo*

PRODUCTION

- The first stage that takes place in the production process is a picture conversion on the computer. Before the image can be sent to the cutter, the composition of lines which form the words and pictures must be changed so that the cutter will cut halfway through the width of the lines.

- If a picture or image is specified that is not on the computer (e.g. a company logo), then this is scanned into the system.

- Next the size of the actual lettering and picture must be entered (Figure 7.6).

- If a prototype needs to be made for the sign, a pen can be used in the vinyl cutter instead of a drag blade and paper can be used instead of vinyl. This will produce an exact replica of the sign so that the customer can check that this is going to fulfil their needs.

- When the design has been checked, it can then be produced. The cutter is set up with a roll of vinyl. The image on the computer is then sent to the cutter which automatically cuts out the design on the screen to the exact shape and size required. The blade is set so that it only cuts through the vinyl and not the backing sheet.

- Once this is complete, the vinyl is cut off the roll and placed on a flat workbench. It is then carefully 'weeded' out by hand with a scalpel and tweezers (the excess vinyl from between the letters etc. is taken out).

- A tacky backing sheet is cut and smoothed over the surface of the vinyl. The sticky backing of the vinyl is peeled off and the design is pressed firmly onto its intended surface. The backing sheet is then removed.

- The production of self-adhesive vinyl signs, lettering and symbols can be carried out in a school situation using CAM cutter/plotters such as Roland CAMM 1 machines, Lynx & ultra Cutters and Stika machines.

- The process is the same as that described for the commercial production of vinyl signs. Some of these CAM machines can also be used to cut paper and thin card. This is useful for the manufacture of nets for packaging.

7.7 *Installing the logo on site*

CHECK YOURSELF – EXAM QUESTION

2 The drawing shows an incomplete design for a stencil to be used in the manufacture of signs to show people where the toilets are in a school.

Another method of adding the symbols to the signs would be to make them from self-adhesive vinyl. Name a piece of computer aided manufacturing (CAM) equipment that could be used to cut out the vinyl symbols. *(1 mark)*

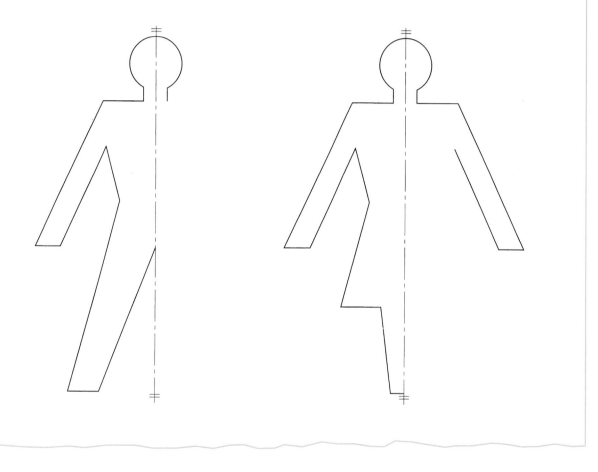

Desktop publishing

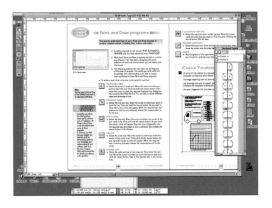

7.10 *Screen showing a page design using QuarkXpress*

You should understand that Desktop Publishing or DTP is what designers use to arrange words and pictures together on computer screen.

- You need to know the following:
  - How to use a DTP program such as QuarkXpress, Pagemaker or Microsoft Publisher.
  - These types of program are used to design graphic products such as magazines, posters and books.

- In DTP all the text is in boxes – see Figure 7.10 (remember these do not show on the final printout).

- Pictures and photographs are also put into boxes.

- You can create more complicated shapes and special effects than in Word. For example, you can curve and stretch text (Figure 7.11) and put pictures into round and elliptical shapes.

Stretch
Stretch

7.11 *Stretching using QuarkXpress*

✎ Clip Art

- Most word processing packages come with a selection of Clip Art. Clip Art is the name given to files of pictures that you can use in your work.

- To access these files you need to click on Insert on the menu bar. Select Picture and then Clip Art. You will see a box of clip art pictures organised into topics. Select the topic you require and choose the piece of Clip Art you want to use (Figure 7.12). Click on it and select Insert, then the image will appear in your work.

- If you click on the picture you will see that it is in a box. You can drag the picture with the mouse to move it around. You can make it bigger or smaller by clicking and dragging the corners of the box.

7.12 *Examples of Clip Art images*

Navigation Contr...

Office

People

People at Work

Photographs

Places

Plants

Religion

Science & Tech...

Seasons

Shapes

Signs

Special Occasions

Sports & Leisu...

Symbols

Transportation

Travel

Weather

Web Backgroun...

Web Banners

Web Bullets & ...

✎ Scanner

- A scanner is useful when you want to import your own artwork and photographs into a computer system. You need to be able to explain how an image is scanned into a computer system.

- The most common type of scanner is a flatbed scanner (Figure 7.13). To operate it, open the lid and place the image you want to scan face down on the scanner window.

7.13 *Flatbed scanner*

- You use the on-screen setting to select the quality of resolution of your scan and to choose colour or black and white. Most scanners do a test scan first and show you a preview so that you can move the picture or select just one part of it to scan.

- Once you are satisfied, click on Scan or OK to do the final scan. You can then name and save the image as a picture file.

- Almost all scanners will enable you to save it as a **bitmap** (bmp) file, which is what you need if you want to import the image into Word.

CHECK YOURSELF – EXAM QUESTION

3 The drawing shows a part finished advertisement for 'FOLO MINTS'.

   (a) Add pencil shading to the isometric drawing of the letter O to enhance the 3D appearance.

        (2 marks)

   (b) Complete the isometric drawing of the word FOLO.

        (4 marks)

   (c) Explain how the hand drawn isometric lettering could be imported into a computer system.

        (2 marks)

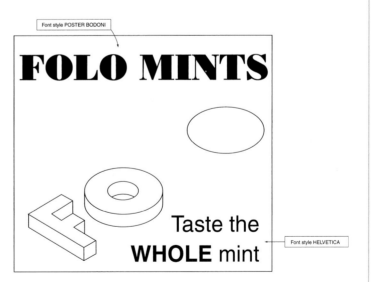

   (d) A computer system has been used to add the slogan 'Taste the WHOLE mint'. Describe how the same system could be used to add the product name 'FOLO MINTS'.

        (2 marks)

Paint and Draw programs

You need to understand how to use a Paint and Draw program to produce original artwork, including lines, texture and colour.

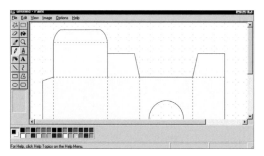

7.14 *Paint screen*

- Suitable programs to use include PAINT, AUTOSKETCH, PAINTBOX and, for more advanced work, PRODESKTOP.

- Most basic Paint and Draw programs operate in a similar way (Figure 7.14). They have a drawing area and a selection of tools and colours which you can select with the mouse.

- The following outlines the main (but *not* all) features of this type of program. It provides you with sufficient knowledge and understanding to be able to answer exam questions on basic Paint and Draw programs.

- To select a tool, click on its icon in the panel (or tool bar).

FREEHAND LINES
- Select the pencil or brush tool. Move the cursor to where you want to start the line. Click and hold the mouse button. Then move the cursor to draw the required freehand line. Releasing the mouse button fixes the line. You are able to select different types and thickness of line.

STRAIGHT LINES
- Select the line tool icon. Move the cursor to where you want to start the line. Click and hold the mouse button. As you start to move the cursor, a line will appear. When the required size and position for the line are achieved, release the mouse button to fix the line.

BOX SHAPES
- Select the box tool. Move the cursor to where one corner of the box needs to be. Click and hold the mouse button. As you move the cursor, a box will appear. Drag the cursor diagonally until the required size and shape of box is achieved, then release the mouse button to fix the box.

CIRCLES
- Select the circle tool. Move the cursor to where you want the centre of the circle to be. Click and hold the mouse button. As you move the cursor, a circle will appear. When the required size of circle is achieved, release the mouse button to fix the circle.

ADDING TEXT
- Select the style and size of text required. Then select the text tool. Move the cursor to where you want the text to start and click the mouse button. Type in the required text in the normal way.

Hint:
The best way to find out how all the different tools work is to experiment with them.

QUESTION SPOTTER

▸ Generally you will not be asked questions about specific software such as Prodesktop, 2D Design or Corel Draw, as not all students have access to these programs.
▸ If, however, you feel that your answer to a question could be enhanced by applying your knowledge and understanding of such software, then do it.
▸ You must, however, take care to ensure that the details are relevant to the question.

COLOUR AND TEXTURE
- Select the required colour and/or texture. Move the cursor inside the area that you want to fill with colour. Clicking the mouse button fills the area.

ERASING MISTAKES
- Select the erase tool. Click and hold the mouse button, then move the cursor over the area that you want to erase.

GRIDS
- Most programs of this type have a grid facility which enables you to position and size your drawings more accurately.

CHECK YOURSELF – EXAM QUESTION

4 A series of instructions are required which explain to children how to use a computer to draw the lorry shown in the sketch below.

The stage explaining how to draw the body of the lorry has been completed.

Use drawings and text to explain the remaining four stages required to complete the computer drawing of the lorry.

Use your judgement for any sizes not given.

(10 marks)

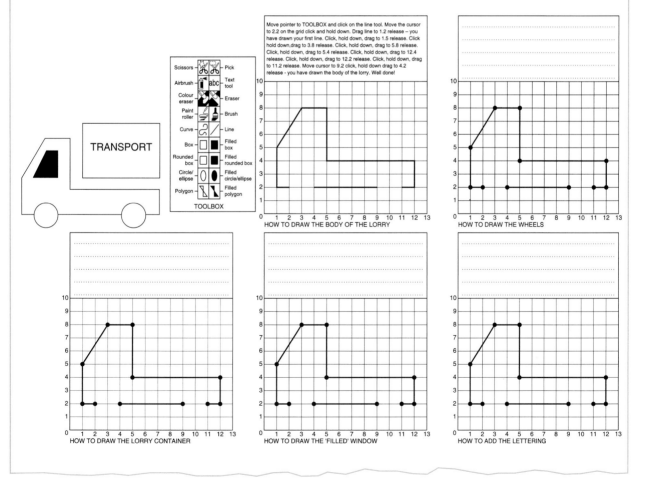

Researching and communicating information

You should be able to gather and edit research material and communicate information using:
- databases
- the Internet
- e-mail.

✎ Databases

- A **database** is a system for storing, modifying and retrieving information. The information can be modified by adding, removing or changing the details.

- A telephone directory, Teletext or the Yellow Pages are examples of databases. A school or club might use a database to keep information about its members.

- You need to know how to use a computerised database to obtain information.

- Each type of data is called a **field** (e.g. names and addresses).

- A single piece of data is called an **entry**. Some databases help you to enter additional details by giving you a **form** – a screen where you fill in a collection of entries, called a **record**, about one particular thing (Figure 7.15).

7.15 *A database screen*   *Fields*   *Entry*

Stock ID	Stock description	Stock type	Date received	Selling price	Cost price	Re-order level	Amount ordered	Quantity in stock	Supplier ID
1	P4 1.8GHz	computer	23/04/2003	£399.00	£259.00	4	8	12	2
2	P4 2.0GHz	computer	02/05/2003	£459.00	£359.00	3	8	1	2
3	P4 2.3GHz	computer	10/03/2003	£579.00	£459.00	3	6	8	7
4	Epson 62B	printer	23/03/2003	£89.99	£49.99	2	12	12	4
5	HP Deskjet 90	printer	02/05/2003	£125.00	£79.00	7	6	12	3
6	Canon 340C	printer	10/03/2003	£109.99	£69.99	5	8	20	5
7	128Kb RAM	memory	12/03/2003	£25.00	£10.00	6	10	15	14
8	256Kb RAM	memory	12/03/2003	£45.00	£18.00	6	12	20	14
9	Maxtor 80Gb HD	hard drive	15/03/2003	£95.00	£45.00	5	15	10	8
10	19" Monitor liama	monitor	20/03/2003	£225.00	£125.00	2	5	8	9
11	15" TFT Mitsubisi	monitor	21/03/2003	£259.00	£129.00	3	5	2	8
12	Maxtor 120Gb HD	hard drive	22/03/2003	£119.00	£58.00	5	12	4	8
13	17" TFT Mitsubisi	monitor	23/03/2003	£299.00	£149.00	2	5	7	8
14	P4 2.5GHz	computer	30/03/2003	£999.00	£599.00	3	8	5	7
15	L&G 56k	modem	01/04/2003	£59.00	£29.00	5	5	5	11

- The way the fields and records are organised is called **data hierarchy**.

- Most computerised databases will have visual data as well as text. A **search function** can find particular entries in a database and a **sort function** can sort out data into different orders such as alphabetical. A **filter function** sorts data into groups (e.g. you could use a filter to make a list of all the students in a school who lived in the same street).

- **Videotex systems**, such as Teletext, use a database to store information. You can see the data on your television screen using a remote control keypad to change from one page (screen) of data to another.

- Businesses use **data warehousing** (accessing various databases) to build up a picture of business conditions and market trends.

- Some databases are stored on **CD-ROMs**. Most CD-ROMs are interactive and enable you to take part in what happens and choose the things you want to see and hear.

✎ The Internet

- You need to know how to use the **Internet** to visit appropriate **websites** in order to view and possibly print relevant research material.

- The Internet is a global network of interconnected computers that communicate with each other via the existing telecommunications networks.

- The 'Web' uses the internet network to access and link websites. To access the Web you need a computer connected to a telephone line using a **modem**. You also need an account with an **Internet Service Provider (ISP)** who connects you to the Web via their powerful computer systems.

- Through your modem and your ISP you can explore what is available on the Web using a program called a **web browser**. You view the contents of a Web page in your browser's window (Figure 7.16).

- Each Web page has a unique address which tells your computer exactly where to find it.

- To view a page for which you have an address, connect up to the Internet and launch your browser. Type the address in a box in your browser's window. It is usually called something like the Location, Go To or Address box, depending on which browser you use. Then press the Return key or click on the confirmation button. It is usually called Send, OK or Go.

7.16 *A Web page*

- If you do not have the address, you can use a facility called a **search service** to look for Web pages on a particular topic. Your Web browser should have a Search button which enables you to view a list of search services. Click on one to go to that page. Most search services allow you to type in a key word which describes the topic you want to look up. You will need to follow the instructions given by the specific service that you are using to find out exactly what you need to type. Click on the Search button to start the search.

- A list of pages containing your key word will appear. Find a page that you want to view and click on its hyperlink to look at it.

E-Mail

■ You can send electronic messages – known as **e-mail** – to anyone else with an Internet connection.

■ Everyone connected to the Internet can have a unique e-mail address, like a personal mailbox, where they can send and receive messages.

■ To send an e-mail you need an e-mail program. Most service providers supply one of these with your Internet software package. Launch your e-mail program. Click on **Option** or the button that allows you to compose a new message. In the window that appears, type your message and the address of the person you want to send it to.

■ You can also send things like pictures and sounds with your e-mail. Most e-mail programs have a button labelled **Attach** or something similar. This attaches the picture or sound to the e-mail message. When you attach something to an e-mail, your mail program encodes the picture or sound. Now it can travel with the main text until it reaches its destination computer where it is turned back into sound or pictures.

■ To send your e-mail connect up to the Internet and click on the **Send** button. Disconnect when your message has been sent.

CHECK YOURSELF – EXAM QUESTION

5 The image below was taken from a point of sale manufacturer's website. It shows examples of point of sale models produced by the company.

Complete the block diagram to show how the image could be captured from the website, put into a Desk Top Publishing application and then re-sized.

(4 marks)

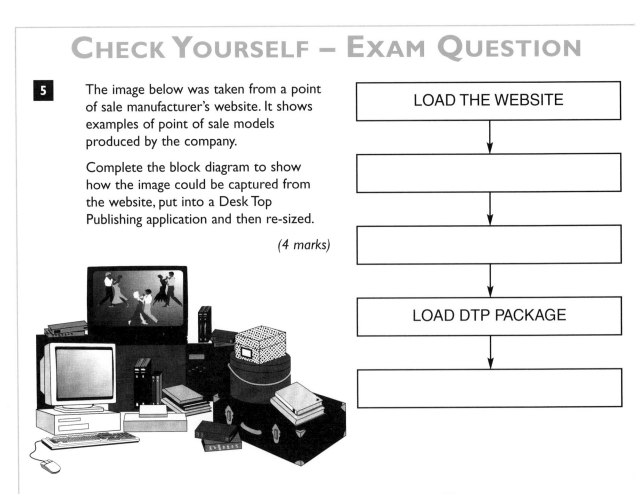

LOAD THE WEBSITE

↓

[ ]

↓

[ ]

↓

LOAD DTP PACKAGE

↓

[ ]

Tables and spreadsheets

You should be able to present data and information using:
- tables
- spreadsheets
- graphs
- charts.

✎ Tables

■ There are two main ways of producing a **table** using Word.

Method 1

■ Select Table at the top of the screen and go down to **Draw**.

■ Select your starting point. Click and drag diagonally to draw a rectangle – the shape and size that you want your whole table to be.

■ Draw in the required number of columns and rows.

■ Add the text required in each of the boxes.

Method 2

■ Select Table and go down to Insert and across to Table.

■ Select the number of columns and rows you require. Click on **OK**.

■ Add the text required in each box (Figure 7.17). The box size will automatically alter to fit the amount of text required.

Age (years)	17	18	19	20	21
Frequency	23	13	4	0	1

7.17 *A simple table*

✎ Spreadsheets

■ When you use a **spreadsheet**, the computer screen becomes a table or grid of boxes. You can type words or numbers in the boxes and then perform sorting or calculations with them. For example, you can use a spreadsheet to work out the cost of a project and to help plan the materials that you will need for it.

■ Business people use spreadsheets to help them calculate expected profits or losses. 'Modelling' a project in this way helps them to see if the project is worth pursuing.

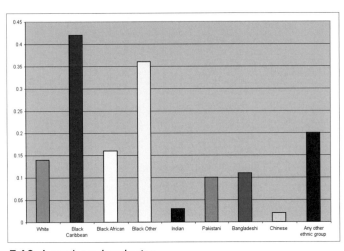

7.18 *A graph produced using information from a spreadsheet*

■ It is possible to produce graphs and charts from the data presented in a spreadsheet (Figure 7.18).

■ The following explains how to produce a simple spreadsheet which gives details about the materials that you buy to make a graphic product.

■ One of the most common programs used to produce spreadsheets is **Excel**. This comes as part of the Microsoft Office package. To start your spreadsheet, launch Excel. You will see a blank table made up of rows and columns.

■ The individual boxes in the table are called **cells**. Click in the first cell in the first column. This is cell A1. Type 'Material'. Use this column to list all the materials and components that were purchased to make your product.

■ At the end of the list type in TOTAL. Click in cell B1 and type Cost. In this column, note the cost of each of the items in column A.

■ Click in the cell beside TOTAL. Move the cursor over the AutoSum tool on the toolbar and click on it. It looks a little like a capital E (Σ). A flashing dotted line appears around the cells containing the numbers you are adding. A formula appears in the cell beside TOTAL. Instead of a plus sign this formula has a colon sign (:). The colon means that all the numbers in column B will be added.

■ Press Enter (↵). The total appears in the cell you clicked in.

■ If you run out of space, you can widen a column by clicking on the edge of the label at the top of the column and dragging it.

■ Click on column heading **B**. Select Cells on the Format menu. Click on the Number tab. Select Currency from the Category list and click on OK (Figure 7.19). This tells the computer that you are typing in money values.

7.19 *A simple spreadsheet in Excel*

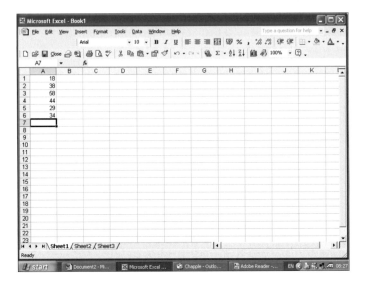

✎ Graphs and charts

- You should be able to produce computer-generated graphs and charts using data from tables and spreadsheets. The examples explained here illustrate the number of Year 11 students in a school who like each of eight different kinds of music.

CHOOSING A CHART

- You will find some charts better than others for displaying certain kinds of information. For example, a **pie chart** is a good way of displaying just one column of numbers. If you want to compare more columns or rows, a **bar chart** (or **column chart**) is the best. **Line graphs** are a good way to show how something changes over time.

MAKING A PIE CHART

- Pie charts display each number on a list as one section of a circle. Open Microsoft Excel. Before you go any further, make sure you only have one column of numbers on your screen (Figure 7.20).

  - **Stage 1:** Select the cells that contain the information you want to display. You do not need to include any headings or totals, just the data.

  - **Stage 2:** Click on the Chart Wizard tool on the toolbar and the first Chart Wizard box appears. At the top of the box click on Standard Types (Figure 7.21).

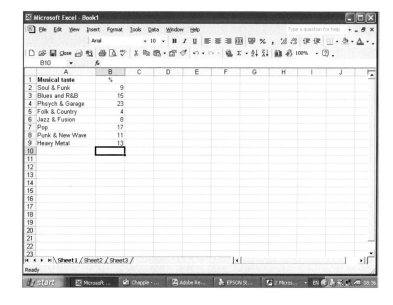

  - **Stage 3:** On the left-hand side of the box you will see a list of charts. Click on Pie so that a range of pie-chart designs appear in the box.

7.20 *Data in Excel before making it into a pie chart*

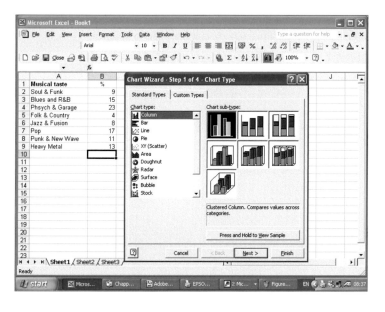

7.21 *The Chart Wizard panel*

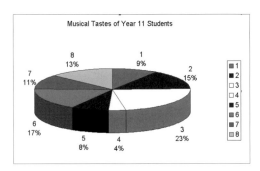

7.22 *A pie chart in Excel*

- **Stage 4:** Choose one of the pie chart designs. Click on it to select it. To see the next Chart Wizard box, click on **Next**.

- **Stage 5:** The second Chart Wizard page should display the data presented as a pie chart of the form chosen in Stage 4. If it doesn't, then click on the words **Data Range** near the top of the box.

- **Stage 6:** The numbers on your spreadsheet are in columns so there should be a black dot beside **Columns**. If it is not there, click so that a dot appears.

- **Stage 7:** Click on **Next** so that a third box appears. Click on **Titles** at the top of the box. Click in the title box, then type a title.

- **Stage 8:** To add labels or percentages beside each section of the chart, click on **Data Labels** for more options. When you are happy with your chart, click on **Finish** (Figure 7.24).

MAKING A BAR CHART

- In computer programs this type of chart is generally called a **column chart**. The process is the same as for a pie chart, except for **Stage 3**. Here you choose **Column** and a range of column-chart designs appear in the box. When you click on your choice of column-chart design, the data is transformed into a bar chart (Figure 7.23).

- It is possible to produce a range of other charts and graphs using Chart Wizard.

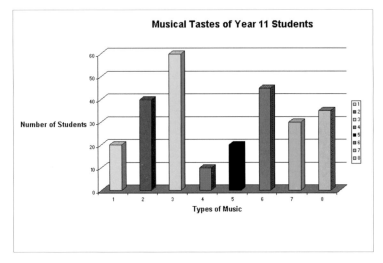

7.23 *A bar chart in Excel*

CHECK YOURSELF – EXAM QUESTION

6   Part of a chart showing daily attendance figures at an international exhibition is shown below.

Monday	♦	
Tuesday	♦♦	
Wednesday	♦♦♦	
Thursday		2,500

Each symbol on the chart represents 1,000 people.

State why it is quicker to produce this type of chart using a computer.

(2 marks)

Computers have a range of functions that make them ideal for testing and trialling graphic products.

- Computers make design easier because you can change and modify aspects of your designs – such as size, colour and layout – as much as you like on the screen without having to re-draw everything each time.

- When you use design software, you can **manipulate** (change around) your designs using a range of different functions called **tools**.

✎ Copying and moving text and images

- You can select a piece of text or a drawing and **cut and paste** it (move it to another part of the document or another file) or **copy** it (repeat or duplicate it). For example, by copying a net several times you can test how many would fit onto a piece of card of a certain size.

- You can cut and paste text and move it to different positions on the net to test which is the most suitable.

- Different colour combinations for the background and the text could be trialled.

✎ Computer animation

- You can use computer animation:

  - to test that the moving parts on products, such as boxes and pop-up cards, operate in the way intended

  - to visualise a design behaving like the real product (Figure 7.24).

- This enables problems to be identified before actual manufacture starts. Software programs such as Pro Desktop include this function.

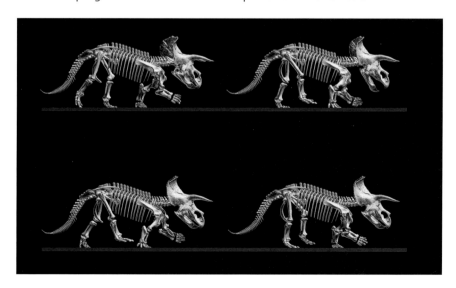

7.24 *Computer animation programs can be used for anything from pop-up cards to moving dinosaurs.*

✎Computer aided testing (CAT)

- You need to be aware that industry standard software is available which simulates products being used. This type of program allows analytical tests to be carried out related to factors such as stress and fatigue.

✎Flow charts and production plans

- You should be able to use ICT to produce **flow charts** and **production plans**.

- Both flow charts and production plans can be produced in the same way using Word; the only difference will be the shapes of the boxes used.

- Select View at the top of the screen.

- Go down to **Toolbars** and drag across to **Drawing**. Click on **Drawing**.

- Select **AutoShapes** at the bottom of the screen.

- Go to **Flowchart** shapes and select the required shape.

- Position the shape in the correct place on the screen and drag to the required size.

 - To add text, select the text box from the bottom of the screen and position inside the flow chart shape. Type in the required text.

- Arrows and lines can be added between the shapes by selecting line or arrow from the bottom of the screen and drawing them in the correct position (Figure 7.25).

7.25 *A flow chart*

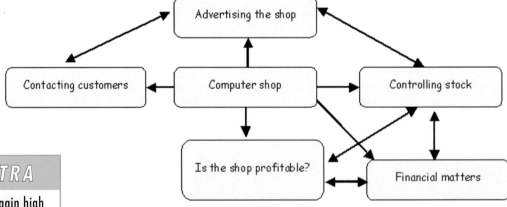

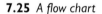
✎Web pages

- You need to have a general understanding of what is involved in the process of designing a Web page.

- You should plan a layout for your page before you turn it into an actual Web page.

- Sketch a layout for the page on a piece of paper. Make a note of the pictures, text and other information that you want to include.

- The easiest way to arrange, or build, a Web page is by using a program called a **Web Editor**. Many of these are suitable for complete beginners. Your service provider may supply one. If not, there are lots that you can download from the Web or you could buy one from a shop.

- With most simple Web Editors you can build up a page by selecting the type of item you want to include and then supplying more details about it. For example, to add text you select the Text Option. Usually a box appears and you can choose from different font styles and sizes and then type in your text.

- You can add background colours, pictures and headings using the same technique (Figure 7.26). If you select the hyperlink option, you will need to type in the address of the Web page you want to link your page to.

7.26 *Starting a Web page*

✎ Manipulating text and images

- You need to know how to mould and size text and/or graphics to suit a particular situation.

- Word will enable you to do a range of different things with text in order to make it look more interesting. You can create coloured text, shadows, outlines and special effects, and you can even curve text around pictures.

TEXT STYLES AND COLOURS

- Start by opening a new Word document. Write a word and highlight it with the cursor. Click on Format in the menu bar and select Font. You will see a box that provides you with a lot of options to try.

WORDART

- This is a facility for making text effects. It is very good for producing headings, posters and stickers. To access WordArt click on Insert in the menu bar, select Picture and then choose WordArt.

- You will see a selection of WordArt styles. When you pick one, a box will appear in which you have to write your text and select the font and font size.

- Click on OK and the text will appear in your document.

■ It is possible to **manipulate** (change around) your designs using a range of different functions called **tools**.

7.27 *You can use WordArt to manipulate your text in order to create different effects.*

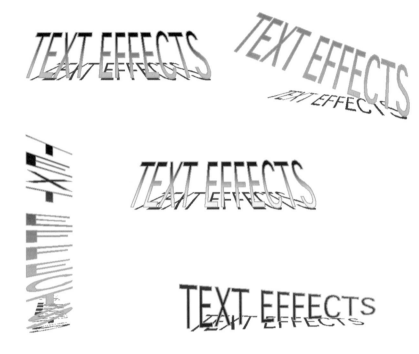

■ You can Resize a picture or text box. You can also Rotate (spin), Skew (twist), Crop (trim) and Stretch pictures and text boxes (Figure 7.27).

■ **Text wrapping** or **Wrapping** allows you to arrange text in a shape that fits neatly around a picture.

UNIT 8: INDUSTRIAL APPLICATIONS

Commercial production

You will need to have an understanding of the following commercial production methods:
• job production
• batch production
• repetitive flow
• continual flow process.

8.1 *Architect's model of a proposed building complex*

✎ Job production

■ **Job production** involves producing 'one off' products. Every item produced is different. It is a very labour intensive method of production.

■ A display model made from card to be used on an exhibition stand is an example of this type of product (Figure 8.1).

✎ Batch production

■ **Batch production** involves the production of a specified quantity of a product (large or small). Batches can be repeated as many times as required.

■ This type of production method is very flexible and can be used to produce batches of similar products with only a small change to the tooling (the setting up of the equipment and machinery required).

■ In school you can simulate this method of production by using stencils, templates, jigs, formers.

■ Equipment such as photocopiers, cutter-plotters and computer printers can also be used as aids to batch production in schools.

⚡ A* EXTRA

▸ You will need to understand how the method of production changes depending on the number of products to be made.

01983 857097
Mobile 07785 222256
www.bigskygallery.com

8.2 *Examples of made-up business cards*

8.3 *Video sleeve*

■ A business card is an example of a product that would be manufactured using batch production (Figure 8.2).

✎ Repetitive flow

■ **Repetitive flow** (sometimes called **mass production**) involves producing large numbers of identical products for a relatively low cost.

■ The production is usually broken down into sub-assemblies of smaller components. This involves the product going through various stages on a production line, where workers at a particular stage are responsible for certain parts of the product.

■ Generally, this production method involves the product being produced for days, sometimes weeks, in large numbers.

■ This form of mass production can be labour intensive or completely automated, depending on the product being manufactured and the facilities available.

■ The packaging for a CD or video are examples of products that would be manufactured in this way (Figure 8.3).

8.4 *Soup carton*

✎ Continual flow process

■ **Continual flow** involves uninterrupted production of basic commodities 24 hours a day. This sort of production often results in the product being relatively inexpensive to produce, but the process is expensive to shut down and then re-start.

■ Only a small workforce is needed to maintain the process.

■ A soup carton is an example of a graphic product that would be manufactured using this method of production (Figure 8.4).

CHECK YOURSELF – EXAM QUESTION

1 'AQACO' wished to 'trial' your design by printing a limited number.

Circle the method of production which is most appropriate for a print run of 5,000 copies.

one-off   batch   mass   continuous

(1 mark)

Manufacturing systems

You will need to have an understanding of the following systems by which the manufacture of products is organised:
- cell production
- in-line assembly
- just in time
- logistics.

✎ Cell production

- **Cell production** involves a number of work stations grouped together to produce a single component (Figure 8.5).

- Many components require a number of processes to be carried out before they are complete.

- Each work station carries out one stage of the manufacturing process and the product passes to the next work station. This is repeated until all the stages of manufacture are completed.

- The production cell team are responsible for every aspect of the production, including quality control and scheduled maintenance.

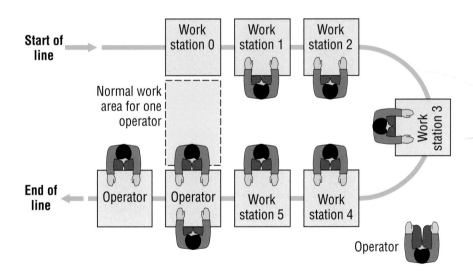

8.5 *Here is a typical arrangement for cell production. The operators may move from one work station to another as necessary.*

✎ In-line assembly

- **In-line assembly** is used to mass-produce many everyday items.

- Products that have many components are often produced on a continuous assembly line (like a conveyor belt). The product moves along the line and has components added to it until the assembly is complete.

- Many in-line assembly systems are fully automated and require only a few people, to ensure continual flow (Figure 8.6).

8.6 *In-line assembly*

✎ Just in time

- This philosophy requires materials, components and sub-assemblies to arrive from suppliers and other factories '**just in time**' for them to be used in the manufacture of a product. Finished products are dispatched immediately they are made.

- This system reduces storage of stock and allows for changes to the product to be made quickly without the need to use up stock items first.

- However, if the supply of components or materials is stopped or delayed the production has to be halted, which becomes very costly.

✎ Logistics

- You need to understand that the production of products relies upon the availability of materials and components when required. This applies just as much to your work in school as it does in an industrial context.

⚡ A* EXTRA

You should be able to name and briefly describe the various methods of production and manufacturing systems.

Packaging, marketing and advertising

You need to understand the packaging, marketing and advertising implications of a product.

✎ Packaging

- **Packaging** is an important factor in any retail environment and a key item in most marketing strategies.

- Consumers react immediately to packaging shapes and are influenced by them when making decisions about which product to buy.

- Different product categories are often easy to recognise by their characteristic form (e.g. chocolate boxes or milk cartons). On the other hand, a manufacturer of an exclusive product – such as jewellery or perfume – may deliberately choose an unusual, eye-catching design.

- You need to understand that products are packaged:

  - for protection

  - for ease of transportation

  - for security

  - for storage and display

  - to give the consumer information

  - to create the right image and enable consumers to identify the product easily.

8.7 *Packaging*

✎ Marketing

- Marketing and selling are not the same thing. **Marketing** concerns everything from research, product planning, development, to promotion and selling. **Selling** is the process of negotiating and carrying out a transaction. Both are essential to any business.

- You need to understand that marketing involves:
  - knowing your product or service
  - knowing your competitors
  - carrying out market research
  - advertising
  - managing sales and distribution
  - packaging
  - pricing.

- **Target marketing** is aiming your product at a specific area of the market. For instance, you might place your advertisements in magazines read by teenagers.

8.8 *Point of sale marketing*

✎ Advertising

- You need to understand that graphic products such as packaging, printed advertisements and point of sale display stands (Figure 8.8), are designed to:

  - inform people about the product

  - influence, persuade and encourage people to buy a company's products rather than someone else's (Figure 8.9).

8.9 *Advertising*

- **Consumers** today expect a great deal of information about products. This enables them to make informed choices and allows them to compare similar products.

- In some cases, legal regulations exist to ensure that we can tell from the information given on the product or its packaging exactly what we are buying. For example, all pre-packed food must, by law, have the following information on it:
  - name of the food
  - name and address of the manufacturer or seller
  - storage instructions (including 'use by' and 'best before' dates)
  - cooking or preparation instructions
  - weight or volume
  - list of ingredients
  - any special claims.

- Many labels also contain nutritional information, but this is voluntary.

- It is common to find many of the things on this list on the packaging of a wide range of products.

- Most packaging includes a **barcode**. This is used to identify the product for pricing and stock-taking (Figure 8.10).

8.10 *Graphic products showing barcodes*

A* EXTRA

You should know how 'target marketing' and 'gap in the market' identification are used to promote a product.

QUESTION SPOTTER

▸ Questions could ask you to explain the function of packaging in terms of protection, transportation, storage, security, display and giving customer information.

CHECK YOURSELF – EXAM QUESTIONS

2 A drawing of a glass perfume bottle is shown.

The glass bottles are to be packaged in individual card boxes.

Besides 'the protection of the glass bottle' list two further specification points related to the transport and storage of the card box.

(2 marks)

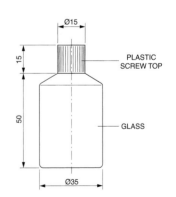

3 An image of an owl is shown.

The image is to be used as part of the packaging for children's confectionery.

Explain why the company feel it is necessary to use such a character in the design of their packaging.

(2 marks)

Quality assurance

Quality assurance involves all aspects of manufacturing performance from design to delivery.

- The quality of a product, in terms of its design, appearance, manufacture and performance, is often the main reason why one product is chosen in preference to another.

- There are laws, standards and regulations which aim to protect the rights of designers, retailers and consumers. A number of these are concerned with the quality of the product and the accuracy of the information given about the product when it is being marketed.

- There are a number of 'marks' and 'symbols' which are used on products and their packaging to inform consumers about quality etc. The ones that you will need to have some knowledge of are explained below.

ISO 9000

- This is an International Standard of Quality that is awarded to companies who demonstrate the highest standards of quality throughout their organisations.

8.11 *The BS kite mark*

Kite mark

- The **kite mark** is the official mark of quality and reliability on articles approved by the British Standards Institution (BSI). The BSI kite mark (Figure 8.11) is only attached to products which the BSI has tested and found to be satisfactory.

- Kite marking has now been largely replaced by European Union (EU) regulations.

- Under the EC 'Declaration of Conformity', **CE markings** (Figure 8.12) should be put on products to show that it meets European standards on health and safety.

$$C\epsilon$$

8.12 *The CE mark*

Copyright mark

- This is used for literary, dramatic, musical and artistic work (Figure 8.13). Once the work has been created, it has **copyright** and cannot be copied without permission or other special arrangements. It can last for up to 50 years after an author's death.

8.13 *Copyright mark*

Trade and service marks

TM

8.14 *Trademark symbol*

- A business can acquire the right to its mark simply by using it or by officially registering it with The Trade Marks Registry. A **trademark** is a word or symbol telling the origin of goods (Figure 8.14). It cannot be used in any form without the permission of the business or company who has the right to it.

✎ Patents

- The **patent** protects every aspect of a new idea anywhere in the world.

- To obtain a patent you must go through the Patent Office. EU patents can also be obtained.

✎ The e mark

- Many products must display a weight or volume (in grams or litres). The large **e** place alongside the amount indicates that it is an average quantity (Figure 8.15).

8.15 *The e mark*

✎ Quality control

- You need to understand that **quality control** is part of the quality assurance process. It is an essential aspect of production and marketing.

- Quality control:
  - helps to ensure that the customer is satisfied with a product
  - is about meeting agreed standards and monitoring these standards from the raw material through to the finished product.

- In the school situation this often involves checking that graphic products you make meet the criteria listed in their specification.

- The monitoring process involves **inspection** and **testing**.

INSPECTION

- This involves examining the product and the materials from which it is made to determine if they meet the required standards.

- In industry it would take too much time if every product was individually inspected, so a sample – such as one in every 50 products – is looked at.

TESTING

- This is concerned with the functional aspects of a product.

- Physical tests are carried out to see if the product functions in the correct way. These tests are often repeated many times in order to determine if the product will continue to function well over its expected lifetime.

- In some cases, **destructive testing** is carried out which pushes the product to its limits in order to determine under what conditions it would fail. Most testing, however, is **non-destructive**.

CHECK YOURSELF – EXAM QUESTION

4 Packages have symbols to communicate information to the retailer and the buyer.

Below are two such symbols. Name each and state its function.

(6 marks)

ISBN 0-00-715917-X

e

9 780007 159178

Commercial printing methods

You need to understand the basic principles of the following commercial printing methods:

- letterpress
- gravure
- lithography – sheet fed offset, web fed offset.

Letterpress printing

- Until the mid 1970s, **letterpress printing** was the printing process most widely used throughout the world. It is still used to a limited degree for the special effects it can produce and for its flexibility.

- To print traditional letterpress, lines of type are placed in a chase, or page format, and laid on a press (Figure 8.16). Ink is applied to the raised surface, which is then pressed onto the paper.

- Images other than text are produced using photo-engraved metal plates or ones made from a synthetic substance.

- It is possible to print letterpress on to any paper or board and, with care, on to some plastics.

- The main advantage of letterpress is that it offers the facility for late changes to the text. A line of text can be taken out of the chase and replaced with another line while on the press.

- It is a costly process and is now only used for high-quality books and stationery, generally in short production runs.

8.16 *Making up the day's sports page for letterpress printing, 1942*

✎ Gravure printing

- This is the printing process that gives the highest quality print and the greatest level of consistency across a print run.

- However, the costs of the process mean that it is not viable for anything less than long print runs, typically 500,000 to 1 million. The **gravure plate** is made photographically. Images are etched into a plate through a screen which breaks them up into a series of dots.

- These dots are etched into the plate as recessed 'cells'. The darker parts of the image have deeper cells than the light areas. This enables different tones to be produced when the image is printed.

- Ink fills the dot cells, the excess ink is removed and rubber-covered cylinders press the paper into the cell holes creating a printed image.

- Gravure printing is used for the high-quality reproduction of photographs and paintings, as well as the printing of full colour books and magazines.

- Gravure can print on to low- or high-quality paper and board, unsupported foil from 7 microns thick, tissue paper, PVC, polythenes and almost all flexible packaging materials.

- It is easy to laminate or varnish on to gravure. This is often done on the press, with one of the printing units converted to a coater for the run.

- The main disadvantages of gravure printing are that the plates are expensive to make and it is difficult to alter colours.

✎ Lithography

8.17 *Lithographic printing*

- This is a type of **planographic** (or flat plate) printing. It is one of the most widely used of all printing processes.

- In this type of printing, the image on the printing plate attracts grease (the ink) and rejects water. The areas which are not being printed reject the ink and attract the water.

- The best offset litho machines will print full colour on both sides of the paper in one go (Figure 8.17). To do this they use a four-colour process involving yellow, cyan (a shade of blue), magenta (a shade of red) and black. This is known as the **CYMK Process** (see page 167).

- Filters are responsible for the **colour separation** and a screen converts the separate colours into individual dots which eventually form the final printed image. The process has a printing plate with the image in relief. The plate is free to rotate.

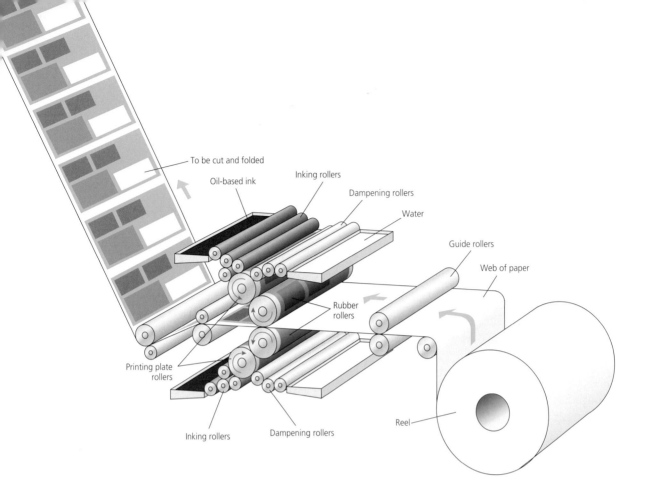

To be cut and folded

Oil-based ink

Inking rollers

Dampening rollers

Water

Guide rollers

Web of paper

Rubber rollers

Printing plate rollers

Inking rollers

Dampening rollers

Reel

8.18 *The process of web offset lithography*

- Ink is applied to the printing plate which is dampened (Figure 8.18). This repels ink from the areas not to be printed. The printing plate then transfers an inked image onto the rubber blanket cylinder which, in turn, presses the image onto the paper or card as it is fed through.

- There are practically no images that cannot be reproduced by lithography so long as they are printed on paper or board (Figure 8.19). It is also possible to print on to plastic and metal, but this is more difficult.

8.19 *Selection of printed material*

SHEET FED

- This process prints on to single sheets of paper which can be from A4 to double A0 in size (see page 176). The minimum print run will depend on the type of work. For a single-colour letterhead using a small machine and disposable printing plates, 100 copies might be economical. Generally, runs of around 5,000 are considered to be commercially viable.

- Quality control can be monitored by inspection. It is important to check whether the registration marks and colour codes on the printed sheet are lined up correctly.

WEB FED

- Web fed machines run from a continuous roll of paper, which is cheaper than pre-cut paper (see Figure 8.18).

- However, it takes a long time to set these machines up, therefore it is only economical for large print runs. Leaflets, advertising literature, magazines and anything that needs to be printed by the tens of thousands are ideal for **web offset printing**.

✎ Digital printing

8.20 *Digital printing*

- This is a modern system of printing which links computers direct to printing presses (Figure 8.20). It eliminates the need for making traditional printing plates.

- The original just has to be scanned in. Digital printers use laser technology to print high-quality text, photographs and graphics on a range of media.

- They can print at a rate of 250 copies per minute. The printers come with a full range of image handling capabilities including image clean up, reduction and enlargement, photo screening, cropping, masking, rotating and the moving of text and graphics.

✎ Producing a printing plate

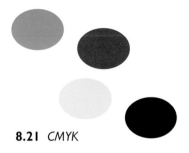

8.21 *CMYK*

- When producing a full-colour print all of the colours are produced from four basic colours: cyan (blue), magenta (red), yellow and **black** (Figure 8.21).

- These are known in printing technology as the 'process colours' and are referred to as CMYK for short. They represent the three primary colours plus black. From these four colours all of the other colours can be produced.

- To produce a full-colour print, the four colours are printed separately one on top of the other. This requires the production of four different **printing plates** of the same image, one to print each colour.

8.22 *Four printing plates are required to print a full-colour photo.*

- When making these plates, the printer uses a process called **colour separation**. The original full-colour image is photographed four times through four different coloured filters to create four half-tone negatives (Figure 8.22).

- The most common methods of colour separation are to use a **process camera** or a special scanner that has built-in colour filters. The image is produced through a screen so that each colour is broken up into dots.

- The scanner or the process camera produces four separate pieces of film. The printing plates are made using this film. A thin metal plate, usually made from aluminium and coated so that it is sensitive to light, is put into a vacuum frame.

- **Ultraviolet light** is shone through the film and, when the plate is developed, the text or image can be seen on the surface of the plate (Figure 8.24). The image on the plate is a layer of greasy substance which repels water but attracts ink, while the non-image area (the background) will repel ink and attract water. This means that the right colour will be in the right place and nowhere else.

5 All colour pictures printed in **books and magazines** are made up of four process colours.

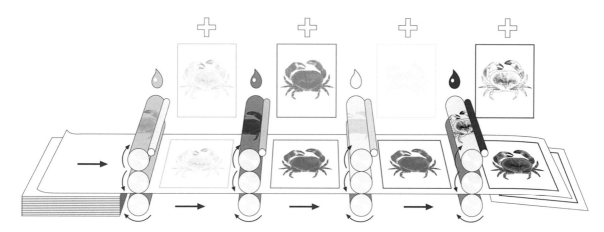

(a) List the **four** process colours. Name each and state its function. *(4 marks)*

(b) What is the full name of the printing process shown above? *(2 marks)*

(c) Why is black usually the last colour to be printed? *(1 mark)*

(d) Give **two** reasons why it is necessary to check the first pages which come off the printing process? *(2 marks)*

6 A drawing of a logo design is shown below.

To print this logo, three printing plates are required (one for BLACK, one for MAGENTA, one for CYAN). The BLACK printing plate is shown completed.

(a) (i) Complete the MAGENTA plate.

Show clearly the areas to be printed magenta and those to be masked off. *(3 marks)*

(ii) Complete the CYAN plate.

Show clearly the areas to be printed cyan and those to be masked off. *(3 marks)*

(b) Give the more common names for CYAN and MAGENTA. *(2 marks)*

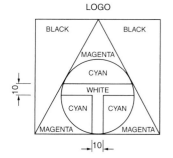

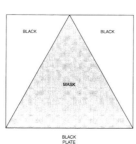

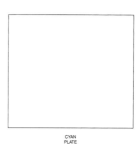

UNIT 9: GOOD WORKING PRACTICE

When planning work, you should be able to devise and record strategies to make effective use of the available resources – such as tools, equipment, materials and time – and to make a risk assessment.

Process and block diagrams

A* EXTRA

As Graphic Products is a visual subject, use diagrams and pictures to show your planning, rather than 'essay type' text.

QUESTION SPOTTER

▸ Generally questions in this section will ask you to show how you would manage the necessary materials, tools, equipment and other resources in the correct sequence in order to carry out a specified procedure.

- When you plan work you have to work out and show how you are going to manage the necessary materials, tools and equipment and other resources in the correct sequence, in order to carry out the required task in the time available.

- The simplest way of showing the sequence of work is to use a **block diagram**. Each key stage in the process is contained in a block. Each block is usually rectangular in shape.

- The diagram places the processes that need to be carried out in the correct sequence. Each block links to the next using arrows that show the order in which the stages have to be carried out (Figure 9.1).

- The advantage of this type of diagram is that it gives a quick visual overview of what has to be done and when it has to be done.

- When producing a block diagram you must:

  - identify the materials, components, tools, equipment and facilities required to carry out the work

  - establish an order for the work, identifying sub-tasks that need to be done first

  - organise the work to maximise the use of time and resources.

| Draw out net for box using template and pencil | → | Cut out net using craft knife, safety rule and cutting mat | → | Score fold lines using scissors and safety rule | → | Fold edges, assemble box |

9.1 *Block diagram showing process for making a net*

CHECK YOURSELF – EXAM QUESTION

1 A Transport Activity Pack is to include a cut-out card model of an articulated lorry.

The drawing shows the net (development) required to make the tractor unit.

An incomplete instruction sheet for making the model of the tractor unit is given below.

(a) Use instructions to complete the full-size isometric drawing showing the outline shape of the tractor unit and its rear wheel. It has been started at point A.

Sizes should be taken from the given net (development).

Do not add the surface detail such as windows, lights etc.

(6 marks)

(b) Complete the block diagram to explain the stages in making the tractor unit.

(4 marks)

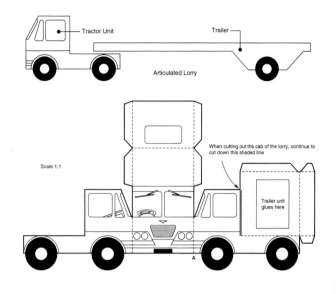

Tractor Unit   Trailer

Articulated Lorry

Scale 1:1

When cutting out the cab of the lorry, continue to cut down this shaded line

Trailer unit glues here

A

A

Isometric view of assembled tractor unit

Applying colour	Cutting out	Scoring and folding	Gluing and assembly
Equipment – _____ _____ _____	**Equipment** – scissors or craft knife, safety rule and _____	**Equipment** – scissors and safety rule _____ _____	**Equipment** – _____ _____ glue
Process – colour in the cab red, lights and window light blue and the centre of the wheels grey.	**Process** – cut round all **bold** solid lines.		**Process** – put glue on each tab and fix in position.
	Quality control check –	**Process** – colour in the cab red, lights and window light blue and the centre of the wheels grey.	**Quality control check** –
Quality control check – make sure you do not colour over the edge of each part.	_____ _____ _____	**Quality control check** – _____ _____ _____	_____ _____ _____

Flow charts

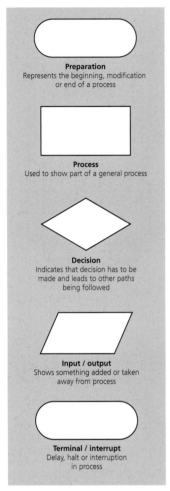

Preparation
Represents the beginning, modification or end of a process

Process
Used to show part of a general process

Decision
Indicates that decision has to be made and leads to other paths being followed

Input / output
Shows something added or taken away from process

Terminal / interrupt
Delay, halt or interruption in process

9.2 *Symbols used in flow charts*

Generally, block diagrams do not take into account the fact that work needs to be checked at various points to ensure that things are correct before progressing to the next stage. A flow chart, however, shows where these checks (or choices) need to be made.

■ A **flow chart** uses standard symbols for each type of activity that takes place when carrying out a particular task (Figure 9.2).

■ The symbols (or boxes) are linked together by arrows which indicate the correct sequence of events.

■ Most flow charts include 'feedback loops' (Figure 9.3). These allow quality control checks (or choices) to be made at various stages and indicate how problems will be resolved. Generally, this involves repeating part of the sequence.

■ In Figure 9.3, the flow chart identifies the stages in the process of reducing the size of a drawing using a photocopier so that it will fit a required space in a leaflet. It includes a feedback loop which enables the size of the copy to be controlled.

■ If the first copy was the wrong size, you would return to stage 1 and adjust the size.

■ If the next copy was still not right, you would again return to stage 1 and adjust the size.

■ You could repeat this until the copy you produce was correct.

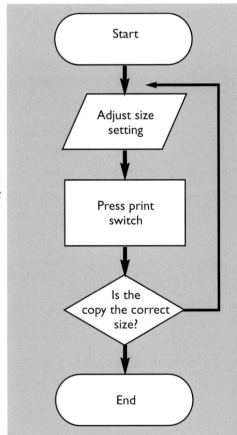

9.3 *A flow chart*

CHECK YOURSELF – EXAM QUESTION

2 A manufacturer packs mobile phones for a supermarket.

The instructions for the packers are shown below.

a. Pick up flat pack card box.

b. Assemble box.

c. Check card box opens and closes.

d. Fill with correct items.

e. Check all items are correct.

f. Close box.

g. Add sales sticker.

h. Place in cartons.

(a) Complete the flow chart for the packers' instructions.
Marks will be awarded for a well-drawn chart.

(6 marks)

(b) Explain why the mobile phone is pre-packed in a
plastic bag before being put into the moulded tray.

(2 marks)

(c) (i) Name a suitable material for vacuum forming the
thin plastic tray.

(1 mark)

(ii) Why are the sides of the plastic moulded tray at a
slight angle?

(1 mark)

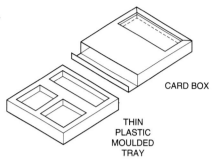

CARD BOX

THIN
PLASTIC
MOULDED
TRAY

FLOW CHART OF THE INSTRUCTIONS FOR THE PACKERS

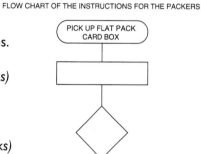

PICK UP FLAT PACK
CARD BOX

Time plans and work schedules

✎ Time plans

- In the school situation, most **time plans** are based on the estimated use of time as, generally, a product is only manufactured once.

- It is always useful to record how long each part of a manufacturing process takes so that this information can be used when producing time plans in the future that involve similar activities: for example, knowing how long it takes to screen print a design (Figure 9.4).

9.4 *Time plan for screen printing*

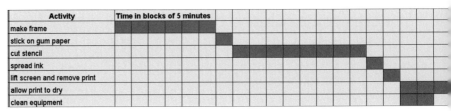

- Sometimes tests and trials that you undertake as part of the product development stage of your work can help you to be more realistic when producing a time plan for the actual manufacture of your product.

- In industry, a **prototype** of the product would be produced (see page 8). This would help:

  - to identify any likely production problems

  - to ascertain the time required for each stage of manufacture prior to the main production run starting.

✎ Work schedules

- A **work schedule** is usually presented in the form of a table or chart.

- Work schedules contain more information than block diagrams and flow charts. They have more detailed quality control and safety checks built into them.

- Most work schedules contain at least the following information (Figure 9.5):

Stage or task – this should be a brief outline of the work to be undertaken.

Materials, tools and equipment – this should detail the resources required for each stage.

Accuracy required – this should state how close to the actual size you are prepared to accept (this is called the **tolerance**).

Time needed – this should be a realistic forecast of the time required to complete the work.

Quality control – this should explain how you are going to check the accuracy and quality of this stage of your work.

Alternative methods – this should suggest alternative ways of completing this stage if problems occur or things go wrong.

Health and Safety (risk assessment) – this should identify potential hazards that could occur while carrying out this stage of the work and the precautions that need to be taken.

9.5 Work schedule

Stage or task	Materials, tools and equipment	Accuracy required	Time needed	Quality control	Alternative methods	Health and safety (risk assessment)

The production and use of detailed work schedules and time plans can help to set realistic deadlines for the various stages involved in the designing, making and marketing of a graphic product.

CHECK YOURSELF – EXAM QUESTION

3   A company publishing greetings cards requires a **time plan** to work out the time taken from the initial design work until cards appear on sale.

(a) For each activity, identify and list the operation on the chart.

Four operations have been completed for you.   *(3 marks)*

(b) Using the information, complete the **time plan** chart to show when each operation starts and how long it lasts.

The first two have been completed for you.   *(6 marks)*

(c) State the **least** number of weeks before a card will appear on sale in a shop.

(1 mark)

Activity	No.	Operation	1	2	3	4	5	6	7	8	9	10	11	12	13	14	15	16
Design team prepare the design concepts of the cards	2	Preparation of design concepts																
3D mock-ups made at same time as design concepts	2	3D mock-ups																
1 week after the design work begins, market research starts	4																	
Once all design work and market research is complete, approval given for best design	1																	
Artwork is prepared and produced on computer	1	Computerised artwork produced																
Card and other materials are ordered during same week that artwork is produced	1																	
Printer's proofs are prepared and sent for final approval	Between 1 & 2																	
Batch production begins immediately approval is given. Five batches to be produced	1 batch per week																	
As soon as 1st batch is complete, it is dispatched to shops	Half a week																	
Cards are received and arranged for sale in shop	Half a week	Cards arranged for sale																

UNIT 10: MATERIALS

You will need to know which material is suitable for a particular situation. In order to do this, you need to be able to identify the properties that materials (including any surface finish that could be applied to them) should have in order to fulfil an identified purpose.

REVISION SESSION 1

Paper

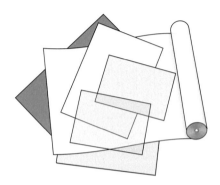

■ You need to experience using a range of different types of paper and be able to select the correct type for a given task.

■ When deciding which paper would be suitable for a specific situation there are five important aspects to consider:
- size
- weight
- surface finish
- plain or pre-printed
- colour.

✎ Size

■ You need to know about **paper sizes** between A5 and A2.

■ The most commonly used sizes of paper are classified in this 'A' series. The larger the A number, the smaller the piece of paper.

■ The paper size doubles every time the A number is reduced (Figure 10.1). For example, two pieces of A4 paper would fit on to one sheet of A3.

10.1 *Paper sizes*

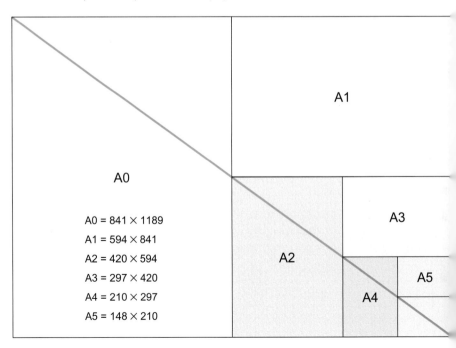

A0 = 841 × 1189
A1 = 594 × 841
A2 = 420 × 594
A3 = 297 × 420
A4 = 210 × 297
A5 = 148 × 210

✎ Weight

- The **thickness** of paper is determined by its weight. The weight is measured in grams per square metre (**gsm**).

- The weight of most of the drawing paper you will use is between 94 gsm and 155 gsm. Remember, the heavier the weight the thicker the paper.

✎ Surface finish

- Some papers, such as layout paper, are very smooth; while others, like sugar paper, can be rough.

- A range of textured papers is available.

✎ Plain or pre-printed

- You will generally use **plain paper** for design work and working drawings.

- **Pre-printed grid papers**, such as isometric or squared papers, are useful for producing both three-dimensional and orthographic drawings.

- Some papers have pre-printed borders etc. These are particularly useful when used in conjunction with a computer printer.

✎ Colour

- Paper is available in a wide range of solid colours, tonal shadings and patterns. You can use coloured paper for both drawing on and mounting work. This type of paper can also be glued to card and board to create a cheaper alternative to buying coloured or patterned versions of these materials.

- When large areas of colour or pattern are required, it is often better to cut out and use a piece of coloured or patterned paper than to spend time colouring the area by hand.

- You should always carry out tests on any paper that you intend to use in order to establish that the materials (pens, markers etc.) are suitable for that particular type of paper.

✎ Cartridge paper

- This good-quality paper provides a slightly soft surface.

- It is suitable for use with most graphic media, including pencils, pens and markers. Some marker pens do, however, tend to 'bleed' on this type of paper.

- Cartridge paper tends to be rather expensive for general school use. Its use is best saved for high-quality presentation or working drawings.

Square grid (1 mm)

Square grid (2 mm)

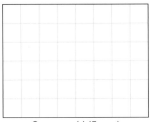

Square grid (5 mm)

Isometric grid (5 mm)

10.2 *Isometric paper and square grid paper*

✎ Tracing paper

- Good-quality tracing paper is transparent. It has a hard, smooth surface and is strong. Its translucency makes it ideal for tracing fine detail.

- Stencils can sometimes be made from good-quality tracing paper.

- Tracing paper is, however, expensive. Cheaper tracing paper, while not as strong or transparent, is perfectly adequate for most work carried out in schools.

✎ Layout paper

- This is sometimes referred to as **detail paper**. It is a thin, fairly transparent white paper which provides a cheap medium for students to use for their design work. It can also be used to trace images.

✎ Bleedproof paper

- This has similar qualities to cartridge paper but is particularly good for use with water-based paints and pens. It prevents these mediums from 'bleeding' (running) into areas where you do not want them to go.

- Some types of bleedproof paper are rather thin and care needs to be taken to prevent them getting torn.

✎ Coloured paper

- Various weights, textures and colours are available.

- Coloured paper has a wide range of uses. You can use it:
  - to draw on with coloured pencils
  - to mount work on
  - in the manufacture of graphic products – for example, it can be glued to card and used to make nets etc. This can sometimes be cheaper than buying coloured card.

- Wrapping paper and wallpaper can be used in a similar way.

✎ Grid paper (square and isometric)

- Various types of grid paper are available. The two that you will use most are **isometric paper** and **square grid paper** (Figure 10.2).

- **Isometric paper** has lines printed on, some of which slope at 30 degrees and others are vertical. Usually, the lines are printed in green to make them easy to draw over.

- The grid is in 5mm sections so that drawings can often be done without the need for measuring. Isometric grid paper helps you to do isometric sketches and drawings quickly.

- **Square grid paper** has horizontal and vertical lines printed onto it, usually in light blue. It comes in a range of sizes. Squares of 2 mm, 5 mm and 10 mm are the ones that you will use the most. This type of paper is particularly useful for producing orthographic drawings.

Card and board

You need to understand the thickness of cards and boards in relation to appropriate construction techniques.

- The thickness of these materials can be determined in the same way as for paper, i.e. by its weight. Sometimes, however, it is measured in **microns**. A micron is one millionth of a metre. Therefore card which is 200 microns thick could be considered as 'thin', while 1,000 micron card could be referred to as 'thick'.

- You also need to understand that some materials are more suitable for manufacturing techniques involving nets, while others are more suited to those involving fabrication. As a general rule, thin sheet materials are best suited to nets while the thicker ones are better where fabrication is required or involved.

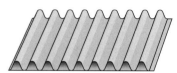
Single face corrugated

- Whenever possible you should carry out tests with a particular material to determine if it is suitable for its intended use.

✎ Corrugated card

- This has two or more layers of card with a fluted inner section to add strength with very little increase in weight (Figure 10.3).

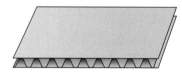
Single wall
(double face corrugated)

- Corrugated card is very strong, lightweight and is recyclable. Its main use is for packaging items which need protection during transportation.

10.3 *Corrugated card*

✎ White board

- This is a strong material which has a bleached surface.

- It is excellent for printing on and is used in the manufacture of graphic products, such as book covers and high-quality packaging.

✎ Duplex board

- The term 'duplex' means that two different boards have been joined together. Duplex board is found on boxes where one surface is bleached white for printing and the other is left as pure wood pulp. It provides a less expensive alternative to white board.

- Duplex is used in the packaging of food products such as breakfast cereals (Figure 10.4).

10.4 *Cereal packet*

✎Cardboard

- This is a cheap, recyclable, rigid board which has a good surface to print on.

- It is used in the manufacture of packaging, boxes and cartons.

✎Ink-jet card

- This type of card is treated so that it can be passed through ink-jet printers. It is a material that can be used in schools to achieve high-quality print finishes.

✎Coated boards

- The properties of boards can be enhanced by the application of various coatings. The two most common are cast coated boards and foil lined boards.

- **Cast coated boards** are similar to bleached white card, but the cast coating achieves a heavier and smoother surface. They are used in the manufacture of luxury products. The surface is excellent for printing and the application of decorative effects such as varnishing and embossing.

- **Foil** can be laminated to board to provide a waterproof liner. This type of material is used in the manufacture of products such as drink cartons and pre-packed food packages (Figure 10.5). The foil can have either a gloss or matt finish.

10.5 *Foil lined board used for a drinks carton*

✎Oiled card

- This is manila card which has been soaked in linseed oil. It is used to make stencils and is, therefore, sometimes called **stencil card**. The linseed oil makes the card tough and pliable so that it can be bent round curved surfaces. The oiled card is, to some extent, waterproof.

✎Foamboard

- **Foamboard** is constructed from polystyrene foam laminated between card (Figure 10.6). It is a strong, lightweight material which resists warping, denting and crushing.

- The surface is very easy to print on.

- Foamboard can be easily glued with PVA glue. The most common thicknesses are 3.5 mm, 5 mm and 9 mm. It is used in the manufacture of products such as display boards, large advertising mobiles, point-of-sale display stands and video advertising materials.

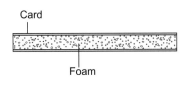

Card

Foam

10.6 *Foamboard*

■ Thin sheet plastics ■

You will need to know how a range of plastic materials can be used in the design and manufacture of graphic products.

You should know that some plastics are non–biodegradable but can be recycled.

✎ Polystyrene

■ Polystyrene is a type of thermoplastic. **Thermoplastics** will soften when they are heated and can be shaped when hot. The plastic will harden when it is cooled, but can be reshaped if heated up again.

■ Polystyrene sheet is ideal for vacuum forming and line bending (see pages 125–6).

■ Sheets are available in a range of colours and thickness. Generally, the most useful thicknesses are between 1.5 mm and 4 mm.

■ It is also possible to get clear and mirror finished polystyrene sheet.

■ The material has good resistance to impact and moisture but has poor weather resistance as it can be broken down by ultraviolet light.

✎ Corrugated plastics

■ This material is sometimes called **corriflute** or **correx**. Corrugated flutes are sandwiched between two thin sheets of plastics.

■ It is tough, lightweight, rigid and available in a range of colours. The most common thickness is 3 mm.

■ It is easy to cut and fold, particularly in the direction of the corrugated flutes (Figure 10.7). The most common methods of fixing are glue, slots and tabs, and 'click' rivets or fasteners.

■ This versatile material is ideal for making products such as drawing folders, containers and house for sale boards. It provides a waterproof surface which can be screen printed.

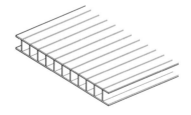

10.7 *Corrugated flutes*

10.8 *Regular forms of formed plastics*

✎ Formed plastics

■ Lengths of plastic are available from suppliers in many regular forms, such as flat strip, round and square bar, tube and angle (Figure 10.8).

■ These materials can be used to make part of a graphic product. For example, the pole of a promotional flag given away by a fast food restaurant could be made from round plastic bar or tube.

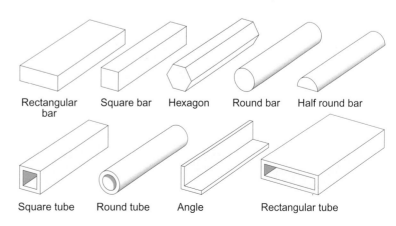

Rectangular bar   Square bar   Hexagon   Round bar   Half round bar

Square tube   Round tube   Angle   Rectangular tube

✎ Acetate

- This is a thin plastic film which is available in a variety of colours and clear. It is possible to print on some types of acetate sheet using a photocopier.

- Several copies from different sources can be made on to clear acetate sheet. These copies can be overlaid (arranged) as required and a final photocopy made which gives the impression that everything has been printed onto one sheet. This technique is shown in Figure 10.9.

10.9 *Photocopying using acetate sheets*

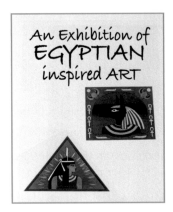
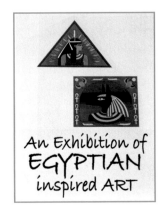

- This shows how a photograph and a piece of text have been copied on to two separate acetate sheets. Three different layouts have been tried by overlaying the two sheets before one has been chosen for photocopying.

- **Acetate sheet** can be used to make 'windows' on items of packaging. If a slightly thicker sheet is used, then complete nets can be made from it; for example, the lift-off lid of a box to hold chocolates.

✎ Self-adhesive vinyl

- You may know this as **'sticky backed plastic'.**

- **Self-adhesive vinyl** is available in a wide range of colours and patterns. When the protective backing is removed and the 'sticky' surface exposed, it can be applied to almost any surface.

- Designs can be cut out by hand with a circle cutter, scissors and craft knives, as well as CAM cutter/plotters such as Roland CAMM 1 machines, Lynx & Ultra Cutters and Stika machines (see Unit 7).

✎ Mylar

- **Mylar** is a translucent plastic film which is used to make stencils. It comes in several thicknesses, but 0.5 mm is fairly standard for home-made stencils. Any thicker is too hard to cut with a craft knife and any thinner is a bit flimsy.

- It is flexible and easy to clean. Commercially produced stencils are laser cut from mylar film.

✎ Low tack masking film

- This self-adhesive film comes in both sheet and tape forms. It is low tack which means that it will stick to your work but can be removed without damaging it.

- The film is used to mask off (cover) specific areas of your work so that colouring media such as airbrushing, spray paint or pastels can be used to apply colour to the areas not masked off. The film can be cut to the required shape using a craft knife.

A* EXTRA

Make sure that the answers you give identify specific materials or components. General answers such as plastic, card, fasteners or clips are often not sufficient to gain full marks.

CHECK YOURSELF – EXAM QUESTIONS
(FOR REVISION SESIONS 1–3)

1   A drawing of three separate parts of a package is shown.

    (a) Explain what a die cutter would be used for in the mass production of the tray insert.   *(1 mark)*

    (b) State why corrugated card would not be an appropriate material for the tray insert.   *(1 mark)*

    (c) Give **one** reason why the packaging might be considered an 'environmentally poor' design.   *(1 mark)*

LID

TRAY INSERT

BASE

45°   45°

2   An incomplete drawing of a direction sign is shown.

    The material for the SYMBOL must:
- be waterproof;
- be flexible;
- require no additional fixing method to the background.

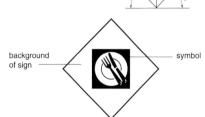

background of sign   symbol

    Name a suitable material for the symbol which satisfies the specification.   *(2 marks)*

3   A charity is planning a collection in support of a local disaster. A collection container is required which shows how much money has been contributed.

    SPECIFICATION

    The collection container should:
- have a method of showing how much money has been collected up to a maximum of £50.00 in £1 coins (a £1 coin is approx. 22 mm diameter x 3 mm thick);
- be free standing on a flat surface;
- be easy to assemble;
- be able to be posted in a 345 x 445 standard protective postal bag;
- allow easy removal of the coins from the container;
- be constructed from appropriate materials and components.

    Use sketches and notes to develop a suitable design for the collection container. Include details of materials, components and joining methods.

           (6 marks)

> **Hint:** £50 in £1 coins weighs approx. 375 grams.

'Smart' and modern materials

10.10 *This kettle changes colour when it boils.*

Most materials that are used to manufacture products have properties which remain more or less constant in use. 'Smart' materials are different as they respond to external factors such as light or temperature levels.

✎ Photochromic inks

■ These are a good example of a 'smart' material that is used in the manufacture of graphic products. **Photochromic inks** change their colour depending upon the temperature. For example, when used in a product such as a plastic mug the design on the mug would change when hot liquid is put into it. (The original design returns when the liquid cools.)

✎ Smart wire

■ This is a **shape memory alloy (SMA)** that changes its length. This creates a good pulling power, when a small current is passed through it.

✎ Thermocolour sheet

■ This is a self-adhesive sheet material printed with thermochromic liquid crystal ink. It changes colour when heated above 27 degrees Centigrade. It can be used for temperature indication/warning, body jewellery and advertising displays.

✎ Polymorph

■ This is a material which becomes easily mouldable (soft) at 62 degrees Centigrade. It can be heated in hot water or with a hairdryer and moulded by hand to create the required shapes (Figure 10.11).

■ In graphic products, it is useful for making prototypes of products such as small bottles, containers, caps, lids etc. It is also useful for making small, reasonably complex, vacuum forming moulds.

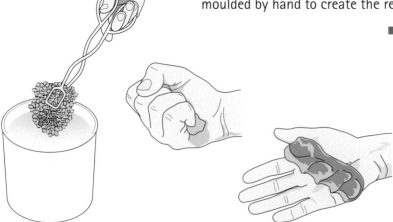

10.11 *Making polymorph plastics*

✎ Klett card

- This is a type of corrugated card which can be fixed together without gluing.

- The series of special corrugations (or grooves) on each piece of card 'lock' into each other when the two surfaces are pushed together, as shown in Figure 10.12.

QUESTION SPOTTER

▸ Most examination papers will have at least part of a question about 'smart' and 'modern' materials.

10.12 *Using Klett card*

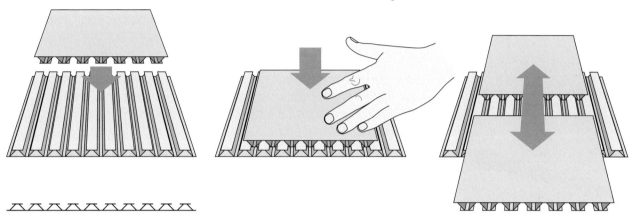

CHECK YOURSELF – EXAM QUESTION

4

The image below was taken from a Point of Sale manufacturer's website. It shows examples of Point of Sale models produced by the company.

The model of a television has a printed image stuck on the front to represent the screen.

Explain how the use of thermochromic inks could improve the visual impact of the model.

(5 marks)

Rigid foam and balsa wood

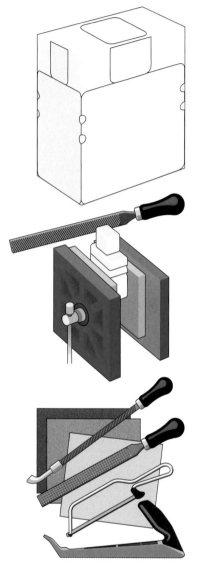

10.13 *Shaping rigid foam*

✎ Rigid foam

- This material is sometimes known as **styrofoam**. It is a dense polystyrene foam which can be cut and shaped easily, using simple hand tools, to form 3D 'block models'. The models are not intended to work but are used for testing or visual reference.

- The foam can be joined with PVA glue or double-sided tape. Certain adhesives and paints will dissolve the foam. Always test a piece of scrap material if you are unsure.

- It is important to mark out the material carefully. A simple method is to draw the front view, end view and plan of the object on a piece of paper. These views can then be stuck to the respective sides of the foam, allowing the required profile to be seen (Figure 10.13, top).

- The foam can be roughly cut to shape using a coping saw or hacksaw. Finer detail can be created using files and abrasive paper (Figure 10.13, middle). Water-based paints are suitable for painting rigid foam.

✎ Balsa wood

- **Balsa wood** is available in a range of sizes and sections including sheet, block and strips (Figure 10.14).

- It is a fairly soft, lightweight wood which is easily cut using a craft knife or junior hacksaw.

- Balsa wood can be glued using balsa cement. Make sure that the glue is used in a well-ventilated area. PVA glue is also suitable but this takes much longer to dry.

- This material can be used to make part of a graphic product. For example, the supporting structure for an advertising mobile could be made from strips of balsa wood.

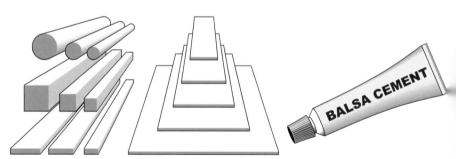

10.14 *Balsa wood*

Joining materials

You will need to be able to display a knowledge and understanding of a range of adhesives and mechanical fixing methods. You will also need to identify the correct fixing method to use in a given situation.

- When selecting an adhesive or fixing method, the following issues will need to be considered:

  - How strong the joint needs to be.

  - The materials that are being joined.

  - If it is a temporary or permanent joint that is required.

  - What size the surfaces to be joined are.

  - Does the join need to be waterproof?

  - Do the separate parts need to move after they are joined?

  - Will the method of joining spoil the appearance of the finished product?

Types of joining materials

PVA ADHESIVE

- **Polyvinyl Acetate (PVA)** adhesive is excellent for gluing card and wood. However, when used on paper it tends to make it wrinkle.

- PVA adhesive is white but dries colourless. It takes about 3 hours to dry.

- This type of adhesive is safe to use, but contact with the eyes and skin should be avoided.

SPRAY ADHESIVE

- This is sometimes referred to as **Spray Mount**. It is an adhesive in an aerosol can which will not stain, soak or wrinkle even quite thin papers.

- Using a spray adhesive is a convenient way of mounting work and photographs. It can, however, be rather messy to use.

- Care needs to be taken to cover the area around the item being sprayed. It should be used in a well-ventilated area or in a spray booth with an extraction system (Figure 10.15).

SOLVENT CEMENT

- This liquid adhesive can be used to glue thin plastic sheets together. It is applied to both surfaces using a small brush or an eye dropper nozzle.

- The liquid welds the two pieces together by causing the plastic to liquidise momentarily before hardening again.

- Solvent cement is harmful to both skin and eyes. Gloves and eye protection should be worn when using it. It should be used in a well-ventilated area or in a spray booth with an extraction system.

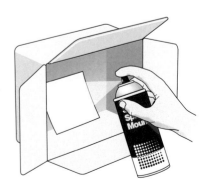

10.15 *Using a spray adhesive*

GLUE GUN

■ Glue sticks are put into one end of the glue gun (Figure 10.16). As they are pushed through the glue gun (either manually or by the use of a trigger), the sticks are heated electronically and softened.

■ The softened glue comes out of the nozzle in the form of a thick liquid. It is best suited on small areas as the glue cools down quickly.

■ The glue sticks are available in various colours.

■ The liquid glue can be used to create decorative effects, as well as gluing surfaces together.

■ Glue guns are available in 'Hot Melt' and 'Cool Melt' versions. Care must be taken as the hot glue can burn the skin if touched.

10.16 *Glue gun*

EPOXY RESIN

■ This product is often called by the trade name 'Araldite'. It comes in two tubes – one containing the glue and one the hardener.

■ The two parts are mixed together to form an adhesive which will create a strong bond between most materials. The quick-setting version of this type of adhesive takes about 5 minutes to set, but longer to harden fully.

■ It is advisable to use this type of adhesive in a well-ventilated area and to wear protective clothing.

GLUE STICKS

■ These are perhaps the most common form of adhesive found in schools. They are cheap, easy and safe to use.

■ Glue sticks produce a fairly weak bond which is fine for gluing paper together but not so effective on card.

SINGLE- AND DOUBLE-SIDED ADHESIVE TAPE

■ The most common form of **single-sided tape** is the transparent form often referred to by the trade name 'Sellotape'. It is cellulose based with a transparent gloss surface which is difficult to write on.

■ Adhesive tape is a useful, quick fixing method when producing card and paper models to test out ideas and concepts. Its use should be avoided on final prototypes as it is often not the most appropriate fixing method to use and can spoil the appearance of your work.

■ A range of coloured tapes are available, in different widths. These are very useful for adding stripes of colour on to designs and products. They are used as a way of adding decoration rather than as a fixing method.

■ **Double-sided tape** consists of a vinyl film coated on both sides with high-tack adhesive and with a wax paper interleaf. It is often used on products that are sent flat pack, such as a display stand, which require quick assembly when they are received by a shop etc. The tape is already attached to the product and only the wax paper has to be removed in order to assemble it.

VELCRO

- The most useful form of **Velcro** as far as graphic products are concerned is the self-adhesive variety.

- This comes in two types:

  - a tape from which the required length can be cut

  - circular 'pads'.

- Velcro is made in two parts – one of which has a series of nylon hooks and the other nylon loops (Figure 10.17). When the two parts are put together, the hooks and loops link together to create a secure fixing method.

- Velcro is used on large flat-pack products such as advertising and display stands where it provides a quick, easy and strong method of assembly.

DOUBLE-SIDED STICKY PADS

- These consist of small pieces of foam coated on each side with a strong adhesive (Figure 10.18). They are ideal for any kind of display work, but their extremely high tack makes them very difficult to remove without damaging both surfaces. They should, therefore, be regarded as a fairly permanent fixing method.

PRESS FIT 'CLICK' FASTENERS

- These press fit fasteners consist of posts and screws manufactured in polyethylene and nylon. The post is simply put through a hole in the pieces to be fastened and the screw pushed firmly into it (Figure 10.19).

- They are a semi-permanent fixing having slotted heads for easy removal with a screwdriver.

- Press fit 'click' fasteners have a variety of uses for fixing together materials such as card, paper, thin plastic, corriflute and fabrics.

CLIC RIVETS

- These are sometimes refered to as **plastic rivets**. They come in two parts which press and 'click' together (Figure 10.20).

- They are ideal for joining together materials such as card, paper, thin sheet plastic, corriflute and fabrics.

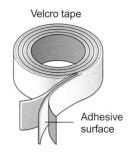

Velcro tape

Adhesive surface

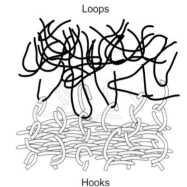

Loops

Hooks

10.17 *Velcro*

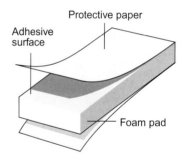

Protective paper

Adhesive surface

Foam pad

10.18 *Double-sided sticky pad*

10.19 *'Click' fastener*

10.20 *Clic rivets*

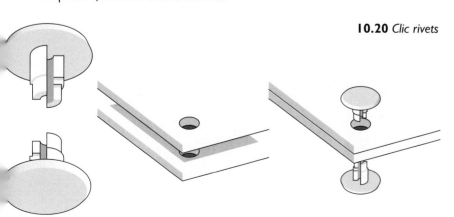

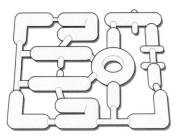

10.21 *Corrijoints*

STAPLES

■ **Staples** are a quick and easy, if not very attractive, way of joining card, paper and thin plastics together. They are frequently used on products such as blister packs and to join plastic bags to backing and information cards.

CORRIJOINTS

■ These are a simple yet effective way of joining fluted plastics, such as corriflute. The shaped pieces of plastic fit into the flutes in the plastic enabling a range of different joints to be made (Figure 10.21).

CHECK YOURSELF – EXAM QUESTION

5   Name the most suitable adhesive for the following uses.

Use	Suitable adhesive
Gluing paper on to paper	
Gluing a photograph on to card (allowing for repositioning)	
Gluing corrugated card on to foamboard	

(3 marks)

Finishing materials

Applying a thin layer of varnish or lacquer to a printed product helps to protect it, as well as making it look more attractive by giving it a glossy finish. The process is carried out after the product has been printed, but before any cutting, folding or joining takes place.

Types of finishing materials

SPIRIT VARNISH

■ This type of varnish requires a special machine to apply it and therefore increases production costs.

■ **Spirit varnishes** are now considered environmentally unacceptable because of the solvents that they contain.

ULTRA-VIOLET (UV) LACQUER

■ **UV lacquer** gives a very smooth, high-gloss finish. It is applied by a roller and then dried with ultraviolet lamps.

LAMINATING

■ This process involves placing a sheet of paper or card between two layers of plastic. Heat and pressure are then used to fuse the layers together (Figure 10.22).

■ Laminating is more than twice as expensive as varnishing but provides a glossier, more durable finish. It is widely used on products such as restaurant menus which are likely to be handled by a large number of people as well as being exposed to moisture.

EMBOSSING

■ Paper and board lend themselves to **embossing**. This is the process by which a design image is made to appear in relief (raised or recessed) to create a sculptured three-dimensional effect.

■ It is achieved by pressing a sheet of paper between a female die and a male bed or counter, both of which are mounted in a press.

■ Embossing is generally used on prestigious products such as the packaging for cosmetics, gift items, high-quality stationery and promotional materials.

■ Embossing will cost roughly the same as the actual printing.

DIE CUTTING

■ The process of **die cutting** involves creating shapes using cutting, scoring and perforating dies (sometimes called cutting formes). These are made from thin strips of steel (sometimes called rules) which are bent to the required shape and wedged into a 15mm thick piece of plywood (Figure 10.24).

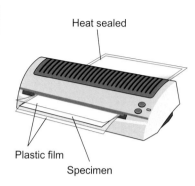

Heat sealed

Plastic film

Specimen

10.22 *Laminating sheets*

10.23 *The embossing process*

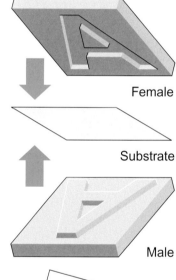

Female

Substrate

Male

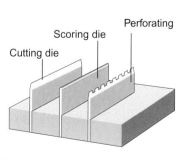

Perforating

Scoring die

Cutting die

10.24 *Die cutting*

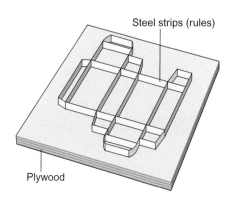

Steel strips (rules)

Plywood

- Most applications would have from 10 to 20 of these dies on one sheet. These are laid out so as to avoid as much wastage as possible. The dies are fixed on to a press. As the printed sheets pass through the press, they are cut and scored by the dies.

- Some small areas are left uncut between the shapes. This allows the machinery to move the cut sheets on to a stack and push out the waste for recycling.

- The most common material for die cutting is board, although you can die cut paper so long as it is not too thin.

- Die cutting is most commonly used for packaging. All cartons, for example, are die cut. Other die-cut products include point-of-sale materials and pop-up books and cards.

LASER CUTTING

- **Laser cutting** uses a device that produces a narrow beam of extremely intense light which can cut out sections of paper and board to a high degree of accuracy and fineness.

- Artwork is scanned into the computer system and from it a laser cuts through the required material.

- Laser cutting works particularly well on most kinds of stationery, such as greeting cards and invitations. This production method produces a sophisticated high-class look.

- The cost of this process works out at roughly double the cost of die cutting.

GUILLOTINE OR ROTARY PAPER TRIMMER

- This a machine used to cut and shape paper and card with straight edges.

⚡ A* EXTRA

It is important that you understand how and why finishes are applied to graphic products.

CHECK YOURSELF – EXAM QUESTIONS

6 A colour leaflet promoting the Valley Leisure Centre is to be distributed in the local area.

The leaflet is to have a gloss surface finish to the paper.

(a) Name **two** printing effects that could be used to give a gloss finish.

(b) Explain **two** reasons why a gloss finish to the paper may be needed. *(4 marks)*

7 A printed brochure advertising a local company is to be produced. It must have a high-quality appearance.

Name **one** printing effect which may give this appearance and describe how it is achieved. *(3 marks)*

8 Name the industrial machine used to cut and shape **batches** of card with straight edges. *(1 mark)*

Standard pre-manufactured components

A component is one part of a product. These are mass produced by a manufacturer. You would buy them to help in the making of graphic products that you have designed. Hence the term 'standard pre-manufactured'.

- When designing and making graphic products you must be able to identify and use a range of pre-manufactured standard components to:
  - simulate surface detail on products and models
  - join materials.

Self-adhesive paper labels and tapes

- A simple way of applying pattern to a surface is to use self-adhesive labels or tapes. These are available in various shapes, colours and sizes and are reasonably cheap (Figure 10.25).

10.25 *Self-adhesive labels*

- The labels can be stuck on top of each other to create a 'deeper' texture effect.

- Computer-generated label designs are a useful way of adding text and information to the surface of a product.

- These types of labels present an easier and cheaper way of putting information on a product than printing directly on the packaging. The information can be changed and updated without having to reprint all of the packaging.

10.26 *Rub down lettering*

Dry transfer lettering

- This is sometimes called **rub down** or **instant** lettering. A wide range of styles and sizes are available.

- The letters are applied by placing the sheet over the drawing or product and rubbing with a blunt pencil (Figure 10.26).

- **Dry transfer lettering** can give professional results, but is rather expensive. Sheets of self-adhesive lettering are also available.

✎ Raised plastic lettering

- **Raised lettering** is used on some products to show company name, logo or other information.

- It is possible to buy injection moulded letters and numbers from a model shop. These are manufactured in various sizes and can simply be glued onto a model or product to simulate moulded or embossed lettering.

✎ Drawing pins

10.27 *Drawing pins*

- **Drawing pins** come in two main types: brass plated and those with coloured plastic caps over the heads (Figure 10.27).

- These come in several sizes, both in terms of their diameter and length. They can be used on models and prototypes to simulate details such as touch control buttons.

- Drawing pins are particularly good for using with foamboard or rigid foam, as they can be pushed easily into these materials and require no further fixing.

✎ Mapping pins

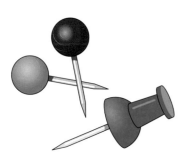

10.28 *Mapping pins*

- These come with various shaped heads. Two of the more common types are shown in Figure 10.28.

- As with drawing pins, **mapping pins** are ideal to use with foamboard and rigid foam. They are available in a range of bright colours. Details such as LEDs (small lights) can be simulated using this type of pin.

✎ Paper fasteners

- Rotating parts in linkage mechanisms made from card can be joined together using **paper fasteners** (Figure 10.29). The two 'legs' of the fastener fold back to secure it in place.

- Care should be taken not to over-tighten the fastener as this will stop the parts moving freely.

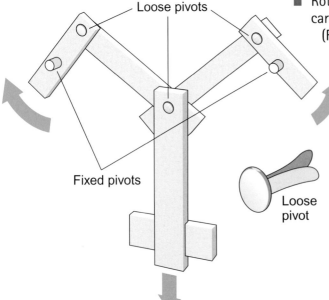

Loose pivots

Fixed pivots

Loose pivot

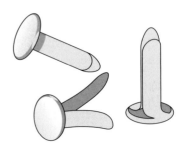

10.29 *Paper fasteners*

Paper clips

- **Paper clips** are available in a range of sizes. They are particularly useful as temporary clamps when positioning and gluing pieces of paper and card together.

Eyelets

- These can be used to join pieces of paper, card and thin plastic together, or to reinforce holes.

- The **eyelet** is secured in place using an eyelet punch (Figure 10.30). This squashes the end of the eyelet and prevents it pulling back through the material. This is shown in the sequence of drawings.

Foamboard hinges, hooks and hangers

- **Foamboard hinges** are used to join two pieces of foamboard together to create a right-angle corner. The foamboard slots into the hinge.

- **Foamboard hooks** have two sharp points which enable them to be pushed into the surface of the foamboard.

- **Foamboard hangers** push into the foam core of the board.

Construction kits

- **Construction kits** which contain gears, wheels and pulleys can be very useful when you are working on designs for graphic products which involve moving parts.

- Simple mechanical models to explain an idea or demonstrate a mechanical principle can be constructed quickly using kits such as Lego or Fisher Technic.

10.30 *Eyelets*

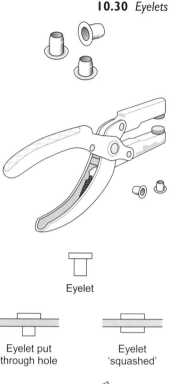

Eyelet

Eyelet put through hole

Eyelet 'squashed'

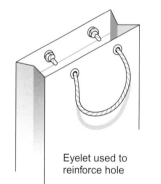

Eyelet used to reinforce hole

Environmental issues

You should be aware of the effects on society and the environment of using materials in terms of pollution, waste and recycleability.

Environmental issues need to be considered at design, manufacturing, distribution and disposal stages in the life of a graphic product. The environment can be effected by both the inputs needed to produce graphic products, e.g. energy (coal, oil, gas etc.), renewable (wood, water etc.) and non-renewable resources (oil etc.), as well as the outputs including waste products, heat and emissions that pollute the air, water and land.

Manufacturers and their suppliers are becoming more committed to reducing environmental impact. For example, they try to reduce their energy consumption and attempt to use less material in the manufacture of graphic products without reducing their performance. Recycled materials are increasingly being used where it is appropriate to do so; for example, in the manufacture of secondary packaging. These issues will be looked at in more depth in the sections on **Quality** and **Health and Safety** in this revision guide (see Unit 12).

9

In order to encourage children to save pound coins for a trip, they are to be given a money box made from card. The pictorial views below give details of the money box.

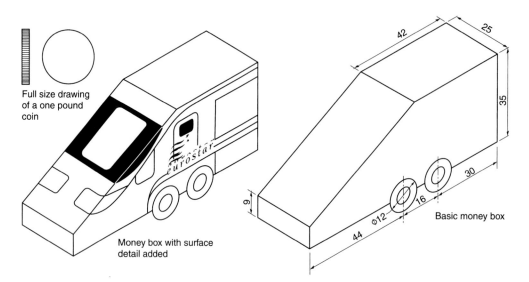

Full size drawing of a one pound coin

Money box with surface detail added

Basic money box

Annotate the given side view of the money box to show how the following could be used to add the surface detail:

- self-adhesive labels

- dry transfer lettering

- CAD.   *(2 marks)*

10

The drawing shows a free gift to be given with each copy of the 'HITS '99' CD. The CD has 12 tracks.

The gift is made from two thin card discs which are fastened at the centre so that they can rotate freely.

As disc B is rotated, the arrow lines up with a track number and details about the title of the track and the artist appear through the holes in disc B.

Name an appropriate fixing method for joining the two discs together.

(2 marks)

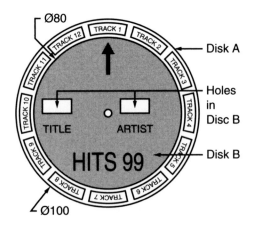

Disk A

Holes in Disc B

Disk B

Unit 11: Systems and control

You need to develop an understanding of control systems.

Control systems

- Any graphic product that includes moving parts, sound or has lights will involve at least one **control system**. A system has three elements: **input**, **process** and **output** (Figure 11.1).

Input → **Process** → **Output**

11.1 *The three elements of a control system*

INPUT
- This is what has to happen in order to start the process working. It can be some kind of movement; for example, moving a lever or opening a pop-up card. Or it may be some kind of change in the environment such as a change in temperature or a change in light levels.

PROCESS
- This changes the input in some way and activates the output. It may involve changing the size of the input or changing one type of input into a different kind of output. For example, movement could be changed into sound.

OUTPUT
- This is what the process makes happen.

- Outputs can be movements; for example, the picture on the page of a children's interactivity book which moves when a lever is pushed and pulled.

- Outputs may also be sounds such as music from a small speaker when a greeting card is opened.

- Outputs may also be lights. An example of this would be LEDs on a point-of-sale display stand, which flashes when people walk past.

Mechanical and electronic systems

- In the context of graphic products, you will need to know about two types of system:

  - **Mechanical systems** – such as those used for pop-up cards and interactive pages in educational and story books.

  - **Electronic systems** – such as those used to produce flashing lights on a point-of-sale display stand.

MECHANICAL SYSTEMS

- A **mechanism** creates movement within a product and is usually made up of a number of moving parts.

- You need to understand that a mechanism transforms (or changes) an input motion and force into a desired output motion.

- Let's look at this in the context of a page from a children's interactive book. The input motion is produced by the user pulling the tab (or lever) that sticks out from the side of the page (Figure 11.2). The output is the arm moving from side to side on the page.

- The mechanism is all of the moving parts. The parts shown in dotted lines in Figure 11.2 would normally be on the back of the page.

Types of control systems

- You will need to be able to:

  - select and use mechanisms to bring about required changes of movement and to control movement

  - identify and describe the following types of motion used in mechanical systems:
    - linear
    - rotary
    - reciprocating
    - oscillating.

LINEAR MOTION

- Linear motion is movement which takes place in a straight line in one direction.

- A basic linear mechanism can make an image move across a surface at any angle. To achieve this effect the user operates a push/pull link or lever (Figure 11.3).

- This type of mechanism is widely used for creating different effects in interactive cards and books. In the example in Figure 11.3, the plane moves forwards in a straight line. This is **linear motion**.

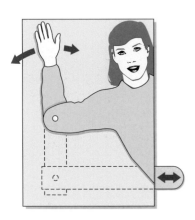

11.2 *Input*

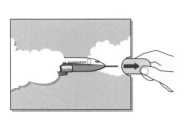

11.3 *Linear motion*

ROTARY MOTION

- This is movement in a circular direction around a central pivot.

- Mechanisms based on this type of movement can be used to show images which move in circles or arcs (part of a circle). These include the path of the sun or a ball, a wheel and the hands on a clock.

- In Figure 11.4, the bow tie spins round and round. This is **rotary motion**.

11.4 *Rotary motion*

RECIPROCATING MOTION

- Repeating backwards and forwards motion in a straight line is known as reciprocating motion.

- In Figure 11.5 the tongue moves in and out of the mouth. This is **reciprocating motion**.

OSCILLATING MOTION

- Repeated backwards and forwards circular movement is called oscillating motion.

- The arm moves in an arc from side to side in Figure 11.2. This is **oscillating motion**.

11.5 *Reciprocating motion*

REVISION SESSION 2 — Levers and linkages

✎ Levers

- Levers are an important part of many mechanisms.

- A **lever** is a long rigid object with a **pivot** (sometimes called a **fulcrum**) somewhere along its length.

- The pivot is a point at which the lever rotates. In the context of graphic products, levers are generally used to increase or decrease movement (Figure 11.6).

11.6 *Movement through a pivot*

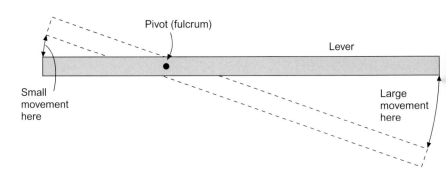

11.7 *Classes of lever*

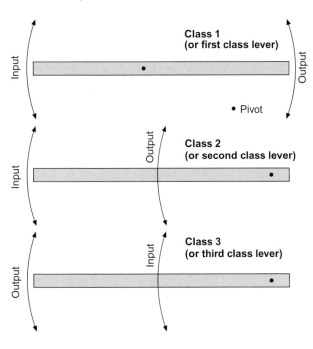

- There are three different kinds of lever each with the pivot, input and output arranged in a different way. The different kinds are called **classes of lever** (Figure 11.7).

✎ Linkages

- When two or more levers are joined together they form a **linkage**. The individual levers are joined using pivots – some of which are fixed to a back surface, while others are moveable (Figure 11.8). Both types of pivot are illustrated and used in the examples that follow.

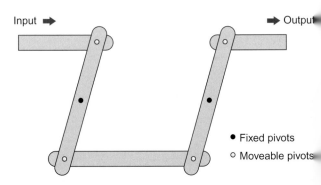

11.8 *Fixed and moveable pivots*

- Linkages are used in many graphic products. They can:
  - create moving images in both educational and children's books
  - add interest to interactive display stands etc.

- It is possible to connect levers together in such a way that they move in opposite directions at the same time (see Figure 11.9).

- It is possible to use levers to change the type of motion. Figure 11.10 shows how reciprocating motion can be changed into oscillating motion.

A* EXTRA

Do not try to invent totally new mechanisms. Try to base your answers on mechanisms that you have made or seen.

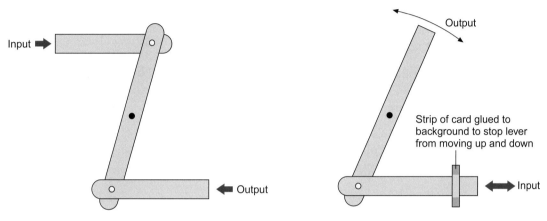

11.9 *Movements in opposite directions*

11.10 *Reciprocating motion turned into oscillating motion*

- You can connect two or more levers together so that they all move together (Figure 11.11).

11.11 *Two levers linked together*

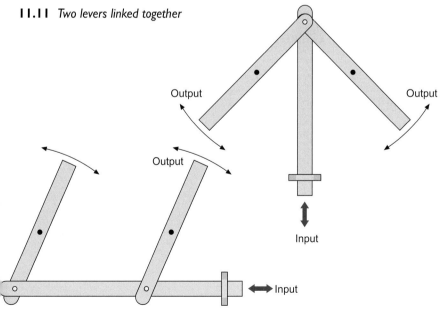

✎ Components

- Components that can be used for the pivots are paper fasteners, eyelets and click or ratchet rivets (Figure 11.12).

11.12 *Components for pivots*

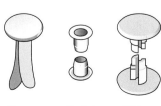

Paper fastener   Eyelet   Click or ratchet rivet

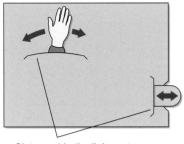

Slots enable the linkage to pass through the background

11.13 *Slots for linkages*

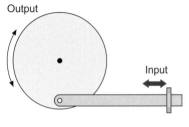

Output

Input

11.14 *Oscillating disc*

- In all linkage mechanisms, the position of the pivot points is crucial. Moving them from one position to another can reverse the direction of the movement, or reduce or increase the distance the mechanism moves.

- It is important that you look at existing graphic products and see what mechanisms are involved in making them work.

- In a graphic product, the linkage mechanism is normally hidden behind the background. This often makes it necessary to have a carefully placed slot so that part of the linkage can pass through the background. The moving image is then attached to the end of the lever, as shown in Figure 11.13.

- Levers can be joined to other shapes such as a circular disc in order to create different types of movement.

- By pushing and pulling (reciprocating motion) the lever, it is possible to make the disc oscillate or rotate – it depends how far you move the lever (Figure 11.14).

- You could use this mechanism to create the effect of a DJ 'scratching' a record. You could use the disc as the input motion and this would make the lever move backwards and forwards.

CHECK YOURSELF – EXAM QUESTIONS

1 The drawing shows part of a page from a pop-up book featuring various types of sport. By moving a lever on the left-hand side of the page, the footballer's right leg moves, along the arc indicated, giving the impression that the footballer is kicking a ball.

(a) Develop a design for a mechanism that would allow this movement to take place.

(b) Using instruments, superimpose a drawing of your chosen mechanism over the drawing of the footballer.

Notes should be used to indicate pivot points etc.

(15 marks)

2 Drawings (i)–(iv) show unfinished designs for a set of 'Matching Cards' to help children learn about motion.

Complete the designs by adding:

(i) an arrow to show the type of motion;

(ii) a description of the type of motion shown;

(iii) the name of the type of motion shown.

(4 marks)

(i)

........**Linear**........ motion

The train moves
in a straight line

(ii)

........**Rotary**........ motion

....

....

(iii)

.... motion

The doors move
from side to side
in a straight line

(iv)

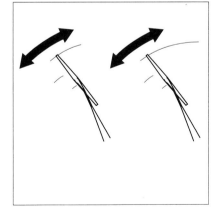

.... motion

The windscreen wipers move
backwards and forwards
following a curved path

Gears and cams

You will need to be able to identify and describe mechanical systems that:
- turn motion through a right angle
- reverse the direction of motion
- change linear motion into rotary motion
- change rotary motion into reciprocating motion.

✎ Turning motion through a right angle

■ Two gears can be positioned at right angles to each other in order to change the direction of motion through a right angle. Such gears are called **bevel gears** (Figure 11.15).

11.15 *Bevel gears*

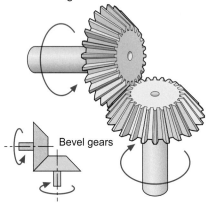

Bevel gears

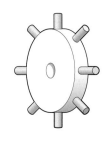

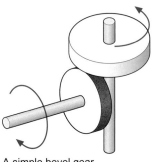

A simple bevel gear

■ Simple gears can be made using foamboard and doweling. Axles for the gears are easily created from straws or doweling.

■ Simple bevel gears can be made by sticking a strip of abrasive paper or an elastic band around the edge of a foamboard disc. A second disc resting on the top of the first will rotate because of the friction between them.

✎ Reversing the direction of motion

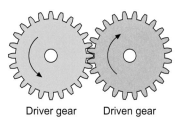

Driver gear   Driven gear

11.16 *Reversing the direction*

■ If two gears are meshed (linked) together the gear being driven (the output) will turn in the opposite direction to the driver (the input, as shown in Figure 11.16).

✎ Changing linear motion into rotary motion

■ Linear motion can be changed into rotary motion using a mechanism called a **rack and pinion**.

■ A rack is a flat strip with teeth cut in it and a pinion is a small gear wheel which meshes with the teeth on the rack (Figure 11.17). When the pinion is turned, the rack will move.

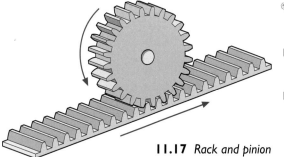

11.17 *Rack and pinion*

Changing rotary motion into reciprocating motion

- A **cam** can be used to change rotary motion into reciprocating motion.

- The cam is fixed to a rotating shaft. A **follower** rests on the edge of the cam and as the shaft is turned the follower moves up and down (Figure 11.18).

- If the cam is egg shaped, then the follower will rise and fall gently as the cam rotates.

- If the cam has a step shape, then the follower will suddenly fall as the cam rotates.

A* EXTRA

‣ Do not try to make your mechanism designs too complicated.

‣ Remember the examples given here show the types of mechanism that you can expect to be asked questions on.

‣ Most designs should be based on the use of materials such as card and foamboard. Avoid using inappropriate materials such as large amounts of wood, plastic and string.

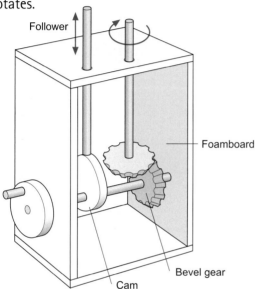

Follower

Foamboard

Bevel gear

Cam

Pear-shaped cam

11.18 *Rotary motion into reciprocating motion*

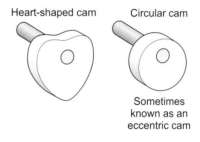

Heart-shaped cam

Circular cam

Sometimes known as an eccentric cam

- The 'mechanical dog' below is made from card. It comes in kit form and is designed for people to cut out and glue together.

- When the handle is turned, it operates both a bevel gear (A) and a cam (B). The follower on the cam makes the dog's mouth open and close, while the bevel gear makes the tail spin round.

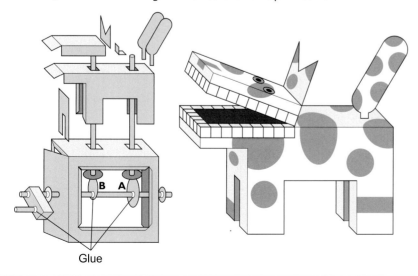

B A

Glue

3 The pictorial drawing shows details of a novelty display stand. The display stand represents a seal bouncing a ball on its nose. A mechanism on the back of the display stand makes the ball move up and down.

Specification points for the mechanism to make the ball move are:

- the input of the mechanism is provided by rotating a card disc on the side of the display stand;

- the output of the mechanism is a 20 mm diameter disc which moves up and down a vertical distance of 20 mm from the nose of the seal;

- the outline shape of the seal is made from 5 mm thick foamboard and is fixed to the back board of the display stand;

- the mechanism must be made from mainly graphic materials or pre-manufactured components.

(a) Use sketches and notes to design a suitable mechanism.

(4 marks)

(b) (i) Complete the front and end views of the display stand by adding your mechanism. Include hidden detail.

(4 marks)

(ii) Show the input and output motions of the mechanism.

(2 marks)

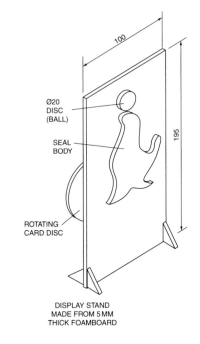

Ø20 DISC (BALL)

SEAL BODY

ROTATING CARD DISC

100

195

DISPLAY STAND MADE FROM 5 MM THICK FOAMBOARD

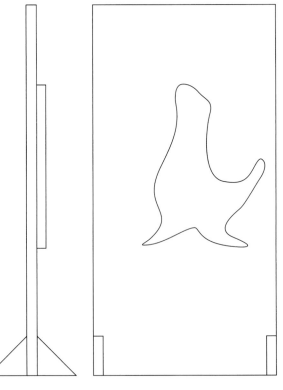

When designing graphic products that include a mechanism you sometimes need to know how much space the mechanism will take up and how far certain parts of the mechanism will move.

- This can be done by making a **prototype** of the mechanism and trying it out.

- It is also possible to establish how a mechanism moves by drawing it. To do this you need to draw the mechanism in different positions as it moves. It is like taking a series of freeze-frame photographs of the mechanism.

- Using this technique, you can plot the path of any moving point on a mechanism to see how it moves. The path followed by any moving point is called the **locus** of the point. The plural of locus is **loci**.

- You will need to be able to determine graphically (this means by drawing) the locus of points on linkages of up to a maximum of four elements (or parts).

✎ Plotting the loci

- The example that follows explains the techniques that can be used to plot the locus of any point on a mechanism. By drawing the mechanism in various positions as it moves, you can determine how long the slot needs to be and establish how point C moves (Figure 11.19).

- For example, if this were part of a moving image on the page you could work out if the image attached to the mechanism at C would remain on the page as the mechanism moved. It can help in the planning of sizes and deciding where things need to go on the page.

- Point A on the mechanism is connected to a disc which rotates around centre X. The locus of A is, therefore, a circle radius X–A.

- Point B moves up and down along the vertical slot. Now let's work out what happens to point C when the mechanism moves.

- Draw a circle radius X–A and divide it into twelve equal parts (1–12) using a 30-degree/60-degree set square. Set a pair of compasses to the distance A–B, put the point on number 1 and make an arc that crosses the vertical line (Figure 11.20). Join the two points and extend the line to point C. Repeat the process to plot the other 11 positions of point C. Draw a freehand curve through the 12 positions to complete the locus of point C.

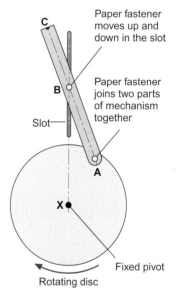

Paper fastener moves up and down in the slot

Paper fastener joins two parts of mechanism together

Slot

Fixed pivot

Rotating disc

11.19 *The loci*

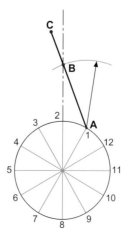

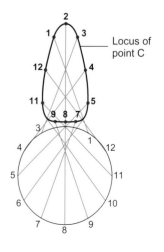

Locus of point C

11.20

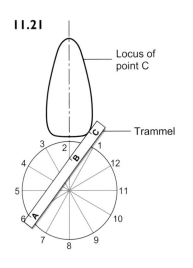

Locus of point C

Trammel

3 2 1
4 12
5 11
6 10
7 8 9

- The locus can also be plotted using a trammel (Figure 11.21). Cut a piece of paper or thin card and mark the lengths A, B and C along the edge. Place A on points 1–12 with B always on the vertical line and mark the 12 positions of C.

- Figure 11.21 shows A at position 6. Finally, draw a freehand curve through the 12 positions of C to complete the locus of C.

CHECK YOURSELF – EXAM QUESTIONS

4 A pictorial drawing of a pop-up card mechanism in its fully open position is shown. When closed, the card is intended to fit inside an 80 mm x 80 mm envelope.

(a) In order to test the design, complete the side view of the mechanism, in the direction of arrow A:

(i) when it is fully open, as shown;
(2 marks)

(ii) when it is half closed.
(2 marks)

20
20
40
80
40
80
corner
Ⓑ
80
'A'

corner
Ⓑ
Side view in direction of arrow 'A'

(b) State the main design fault with the mechanism. *(1 mark)*

(c) Name one property of the card needed to manufacture this mechanism. *(1 mark)*

(d) Name a commercial manufacturing process which is used to cut out batches of card for the mechanism. *(1 mark)*

(e) A pop-up card is a simple type of mechanism control system. State how the input motion is achieved for the pop-up card to work. *(1 mark)*

(f) Explain how **computer modelling** could help in the testing of mechanisms to be used in pop-up cards.

(2 marks)

5 The drawing shows an aircraft undercarriage in the 'down' position and in chain line with the mechanism partly folded. This is to form the moving parts on a drawing for a page in an interactive book about aircraft.

(a) Find, by construction, the position of HJ and GH when the leg FG is horizontal. *(2 marks)*

(b) Show where a slot would need to be cut if the push/pull link was attached to *(2 marks)*

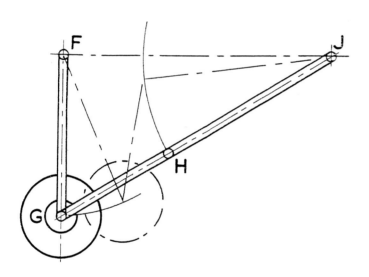

Pop-up systems

Pop-up systems are used in many graphic products such as books, greeting cards, packaging and point–of–sale displays. Pop-ups can create impact and surprise as well as making products more appealing and interesting for the user.

■ You will need to be able to analyse, design and use simple pop-up systems based on the following:

- V-folds

- multiple layers which use a parallelogram action.

✎ V-fold mechanisms

■ The **V–fold mechanism** is one of the easiest and most useful methods of creating a pop-up movement. The mechanism gets its name from the V-shape that it forms (Figure 11.22).

■ The design that is used must be arranged so that it is symmetrical along the centre fold of the card or book. The mechanism works when the card or book is opened or closed.

11.22 *V-fold mechanisms*

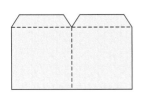

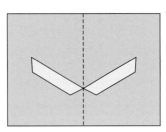

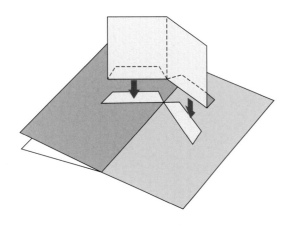

11.23 *Changing the angle at the centre of the V-fold*

90° — Card will stand up vertically when opened

60° — Card will lean backwards when opened

120° — Card will lean forwards when opened

- You can make V-folds stand vertically when the book or card is open or you can make them lean backwards or forwards. This is done by changing the angle at the centre of the V-fold (Figure 11.23). If this angle is 90 degrees, the V-fold will stand vertically. If it is more or less than 90 degrees, then the V-fold will lean.

- You can create a 3D view by using several (sometimes called multiple) V-folds (Figure 11.24). When making multiple V-folds you must make sure that all of the folds are exactly in line, otherwise the pop-up will not close properly.

11.24 *Multiple V-folds*

CHECK YOURSELF – EXAM QUESTION

6

To add a little 'fun' to their Annual Report a company has presented part of the information about its profits in the form of a pop-up bar chart.

The drawing below shows the company's Annual Report open at the page with the bar chart.

Use a series of drawings and notes to show how this final design could have been developed and how the mechanism that is uses works.

(15 marks)

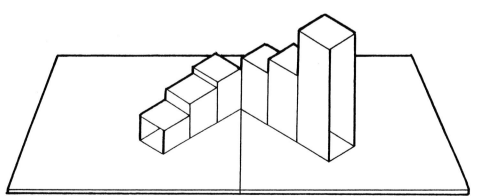

Multiple layers

The multiple layers – parallelogram **mechanism was one of the first to be used for pop-up books. The technique allows you to create vertical and horizontal surfaces raised from the background either one or several at a time.**

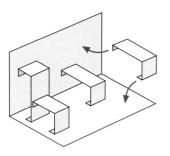

As long as the edges are parallel to one side of the base the card will fold flat

but be sure that the base is big enough

11.25 *Multiple layers*

■ The method is used in books, cards etc. which open to 90 degrees. Each surface is connected to the card or page by tabs which keep it parallel to one of the surfaces when the book or card is opened (Figure 11.25). Several raised surfaces can be used but the more you have the greater the thickness of the mechanism and the harder it is to close the whole thing flat.

■ A number of different surfaces at different distances from the back and base can give the feeling of depth and distance. Images can be drawn or or added to the vertical surfaces (Figure 11.26).

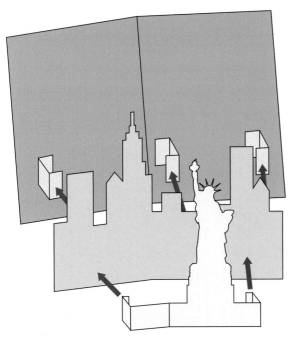

11.26

11.27

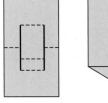

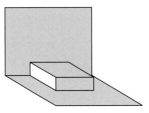

■ It is not always necessary to make this type of pop-up from separate pieces. It is possible to cut out the shapes from the background, as shown in Figure 11.27.

7 An activity sheet, in the form of a visual flow chart, is required to show children how to make a pop-up card of their trip to Paris.

(a) Complete the flow chart by adding:

    (i) the missing text to stages 3 and 5;   *(2 marks)*

    (ii) the missing diagrams to stages 2, 4 and 8.   *(4 marks)*

(b) All of the pieces required to make the pop-up card are to be cut from one piece of thin card. Use notes and drawings to calculate the minimum size of thin card required.   *(2 marks)*

(c) Identify **one** potential hazard with children using any of the tools and equipment and state how the hazard could be overcome.   *(2 marks)*

HOW TO MAKE A POP-UP CARD

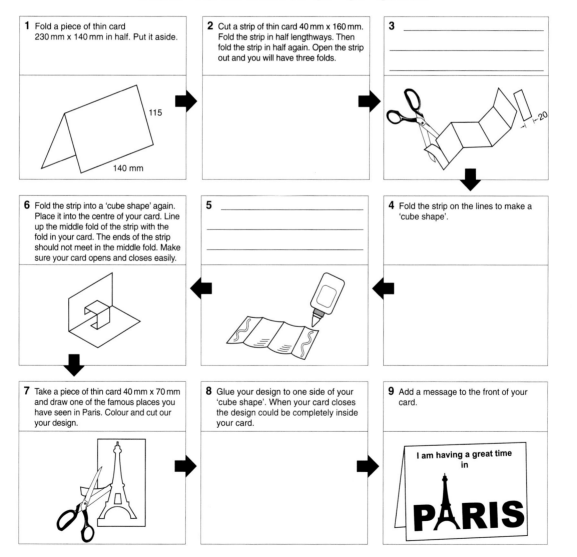

1 Fold a piece of thin card 230 mm x 140 mm in half. Put it aside.

115

140 mm

2 Cut a strip of thin card 40 mm x 160 mm. Fold the strip in half lengthways. Then fold the strip in half again. Open the strip out and you will have three folds.

3 _____

20

6 Fold the strip into a 'cube shape' again. Place it into the centre of your card. Line up the middle fold of the strip with the fold in your card. The ends of the strip should not meet in the middle fold. Make sure your card opens and closes easily.

5 _____

4 Fold the strip on the lines to make a 'cube shape'.

7 Take a piece of thin card 40 mm x 70 mm and draw one of the famous places you have seen in Paris. Colour and cut our your design.

8 Glue your design to one side of your 'cube shape'. When your card closes the design could be completely inside your card.

9 Add a message to the front of your card.

I am having a great time in

PARIS

QUESTION SPOTTER

▸ You will **not** be asked to design electronic systems.
▸ Most questions will require you to draw circuit diagrams based on the information given in the question.
▸ You may also be asked to suggest how certain electronic systems could be incorporated in to the design of graphic products.

A number of graphic products have electronic circuits to enable them to include sound and light in their design.

■ Examples of such products include greeting cards that play a tune when they are opened or the cover for a CD which incorporates a continually flashing LED (light-emitting diodes) in its design.

■ Generally, you will not require any specific knowledge about electronics to be able to answer the type of questions that you will be set in the exam.

■ You will, however, need to have a general understanding of circuits with supporting details of components. Any specific information and details about the components etc. will be given to you in the question.

■ You will need to be able to produce, in response to an identified need, a drawing of a circuit diagram from a series of sub-circuit or block diagrams. All electronic circuits can be shown as block diagrams having an input, control and output. Most electronic components fall into one of these categories, which make the process of circuit design easier to understand.

■ Although you do not require knowledge about specific components and how they work, some of the more common ones are listed in Figure 11.28 to provide you with some useful background information. **Remember you do not have to memorise any of this information.**

11.28 *Electrical components*

INPUTS	
Batteries are used to provide the power for many electronic circuits used in graphic products because they are small.	
Switches come in many different styles. They are used to switch circuits on and off.	
Capacitors are used to store an electrical charge.	
Resistors are used to control and direct the flow of electricity.	
Variable resistors can be adjusted to change their resistance.	
Thermistors sense temperature changes and convert them into voltage changes.	
The **light-dependant resistor** (LDR) senses changes in light and converts them into voltage changes.	
Moisture sensors convert changes in moisture content into voltage changes.	

CONTROLS

Transistors are useful because they allow circuits to work automatically. They act as a switch, reacting to voltage changes in the input.	
Increasingly electronic circuits are being controlled by integrated circuits and programmable chips. This enables circuits to become much smaller in size.	

OUTPUTS

Bulbs are available in various shapes and sizes.	
Light-emitting diodes (LEDs) can be used instead of bulbs. They are much tougher and use less power. They come in three colours: red, green and amber.	Protective resistor
Motors can be used to provide rotary motion.	
Buzzers give a continuous sound.	
Speakers change electronic pulses into sound.	

✎ Electrical circuit diagrams

- Technical illustrators are often required to draw electrical circuit diagrams. For example, most car manuals contain wiring diagrams. These are useful when carrying out repairs or fitting accessories to the car.

- It would be very time consuming for the illustrator to draw every component exactly as it looks. So symbols are used to represent components, with the connections between them shown as lines.

- This type of drawing is often known as a **schematic diagram**. It is a simple method of graphically showing how a complex electrical circuit works (Figure 11.29).

- Electrical circuit diagrams make use of the nationally recognised symbols shown earlier in Figure 11.28. This helps to ensure that the diagrams can be understood by anyone anywhere in the world. Sometimes it is necessary to identify each symbol by using some form of key on the drawing.

⚡ A* EXTRA

- ▸ Remember the wires connecting the components should be drawn horizontal or vertical.
- ▸ Make sure you understand what a schematic drawing is.

11.29 A simple electrical circuit diagram

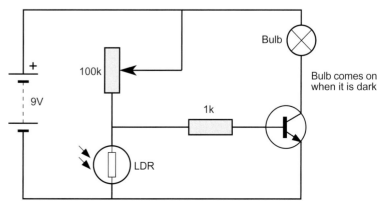

CHECK YOURSELF – EXAM QUESTION

8 A leaflet giving details about a lawn mower is shown.

   (a) Name the **specific** drawing system used in the leaflet. *(1 mark)*

   (b) State different purposes for producing this type of leaflet for use by:

     (i) the customer *(1 mark)*

     (ii) the manufacturer. *(1 mark)*

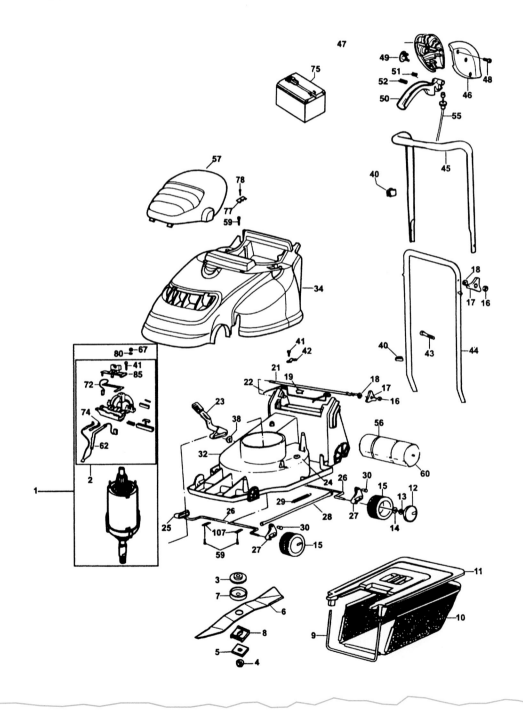

(c) The lawn mower has five different height settings for cutting grass to different lengths.

An incomplete diagram to help customers decide which setting to use is shown.

Height 1 cuts the grass to 60 mm, whilst height 5 gives a shorter cut of 20 mm.

Complete the diagram by graphically showing the relationship between the five height settings and the appropriate length of grass.

Do not use words in your answer.

(3 marks)

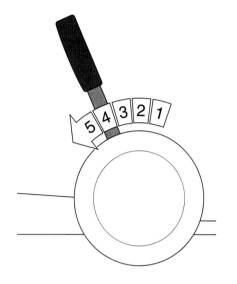

(d) The lawn mower is powered by a re-chargeable battery connected to a hand-operated switch located on the handle of the mower.

Use instructions to draw a simple **2D schematic** diagram of the mower to show both the electrical connections and the relative positions of the motor, battery and switch on the mower.

Use the leaflet shown in **(a)**, the parts list and the pictorial view of the lawn mower to help you.

(4 marks)

PARTS LIST

PART NO.	DESCRIPTION
44, 45	HANDLE
10, 11	GRASS BOX
50	HAND OPERATED SWITCH
57	BATTERY COVER
75	BATTERY
24	MOTOR HOUSING
6	CUTTER BLADE

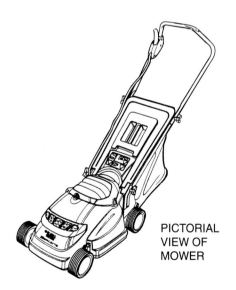

PICTORIAL VIEW OF MOWER

UNIT 12: QUALITY

What is meant by 'quality'?

Quality is generally defined as being 'the mark or standard of excellence'. A good quality graphic product is not necessarily expensive or one that lasts a long time. If a product does what it is supposed to and is safe, then it is good quality.

- For the consumer, a product has to offer good value for money.

- For a manufacturer, quality is about making good products in the most efficient way and for the most economical price (Figure 12.1).

- You should understand how to distinguish between quality of design and quality of manufacture by drawing on your experience and understanding of existing graphic products and their applications.

12.1 A range of graphic products

✎ Quality of design

- Some of the main factors which reflect quality of design are:
  - the product works well
  - the product looks good
  - the product is safe to use
  - the product is environmentally friendly
  - the product can be manufactured easily and economically.

⚡ A* EXTRA

When analysing a graphic product, you must make sure that you can distinguish between the quality of its design and the quality of its manufacture.

✎ Quality of manufacture

- Some of the main factors which reflect quality of manufacture are that the product:
  - is well made
  - meets its specification and performance requirements
  - is manufactured by a suitable safe method
  - is made within budget limits to sell at an attractive and competitive selling price
  - is manufactured for safe use and disposal.

✎ Quality assurance

- **Quality assurance checks** have to be made on the systems that design, manufacture and distribute graphic products.

- These checks ensure that consistency is achieved and that the product is of the required standard.

- Factors such as equipment, materials, processes and staff training all need to be constantly monitored and subjected to quality audits.

- Test results are measured against specific criteria.

- If quality assurance staff find that a product does not match the criteria, the stock is isolated and rechecked before deciding what action will be taken.

- European quality assurance standards, such as ISO 9000, are awarded to companies able to guarantee a consistent high quality of product or service.

Quality control

- This is part of the quality assurance function. **Quality control** is about meeting agreed quality standards and monitoring these standards.

- You will need to have an understanding of the procedures that could be set up during the manufacture of a graphic product to ensure control over its quality.

- In industry, checks are made throughout the entire process of producing a graphic product. This enables the manufacturer to be confident that products leaving their production line are despatched in perfect condition.

- In a school situation, the use of systems such as templates, stencils, jigs, ICT and CAD/CAM will enable you to control the quality of the graphic products that you design and manufacture.

A* EXTRA

You should be able to explain how and why quality checks need to be made when designing, making and distributing a graphic product.

CHECK YOURSELF – EXAM QUESTION

I Use sketches and notes to design a template to allow 50 nets (developments) of the leaflet holder to be quickly marked out.

The design of the template should include a method for marking out the fold lines as well as the outer shape of the leaflet holder.

(3 marks)

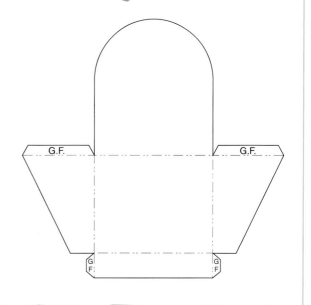

■ The most important reason for designing something is to solve a problem or satisfy a particular need.

■ A successful product must, therefore, **function** properly. It must do the job for which it was designed.

■ If you consider this in terms of a box to hold chocolates, the main function of the box is to hold and protect the chocolates. This is called the **primary function**.

■ However, it is important that the box is attractive to look at, easy to open and get the chocolates out, easy to display in the shop, informs the customer about the product and so on.

■ These functions which enhance the product's use are called **secondary functions**.

■ You should be able to analyse how far existing products satisfy their intended needs and fulfil their purpose. Testing a product against its **specification** measures its fitness for purpose and can give you guidance for suggesting improvements and modifications.

CHECK YOURSELF – EXAM QUESTION

2 Details are given about a sleeve to hold a cassette tape.

It has been found that the tape can easily fall out of the sleeve shown in part on the right. The design shown below helps to overcome this problem.

(a) Explain why the change shown at X has been made.

(2 marks)

(b) Give **two** reasons why this design would be more expensive to manufacture than the card sleeve shown in the first part above.

(2 marks)

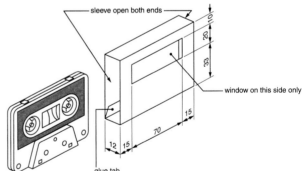

sleeve open both ends
window on this side only
glue tab

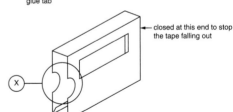

closed at this end to stop the tape falling out

Ergonomics

- Graphic products are designed and made to be used by people. You may touch or hold them, lift or carry them, manipulate, operate or gain information from them.

- The study of the design of products for their safe and efficient use by people is called **ergonomics**.

- When designing for people, three main ergonomic factors have to be considered (Figure 12.2):

  - the **size** of the people that will use the product

  - the **movements** they will make when using the product

  - the **reactions** of the body to the design through our senses of sight, hearing, smell, taste and touch.

12.2 *Finger grip*

Size

- When designing for people you must take into account all of the **measurements** which are important for the safe, comfortable and easy use of the product.

- Because people are different sizes, these measurements are based on the average sizes across a range of people. This is called **anthropometric data**. It is generally presented as a series of tables which are readily available for designers to use.

Movement

- You should avoid designs which cause the body to make unnatural movements.

- Some movements can prove difficult or painful for some elderly people. These should be taken into account in your designs, as should the restricted movements of handicapped users.

- Designs which have to be lifted should be designed for minimum weight and ease of use.

Senses

- By picking up and handling graphic products, you make physical contact with them using your sense of touch.

- You can also experience some of them via your senses of sight, hearing, smell or taste.

- Designs which communicate information visually using symbols, letters and words should:
  - be of an appropriate size
  - be correctly positioned
  - use the most effective colour schemes
  - display good contrast in colour.

CHECK YOURSELF – EXAM QUESTION

3

Pictorial views of a folder to hold activity sheets and games for a trip to Paris are shown.

The folder is made from one piece of card with the front corners glued together.

The drawing below shows a handle which is to be attached to the top of the folder. The handle is made from thin polystyrene sheet. It is to be securely attached to the folder but in such a way that it can be removed easily.

Explain how the given anthropometric data could be used to work out how big to make the handle.

(4 marks)

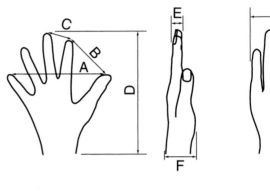

Not to scale

	CHILD	ADULT
A	140	210
B	40	60
C	35	50
D	140	210
E	10	15
F	35	50
G	75	110

Anthropometric Data

✎ Accuracy and tolerance

- When assembling products you should understand the importance of accuracy. For example, when designing a box to hold a bottle of perfume you must make sure that the box is just a little bigger than the bottle (Figure 12.3).

- It is sometimes difficult, however, to make something exactly to size, particularly in a school situation. This is why accuracy is generally linked to a **tolerance**.

- In practice, many manufactured products are made to an acceptable level of tolerance.

- The term 'tolerance' describes the acceptable deviation from the ideal size that you are prepared to accept. In the case of the box for a perfume bottle, the tolerance could be +2mm or +3mm bigger, but obviously it could not be any smaller than the bottle!

- The key question is always: how accurate does it have to be? A design specification should include tolerance limits (e.g. +/-2mm). Generally, the smaller the tolerance the higher the manufacturing costs.

- As part of quality control you would need to carry out accuracy tests at key stages during the design and manufacture of a graphic product. These key stages should be identified in your specification.

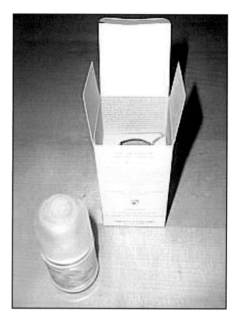

12.3 *Perfume bottle and box*

✎ Appropriate use of materials and resources

- You will need to be able to discuss if appropriate resources and materials have been chosen for a particular graphic product related to its manufacture and maintenance.

- You must also understand that to achieve the best use of materials and components, you need to take into account the relationship between the material, its working properties, the product you want to produce and the intended manufacturing process.

✎ Manufacture and maintenance

- Some graphic products, such as food packaging, are intended to have a short life once the product has been purchased. Therefore, their maintenance is not a major factor that has to be considered.

- Where a longer life expectancy is required, graphic products should be designed to require little maintenance. When maintenance is required, it should be easy to carry out. This will include, for example, the removal and replacement of a battery in a children's book or board game that features light or sound.

- The most basic form of maintenance is cleaning.

- The menu for a fast food restaurant is a good example of where the appropriate use of materials can make maintenance easier. If laminated or encapsulated card is used for the menu it would be much easier to clean than one made only from card (Figure 12.4).

12.4 *Menu*

12.5 *House-for-sale board*

- The use of corrugated plastic for house-for-sale signs makes them easier to maintain than if they were made from foamboard or thick card (Figure 12.5).

Social, cultural and moral implications

- When designing and making graphic products you need to understand that there will be many instances where the values of different types of people will conflict.

- Designers need to make judgements about how to resolve conflicts and find a compromise solution. These conflicts can arise for a variety of reasons.

SOCIAL

- When designing you need to consider an increasing range of users of products in different societies who will have differing needs.

- Some products can have a major impact on the way large groups of people live their lives. Increasingly, ICT is having a major impact on society as work, entertainment and shopping can be undertaken at home. Also, workers using ICT/CAD at home have less social interaction with fellow designers.

- Advanced automation means fewer people are needed to manufacture and distribute goods. This can cause unemployment.

- These diverse and wider needs should be considered where appropriate.

CULTURAL

- People have differing cultural backgrounds and needs. Designers and manufacturers need to be aware of these and be sensitive to them. This is particularly true in respect of religion, traditions and lifestyles.

- Food and clothing and the symbolism of certain shapes and colours all play an important part in maintaining the identity of a particular culture. For example, red is considered as 'danger' in the West, but is good luck for the Chinese community.

- Cultural issues are often related to moral and social considerations. When a product is intended for use by a range of cultures, it is important to identify and recognise the needs of those cultures.

MORAL

- You need to be aware that, in certain situations, a product may have the capacity to injure or harm someone. Cigarettes and alcohol are two obvious examples.

- You should also understand that there are some issues that some people may find offensive because of their views and the values that they hold; for example, the use of certain animal products and images.

CHECK YOURSELF – EXAM QUESTION

4 Many products use names that have no exact meaning in English and have been invented just for that product (e.g. TWIX, Smarties).

Why is it important to check if the name exists in other cultures?

(2 marks)

▰Further issues ▰

✎Economic issues

- You will need to develop an understanding about cost and value for money. For example, some designs may result in products that are too expensive to sell or be used.

- The design and manufacture of some products can have an economic impact on the way groups of people live their lives. For example, automation has reduced the need for a large manufacturing workforce; ICT has allowed people to work more freely.

- All designs have cost implications that must be resolved.

✎Environmental issues

- The **manufacture**, **use** and **disposal** of any product will have both beneficial and detrimental effects upon people, wildlife and the environment.

- Designers and manufacturers are becoming increasingly aware of their responsibility towards the environment.

- You need to be aware of how easy it is to dispose of, or recycle, the materials used in the manufacture of graphic products.

- You should understand how the production of these materials, and the processes that they are subjected to, affect the environment.

DISPOSAL AND RECYCLING OF MATERIALS

- Between 25% and 35% of the waste products we throw away in household rubbish is made up of packaging.

- Making and disposing of packaging requires energy and uses up natural resources such as trees and oil. Some of this waste is sorted and the materials recycled, some is incinerated, but the majority is disposed of i landfill sites (Figure 12.6). Both incineration and decomposition of wast materials produce **pollutants**.

12.6 *Landfill site*

- There is no point in over-packaging a product. For industry, excess materials mean extra costs and consumers generally dislike seeing products which obviously have too much packaging.

- Reducing the number of separate pieces in a package helps to reduce the possibility of them being dropped rather than disposed of correctly. Sweet wrappers are a good example of this type of problem.

- Designers of packaging need graphically to remind and encourage consumers to dispose of packaging materials properly.

BIODEGRADABLE PRODUCTS

- **Biodegradable products**, such as untreated paper, are those which will decompose (rot) more quickly.

- Some materials, such as plastics, do not rot very easily – they are **non-biodegradable**.

- A number of plastics, however, can be recycled and used again. As most plastics are made from oil, which is a non-renewable resource, recycling is becoming increasingly important and necessary.

✎Recycling

- This involves the collection and separation of materials from the waste stream and the subsequent processing to produce marketable products.

- The term 'recyclable' is often used loosely, and sometimes misleadingly, on products. For example, just because a product is 'recyclable' does not mean that it will be 'recycled'.

- Recycling can be expensive in terms of the energy and the cost of collection and sorting. For example, it can sometimes take more energy to recycle a product than to make it from new resources.

- The cleaning that has to take place as part of the recycling process uses chemicals which can cause pollution.

RECYCLED MATERIALS

- The term 'recycled' does not mean that a product contains 100% recovered materials. It means that it contains some recovered materials. The actual amount is frequently stated on the product.

- **Paper and boards** are two of the most frequently used recycled materials. Most recycled papers and boards are generally grey, although it is possible to obtain a white finish but this involves the use of chemicals.

- Recycled paper and board is often dyed to disguise its greyness and you can make good use of the background colour in a design.

- The overriding rule when designing for recycled paper and board is to accept that you will not be able to achieve the kind of result that you would get from, say, glossy art paper. There will be no 'brilliance' in the reproduction as recycled paper tends to be porous and cannot hold fine detail.

QUESTION SPOTTER

▸ Some questions will ask you about the advantages and disadvantages of recycling and using recycled materials.

- Best results are generally achieved from line illustrations and two-colour work.

- Recycled paper-based materials should not be used in situations where they will come into direct contact with food because the impurities in the material can taint the food. For example, the outer card packaging for cereal boxes is often made from recycled materials but the inner packaging has to be made from new (or virgin) materials.

CHECK YOURSELF – EXAM QUESTIONS

5 Why is recycled card not a suitable material for a chocolate box?

(2 marks)

6 A paper bag to be used in a sweet shop is shown.

State **two** aspects of the bag which make it environmentally friendly. *(2 marks)*

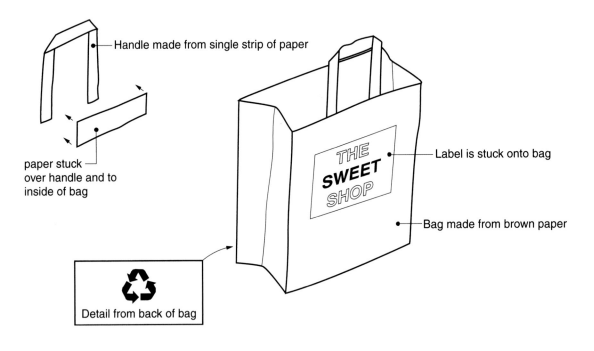

Handle made from single strip of paper

paper stuck over handle and to inside of bag

Label is stuck onto bag

THE SWEET SHOP

Bag made from brown paper

Detail from back of bag

Environmental symbols

- Most manufacturers of graphic products are committed to promoting packaging recycling by enabling easy identification of different materials that can be recycled and by encouraging the use of recycled materials.

- They promote the recycling of their packaging by using internationally recognised symbols (see Figure 12.7).

- You should be able to recognise and understand the symbols and pictograms which are associated with environmental and recycling issues. The examples shown are some of the symbols you may see on products that you buy. They can help you choose the best recycling option.

12.7 *Internationally recognised symbols*

Common symbols on packaging

- The top symbol in Figure 12.7 is for packaging made from **glass** that is recyclable after use. You should use a bottle bank or household collection.

- The second symbol is for packaging made from **steel** that is recyclable after use. You should use a can bank or household collection.

- The bottom symbol in Figure 12.7 is for packaging made from **aluminium** that is recyclable after use. You should use a can bank or household collection.

12.8 *SPI symbols*

SPI symbols

- These symbols are used in Europe and the USA to indicate that the packaging is made from **plastic** which can be recycled after use if suitable collection facilities are available where you live. The numbers 1–7 identify the specific type of plastic used (see Figure 12.8).

1	2	3	4
PETE	**HDPE**	**V**	**LDPE**
Polyethylene terepthalate	High density polyethylene	PVC	Low density polyethylene

Other symbols

MOBIUS LOOP

- This indicates that the product is capable of being recycled (Figure 12.9).

5	6	7
PP	**PS**	**OTHER**
Polypropylene	Polystyrene	All other resins and multi-materials

MOBIUS LOOP WITH A PERCENTAGE

- This indicates that a product contains X% of recycled material (Figure 12.10). However, this symbol is voluntary.

- Some products contain recycled materials but do not carry this symbol. Recycled content does not mean it is necessarily better for the environment and its use is often inappropriate, particularly for packaging used for food, toiletries and cosmetics.

12.9 *Mobius loop symbol*

12.10 *Mobius loop symbol for recyclable cardboard*

A* EXTRA

You should know and understand the symbols associated with recycling.

QUESTION SPOTTER

▶ You could be asked to explain why products are packaged, and the problems associated with the disposal of packaging.

CARDBOARD PACKAGING

■ This indicates that the packaging has been made from at least 50% post consumer recycled material (Figure 12.11).

GREEN DOT

■ This shows that a 'recycling fee' has been paid for this packaging when it is sold in some European countries (Figure 12.12). This fee goes towards the recovery of the packaging after it has been used.

TIDYMAN SYMBOL

■ This appears on many graphic products (Figure 12.13). It aims to encourage people to dispose of their waste carefully and in an appropriate way.

CARDBOARD MADE FROM RECYCLED MATERIALS

12.11 *Cardboard symbol*

12.12 *Green dot symbol*

12.13 *Tidyman symbol*

CHECK YOURSELF – EXAM QUESTION

7 **(a)** The sign on the right is related to recycling.

What is the exact meaning of the symbol?

(2 marks)

(b) Sketch another sign or symbol which relates to recycling.

(2 marks)

(c) What would be an appropriate colour to print this sign/symbol?

(1 mark)

■ Aesthetics ■

- Although it is essential that a product functions properly because we have feelings and emotions and are surrounded by the things we make, it is also important that the product 'looks good'. The appearance of a product can have a big impact on consumer choice – it is one of the first things that attract potential customers.

- The qualities that make a product attractive to look at, or pleasing to experience, determine its **aesthetic** appeal.

- It is through the senses of sight, touch, hearing and smell that the aesthetic qualities of a product, such as its shape, colour and texture, can be appreciated and measured.

- However, one person's ideas about what 'looks good' can be very different from another's. This is because aesthetic judgement is conditioned and influenced by many different factors – some examples of which are described below.

  - **Social influences** – the effects upon you resulting from how and where you have grown up.

  - **Personal experiences** – what you have done, seen and felt in your life, including your physical and psychological interactions with objects, systems and environments.

  - **Peer group influences** – what your friends like or dislike.

  - **Media influences** – the effects of radio, television, magazines, etc. upon you.

  - **Fashion and trends** – 'accepted' styles influenced by some people's ideas of what is 'good design'.

  - **Travel** – visiting other countries and experiencing different cultures.

  - **Education** – thinking about design and gaining experience of materials etc. through your use in designing and making graphic products.

- With the above in mind, you – as a designer, maker and consumer – should take every opportunity to observe, discuss and analyse designs both old and new. This will broaden your mind, help to develop your design skills and enable you to discuss why you feel a particular product is **aesthetically pleasing**.

✎ Signs and symbols relating to quality assurance

- Make sure that you recognise some of the more common symbols and signs which relate to quality assurance. They are an indication that the product meets a required standard established by a recognised authority.

- Details are given about these symbols and signs in the 'Industrial applications' section of this guide.

QUESTION SPOTTER

▶ Knowledge and understanding gained from studying this unit will help you in both product analysis questions and those that ask you to list and/or justify specification points.

UNIT 13: HEALTH AND SAFETY

You will need to have an understanding of health and safety issues in relation to the design, manufacture and use of graphic products.

REVISION SESSION 1

Product safety

- Products should be designed to be both **ergonomically safe** and **technically safe**. Where necessary, you should allow for easy maintenance to ensure their continued safe use.

- A product has to pass a range of tests set against nationally and internationally recognised safety standards, such as those produced by the British Standards Institution (BSI). (See the 'Industrial applications' unit for more details.)

- It is important that appropriate materials and surface finishes are chosen for a product so that they do not endanger the health and safety of the people who have to handle and use the product. For example, recycled-paper-based materials should not be used in situations where they come into direct contact with food.

- Surface finishes such as foil linings can help to prevent contamination and prolong the life of certain products, like fruit juice. Surface finishes should avoid sharp edges and dangerous corners. As an example, make sure there are no sharp corners on a menu which has been laminated.

- Careful consideration must be given to the ways in which people might misuse a product, as the manufacturer can be held responsible for any accidents which occur as a result of poor design or manufacture.

13.1 *Example of an appropriate safety device*

- Appropriate safety devices such as 'childproof tops' should be incorporated into the design of containers for toxic and dangerous substances (Figure 13.1).

- Where appropriate, written warnings, symbols and labels should be used to inform the user of potential hazards when handling, storing or using the product.

QUESTION SPOTTER

▶ Some questions will ask you to identify the precautions that have been taken to ensure that a specified product is safe to use.

A* EXTRA

Avoid stating that 'sharp corners or edges' are the only potential danger that can exist in a product. While it may be relevant and possibly gain you marks, try to go beyond the obvious and probably gain yourself more marks.

---

1 Identify one potential health hazard and one hygiene hazard when choosing suitable materials for the box containing chocolates.

(2 marks)

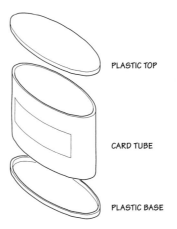

PLASTIC TOP

CARD TUBE

PLASTIC BASE

2 Some customers have complained that the flag shown is dangerous for children to use. Give one possible change to the design that would improve its safety.

(1 mark)

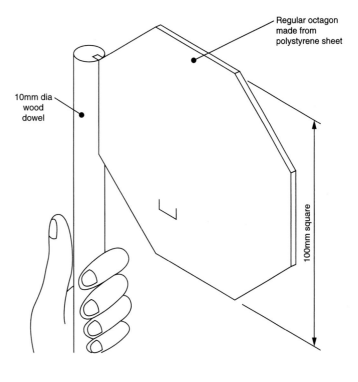

Regular octagon made from polystyrene sheet

10mm dia wood dowel

100mm square

A safe working environment

- In both a school and industrial context, you should know what makes a safe working environment and be able to follow good working practices.

- In a school situation, you should be able to manage your own working environment to ensure the health and safety of yourself and others.

Material, tools and equipment

- Adequate facilities must be provided for the safe storage and use of:
  - tools and equipment
  - materials, adhesives, chemicals, solvents and finishes
  - flammable and toxic substances.

- The use and storage of some materials and substances must conform to **COSHH** (Containment Of Substances Hazardous to Health) regulations.

- Your school should have a list of all such items and you need to be aware of the guidelines provided about their safe storage and use.

Personal safety

- As and where required, adequate facilities should be provided in terms of:

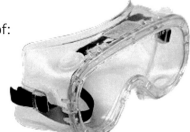

13.2 *Protective gear*

  - protective clothing including eye protection and face masks (Figure 13.2)
  - machine guards
  - dust and fume extraction
  - the disposal of waste materials
  - the provision and use of barrier creams
  - an accident procedure being in place.

> ⚡ **A* EXTRA**
>
> Make sure that your answers are specific. For example, rather than say 'Protective clothing should be worn' identify what items are required. If fumes are involved, your answer should read: 'A face mask should be worn because ....'

CHECK YOURSELF – EXAM QUESTION

3 Give **two** safety procedures which must be followed when using a hot melt glue gun.

(2 marks)

Risk assessment

- When a production involves hazardous situations it is necessary to identify, analyse and assess each particular risk situation.

- It is also important to ensure that adequate precautions are taken to minimise the potential danger. This applies just as much in a school situation as it does in the context of industrial manufacture.

- When producing a production plan for making a graphic product, you should list all the potential hazards you might encounter and write procedures that will minimise the risks (Figure 13.3).

Process	Hazard	Risk assessment	Control	Test	Remedial action

13.3 Headings for a risk assessment table

- You should make use of various information sources when identifying potential hazards, including:

  - COSHH – for example, you could use these regulations to identify hazards linked to the fumes given off by some adhesives

  - the instructions and information given on the labels of products such as Spraymount, impact adhesives and superglue

  - the instructions for using unfamiliar equipment such as a guillotine or a strip heater

  - the recognition and understanding of UK and European safety symbols (Figure 13.4).

13.4 UK and European safety symbols

Corrosive

Highly inflammable

Explosive

Oxidisng

Toxic

- In industry, it is the responsibility of the employer to assess the risks involved in each stage of production. The employer should set up procedures for dealing with them; Health and Safety inspectors will check that the correct procedures are in place and being adhered to.

> ⚡ **A* EXTRA**
>
> Where appropriate, try to mention specific standards and regulations in your answer. This could gain you more marks, if the information is relevant.

Environmental issues and effects

■ You need to understand that the manufacture, use and disposal of graphic products can have adverse effects on the environment which, in turn, can effect people's health and safety.

■ The manufacturing process can result in:

• energy and non-renewable resources being used and sometimes wasted (e.g. the use of plastics diminishing oil reserves)

• soil pollution from inks on paper litter

• solid waste that needs to be disposed of

• liquid waste, including chemicals, that needs to be disposed of (e.g. dyes, inks).

■ Regularly changing styles and fashion leads to people adopting a throw-away approach where products are only used for a short period of time. This increases the need to dispose of redundant products in a safe and environmentally-friendly way.

■ The use and disposal of graphic products can result in:

• litter and pollution

• landfill sites being used to bury rubbish

• emissions to the atmosphere caused by burning rubbish, some of which can be toxic

• wildlife being harmed.

■ See Unit 12 for more details.

CHECK YOURSELF – EXAM QUESTION

4 The packaging industry uses large amounts of wood-based products and plastics. Give **one** environmental consequence of the use of each.

(4 marks)

UNIT 14: PRODUCT EVALUATION AND ANALYSIS

As a result of the knowledge and understanding that you have gained from studying about materials, components, constructional techniques, manufacturing processes, health and safety, control systems and quality assurance you should be able to:

- evaluate your own work
- carry out a product analysis of commercially manufactured products and their applications (what they do and how they work).

REVISION SESSION 1

Evaluating your own work

■ You should be able to:

(a) review your work and apply quality assurance techniques by devising and applying tests to check the quality of your work at critical control points. Testing carried out during manufacture will inform you of your progress towards a successful outcome.

(b) evaluate the proposed product against:

- its specification
- its fitness for purpose
- the design need
- the needs of the intended user(s).

(c) evaluate the proposed product against moral, cultural and environmental issues for the intended user.

(d) review whether you have used materials and resources appropriately.

(e) carry out testing resulting in conclusions that suggest modifications or improvements related to:

- improved product performance
- quality of design
- quality of manufacture
- fitness for purpose
- target market
- larger scale production.

(f) analyse the performance of the control systems that you use to aid batch production and to ensure consistent, quality outcomes. Remember, in a school situation this will involve the use of systems such as templates, stencils, jigs, ICT and CAD/CAM.

QUESTION SPOTTER

▶ Remember product analysis is about looking at a product and establishing how it was made and how it works.

■ You might employ any or all of the following methods of evaluation:

- field testing under working conditions
- testing over extended periods of time
- third party testing
- testing against the product's specification
- testing against external standards and general sensory tests.

CHECK YOURSELF – EXAM QUESTION

1 **(a)** Describe a simple test which could be used to evaluate the desk tidy shown.

(1 mark)

(b) Give **one** reason for using your test.

(1 mark)

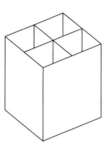

DESK TIDY
WITH FOUR
COMPARTMENTS

■ You should be able to carry out a product analysis of commercially manufactured products and their applications. The process should include:

- establishing the function and application(s) of the product

- identifying the constituent parts of the product and their interrelated functions

- establishing how the product works including any scientific principles involved

- identifying the materials from which the product is made and the production processes used to manufacture the product.

✎ Function and application(s) of the product

■ A well-designed product should successfully do the job for which it is designed.

■ It must fulfil, to a high standard, both the primary function and the range of secondary functions which enhance its use.

■ It must meet the needs of the user.

✎ Constituent parts of the product and their interrelated functions

■ Many graphic products are made of more than one part. For example, the box shown in Figure 14.1 has four parts each one of which has a particular function.

✎ How the product works

■ For example, you might be asked to explain how a particular net (development) 'works' in terms of the shape that it produces when it is folded and assembled.

■ The design of some technical products relies on the application of scientific principles. For example, you could be asked what scientific principles are involved in making the circuit work or the mechanism move in the design of a game that involves electronics or moving parts (Figure 14.2). The type of technology incorporated will depend upon the functions of the product.

> **QUESTION SPOTTER**
>
> As part of a question you may be asked to make an improvement to an existing design based on the product analysis that you have undertaken or problems that have been identified in the question.

14.1 *Packaging to hold chocolates*

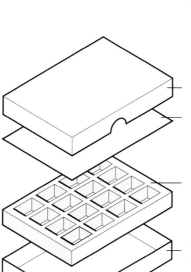

The function of the lid is to enable the user to gain easy access to the contents of the box.

The function of the information card is to give details about each type of chocolate.

The function of the insert tray is to separate each chocolate.

The function of the box is to protect the insert tray and its contents.

14.2 *A game for children*

✎ Materials and the production processes used

- The function, appearance, safety, reliability, durability and overall quality of a product are affected by the materials used.

- It is the material's properties which determine its suitability for a particular product and situation.

- All products should be designed for ease of construction and manufacture. This requires you to have a clear understanding of materials, available components and manufacturing processes.

✎ The intended market for the product

- People belong to different age groups and different cultures. They have different incomes and lifestyles. All of these factors can affect a person's tastes and, therefore, can have an influence on what they buy.

💡 QUESTION SPOTTER

- Some product analysis questions could be based on areas that you were told to study by the Exam Board prior to the exam. In these cases, a 'Theme Sheet' will be sent to schools by the Exam Board well before the exam.
- This sheet will outline the specific areas that have to be studied. Check with your teacher if there are any special areas that you need to study. An example of one of these 'Theme Sheets' is shown.

Product Analysis Theme: Point-of-Sale Displays

Papers 3 and 4 will contain a compulsory product analysis question set on the theme: point-of-sale displays.

The question will be assessed against the skills outlined in Section 7.4 of the syllabus subject content.

However, to assist teachers in the preparation of their candidates for this examination, it is suggested that the following aspects of Point-of-Sale Displays are considered.

- Methods of manufacture in nets.
- Flat-pack assembly.
- Methods of attaching information.
- Suitable printing methods.
- Purpose of Point-of-Sale Displays.
- Methods of transportation of Point-of-Sale Displays from manufacturer to retailer.
- Materials used including cardboard and foamboard.
- Methods of assembly without the use of glue.

Performance of products v. alternative products and solutions

- Most products have to compete against a range of alternative, but similar, products for their 'slot in the market'.

- Brand name, advertising, appearance and price are some of the main factors that will affect a product's competitiveness.

- You will need to establish how the product is different to its opposition and what features it has that could result in its commercial success.

CHECK YOURSELF – EXAM QUESTIONS

2 Give **two** different reasons why companies spend money on producing point-of-sale displays.

(2 marks)

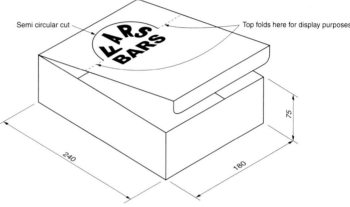

3 The drawing below shows a 'point of sale' display box to hold chocolate bars. The top can be 'folded open' to display the chocolate bars.

(a) State **two** reasons why this type of product is often sent from the printer to the sweet manufacturer in a flat pack form. *(2 marks)*

(b) Part of the instructions for assembling the box are shown.

Explain why this modern method of fixing is used rather than glue. *(2 marks)*

(c) Complete the freehand sketch of the box showing the top in the open 'display' position.

Do not include any of the lettering or chocolate bars. *(3 marks)*

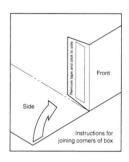

Instructions for joining corners of box

(d) A modification is required which will allow the corners of the box to be joined using slot-in tabs rather than the method shown in part **(b)**.

Use sketches and notes to show this modification to **one** corner of the box. *(3 marks)*

GUIDANCE ON EXAM TECHNIQUE

■ Make sure that you know exactly what you have to revise. Check with your teacher the specific areas of this guide you need to study in order to meet the requirements of the examination course that you are following.

■ Make sure that you know what the layout of the exam paper is like, how long the exam is and how many questions you have to answer. Ask your teacher if you can see past exam papers and if there are any theme-sheets that you need to research.

■ Practise by answering the questions in this guide. Refer to the exemplar answers which follow and ask your teacher for help if you do not understand something.

■ Read each question through carefully before you start your answer. Make sure you are clear what the question is asking you to do.

■ Look at the number of marks you can gain for each question. This will help you to decide how long to spend on the questions and how much detail to include in written answers.

■ Candidates frequently lose marks on exam papers because they misread or misunderstand important words in questions. A list of the most commonly used words is given below.

'GIVE ... / STATE ... / NAME ...'
This generally requires the specific name of an object, process or material to be given. Normally, a one- or two-word answer is sufficient; at the very most, a short sentence. Marks will rarely be given for general terms such as 'glue' or 'printing'.

'LIST ...'
This requires information to be arranged in an appropriate order. It can require single words (e.g. 'List the equipment you would use to make ....') or phrases (e.g. 'List the stages in making....'). Where the order is important, questions will generally read: 'List in order...' or 'List in order of importance...'.

'DESCRIBE ...'
This requires you to give an idea of what an object looks like and how it functions or what is involved in a process. It normally involves a statement or account of something consisting of one or two sentences that make reference to aspects, such as the form, function and properties of the object or process (e.g. 'Describe how a company logo is incorporated into the layout of the graphics on an item of packaging.'; 'Describe how market research can be used to ....').

'EXPLAIN ...'
This normally requires a clear, detailed account of something, including reasons, justifications and examples (e.g. 'Explain how the increased use of ICT in industry has affected employment in this country.').

'COMPARE ...'

A comparison must involve analysis. It is a recording of the similarities and/or differences between two or more similar products. Making judgements and drawing conclusions may form part of this process.

'CALCULATE ...'

This word simply means 'work out'. Marks are usually awarded for both the process and the answer. Candidates who write only an answer will not gain the process marks, even if the answer is correct.

'ADVANTAGES AND DISADVANTAGES ...'

Questions which include these words have marks allocated to each, so candidates must give both to gain access to full marks. For example, 'An advantage of using lithography for the printing of packaging would be that it is the most economical process for general printing, and a disadvantage could be that the plate life is limited to 150,000 copies.'

'USE NOTES AND SKETCHES (ANNOTATED SKETCHES) ...'

This indicates that candidates should answer the question using both sketches and notes to support or clarify particular points in the answer. Marks for such questions are allocated to both methods of communication. Candidates who write continuous prose, or just produce sketches, will not have access to all of the marks. Marks are awarded for the clarity and quality of communication.

'DEVELOP ...'

This means 'to improve upon a basic idea'. You are normally expected to show a workable or worthwhile solution.

'EVALUATE ...'

This involves making informed judgements about products and processes against clear criteria. These criteria may be given in the question or the candidate may be required to formulate them.

UNIT 1: TOOLS AND EQUIPMENT

Using drawing equipment (page 67)

1(a) One mark would be allocated to each of the four straight lines correctly drawn with the dots added. A tolerance of + or – 2mm is usually allowed on questions of this type.

(b) One mark is given for each of four names carefully printed. Always try to do printing between guidelines – it will help to improve the quality. Questions of this type are perhaps more common on OCR papers than other exam boards.

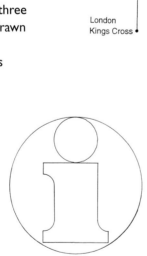

Aberdeen
Dundee
Edinburgh
Newcastle
Durham
Darlington
York
Doncaster
Newark
Peterborough
Stevenage
London
Kings Cross

Using drafting aids (page 69)

2 One mark will be allocated to each of the two circles. The two horizontal lines each has a mark allocated to it, as do the two vertical lines. Each of the three radius 10 arcs correctly drawn would gain a mark. The examiner would mark this question with the aid of a transparent overlay with the correct answer printed on it. A tolerance of + or – 2mm would generally be allowed. Remember: a circle template is a very useful aid when answering this type of question.

Using colouring media (page 71)

3 Drawing the rays of the sun is the most difficult part of this question. At first, perhaps, it is not obvious how wide the bottom of each ray is. A closer study of the information given should enable you to see that the sides of each ray slope towards the centre of the semi-circle. The answer requires the accurate use of a T-square, 45-degree set square and compasses.

Ten marks were available for this question. Two marks would be given for the use of appropriate colour such as yellow, orange or red. There would then be four marks available for each of two possible logo designs. In this type of question, try to keep your ideas simple and use lettering designs which are not too complex. It is important that the lettering style is easy to read. Make sure that you address all of the specification points given in the question; here they are very straightforward, but that is not always the case.

Using tools and equipment for model making (page 72)

4(a) While mylar or oiled card are the most suitable materials for making the stencil, other acceptable materials would be thin sheet polystyrene or acrylic and acetate. Generic terms such as 'plastic' would not be acceptable.

Appropriate reasons for the choice of material include: it is more durable, waterproof and it stays flat

(b) (i) At least two appropriate tools/equipment would have to be named to gain the mark, e.g. craft knife, safety rule, cutting board.

(ii) Up to 3 marks were available for illustrating this stage. A basic attempt to show the process would gain 1 mark, while a good attempt would gain 2 marks. If the process was very clearly communicated, using both sketches and notes, then the full 3 marks would be given.

(c) (i) Again, at least two appropriate tools/equipment would have to be named, e.g. masking tape aerosol spray paint, brush, paint.

(ii) Up to 3 marks were available for illustrating each stage. A basic attempt to show the process would gain 1 mark, while a good attempt would gain 2 marks. If the process was very clearly communicated, using both sketches and notes, then the full 3 marks would be given. If you choose a more complex method of production – i.e. screenprinting – you would still have access to all of the available marks.

Using printing equipment (page 74)

5(a) Two marks were allocated to this part of the question and an explanation is asked for. The examiner would, therefore, be looking for two aspects in your answer – a reason and a justification/explanation. For example: 'It only has to go through the copier once [1 mark] therefore you do not have to worry about lining both sides up [1 mark].'

Remember: always check how many marks are available for a question. This will give you some indication as to how many aspects the examiner is looking for in your answer.

(b) Examples of appropriate answers would be a scanner or a digital camera.

Using photographic equipment (page 77)

6 Film: the key words are develop, scan, jpeg/tiff, save, import.

Digital: the key words are images, download, USB/port, file direct, TWAIN, thumbnail, album, jpeg/tiff, import.

If your explanation showed little or no understanding of the stages involved when images are imported to a computer system, you would score 0 marks. You would gain only 1 mark if your understanding was poor or confused. A second mark would be given for showing some understanding and writing down some key words. The full 3 marks would be allocated if you showed a good understanding of the process involved.

UNIT 2: DRAWING SYSTEMS

Third angle orthographic projection (page 78)

1 Examiners mark questions of this type using a see-through overlay with the correct answer printed on it. They lay this over your answer to see how it corresponds with the correct solution. Marks are then allocated based on your correct interpretation of the two required views and how accurate your drawing is. Each of the dots on this answer scheme indicates where part of a mark would be allocated. Remember: to gain full marks on an orthographic drawing, the views must be in line and in the correct position.

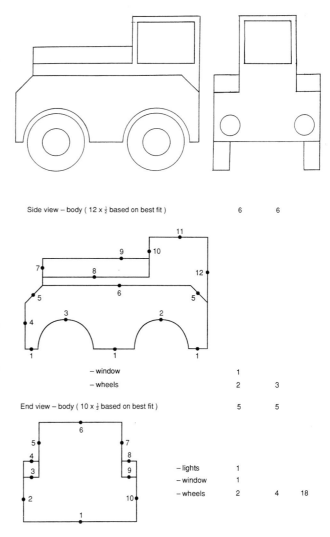

Side view – body (12 x ½ based on best fit)   6   6

– window   1
– wheels   2   3

End view – body (10 x ½ based on best fit)   5   5

– lights   1
– window   1
– wheels   2   4   18

Isometric drawing (page 81)

2 This is another question where the examiner would mark your answer using a see-through overlay. You could gain up to 5 marks for correctly interpreting the information into an isometric drawing and up to 4 additional marks depending on how accurate your solution was. One of the more difficult parts of the question is getting the stick of the lolly in the correct place. An ellipse template would be a very useful aid when answering this question. It would make the drawing of the curves much quicker and more accurate.

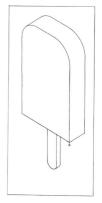

3 You would gain 1 mark if you used the correct method of drawing, i.e. an exploded view. For an answer that had pieces joined but in an inappropriate way (e.g. some pieces glued on), you would gain just 1 additional mark; but if you showed two pieces joined using a halving joint you would gain both of the marks available.

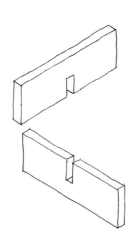

Remember: the examiner's marking is always positive and will give you credit for what you do correctly even if your answer is not fully completed or totally correct. For example, if you presented your answer as a 2D drawing you could still gain up to 2 marks for this question.

Planometric drawing (page 85)

4 (i) One mark would be given for the correct size of each division, i.e. 20mm, 50mm and 5mm. Three accurate semi-circles, drawn with compasses or a template, would each gain 1 mark. Inaccurate compass or template drawn semi-circles could gain up to 2 marks and freehand curves a maximum of 1 mark.

(ii) Three labels on the correct sections would gain 1 mark; if the lettering were of the same height as the given example and a reasonable attempt had been made to curve it round the can a second mark would be awarded.

(iii) If the shading was dark on the edges and lighter towards the middle, 1 mark would be awarded. If a clear highlight was then shown the second mark would be given.

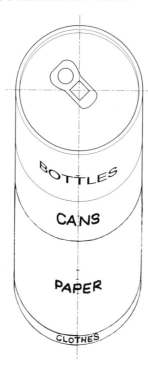

Perspective drawing (page 87)

5(a) Two marks were available for drawing part of the letter L on the horizontal surface, 1 for the height and 1 for the thickness. One mark would be given for drawing the remainder of the L on the sloping face.

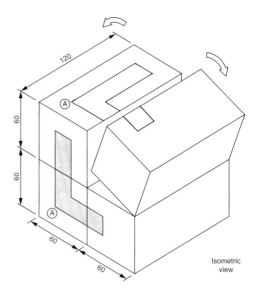

Isometric view

(b) If you drew at least four correct lines back to the given vanishing points you would gain 1 mark. By adding lines to show four boxes in a line and in perspective you could gain 2 additional marks. If your drawing showed evidence of foreshortening – i.e. the boxes getting shorter in length – you would gain the last of the 4 marks.

(c) One mark would be given if there was some appropriate attempt at drawing the letter on the side. If the three parts of the letter were in the correct position, the next mark would be gained. The final mark would be awarded for having consistent proportions to the parts and them being in perspective.

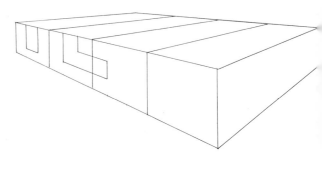

Assembly drawings (page 90)

6 When marking this question the examiner would be looking for the following in your answer:

- a sketch in isometric form (2 marks)
- evidence of card thickness (1 mark)
- outer shapes for the fuselage (3 marks), the wings (2 marks), engines (2 marks) and tailplane
- surface detail, windows, lettering etc. (3 marks)
- colour (1 mark)

If you produced a 2D sketch you could only gain the marks for the surface detail and the colour.

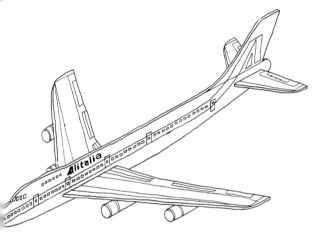

Pictograms (page 92)

7(a) There is no one correct answer to this part of the question. The mark would be awarded based on you saying that your chosen design was clear and easy to understand. Remember: these are the qualities of any good pictogram.

(b) This question asks you to use instruments to produce your answer, therefore the examiner will be looking for a reasonable degree of accuracy when marking your solution. A tolerance of + or - 2mm is common on this type of question. There would be 1 mark for each of the two rectangles, 1 mark for the quarter circle and 2 marks for the finger.

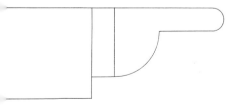

UNIT 3: BASIC GRAPHIC SHAPES

Triangles (page 94)

1(a) There are 11 small **equilateral triangles** and one **trapezium** or **quadrilateral**.

(b) This is a straightforward question targeted at around the F–G grade level. The triangles can all be easily drawn using a T-square and 60-degree set square. Questions of this type are often a lead in to making a modification to the existing design or producing an alternative design.

2 This question involves a more complex logo design based on triangles and would be targeted around the C–D grade level.

(a) The particular type of triangle that has been used in the logo design is an **isosceles** triangle.

(b) There are two ways in which this questioned could be answered. The first method involves drawing the first isosceles triangle and then adding the next on the side of it, and so on until the design is completed. The second method is, perhaps, easier and more accurate. A circle would be drawn with its centre at C and the radius equal to the long side of the triangle. The length of the short side of the triangle could then be stepped off eight times around the circumference and the triangles. Remember: marks are generally based on the outcome not for using a particular method.

Polygons (page 97)

3 This is another question that the examiner would mark using a see-through overlay and where a small tolerance would be allowed. An octagon drawn with a degree of accuracy would gain 1 mark, while an accurate octagon would gain 2 marks. The hexagon would be marked in the same way as the octagon. Drawing the T and the G could each gain you up to 2 marks and the letter A 1 mark.

4 Correct answers are:
  (i) Circle
  (ii) Square
  (ii) Equilateral triangle
  (iv) Octagon
  (v) Rectangle

The ellipse (page 100)

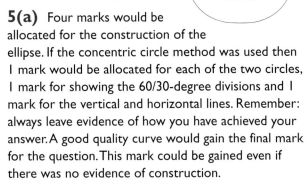

5(a) Four marks would be allocated for the construction of the ellipse. If the concentric circle method was used then 1 mark would be allocated for each of the two circles, 1 mark for showing the 60/30-degree divisions and 1 mark for the vertical and horizontal lines. Remember: always leave evidence of how you have achieved your answer. A good quality curve would gain the final mark for the question. This mark could be gained even if there was no evidence of construction.

(b) One mark would be gained for correctly drawing each part circle.

Shapes formed from combination of circles, tangents and tangrential arcs (page 102)

6 Questions of this complexity are rare on Graphic Products question papers but obviously if you can answer it then more straightforward questions involving circles and arcs should not present you with any problems. Some of the smaller curves could be drawn with a circle template. Always start a question of this type by drawing the centre lines. Then mark in the centres that you are given sizes for and draw the curves (e.g. the radius 120 mm curves). You then have to work out the other centre using the techniques explained elsewhere in this guide. Remember: many questions are like this – they have an easy start and then move on to harder bits. Always try to do as much of a question as you can. Never think 'I can't do this' and make no attempt at all.

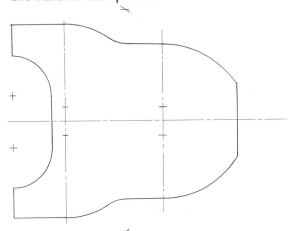

UNIT 4: ENHANCEMENT TECHNIQUES

Use of tone (page 104)

1 This question requires you to add both colour and texture to both materials. Remember: different tones of colour should be used on each surface. Two marks would be allocated to the plastic, one for the colour – a light blue, and one for the texture – representing reflections. The wood is more complex and 2 marks would be given for the appropriate use of tone and 2 marks for the texture – representing the grain lines. The piece of the base that can be seen through the plastic would require a different tone than the remainder of the wood.

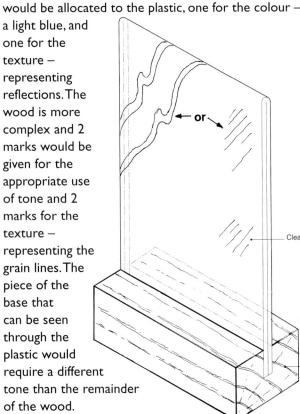

2 (i) At least two tones of colour, or pencil shading, need to be added in order to gain the mark.

(ii) At least two different types of grain would need to be added in order to gain the mark.

UNIT 5: DATA PRESENTATION

Table (page 108)

1 This is a straightforward question and was targeted at a Grade G. One mark was awarded for showing the correct number for each type of property while the second mark was given for indicating the correct names.

Type	Clothes	Cafe	Pubs	Hair-dressers	Shoe	TV	Others	Empty	Vid
No.	3	2	4	5	1	3	8	1	3

Line graphs (page 109)

2 The solution shown below is in the form of a line graph, but other methods of presentation would be equally acceptable so long as the information was clearly and correctly communicated. In this question, 4 marks would be allocated to the 4 pieces of information being correctly represented. The other 2 marks would be allocated for labelling. Remember: on a line graph both axes should be labelled and a title given to the graph.

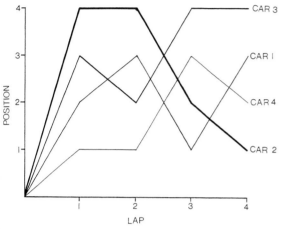

Bar charts (page 110)

3 There are several different ways in which this question could be answered but the given solution is

BALL POSSESSION

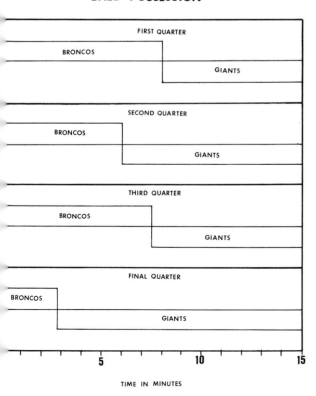

perhaps the most appropriate. While the presentation of the data is the most important aspect of the question, you should not overlook the fact that marks would be awarded for the effective use of colour and a suitable key. Appropriate labelling would be acceptable in place of a key.

Pie charts (page 111)

4(a) Dividing the circle into five appropriate sectors gained 1 mark and correctly labelling the sectors the second mark.

(b) Drawing a reasonable isometric circle would gain 1 mark, adding the five divisions up to 2 marks and the labelling 1 mark. A key could be used in place of the labelling but it would possibly take longer to produce.

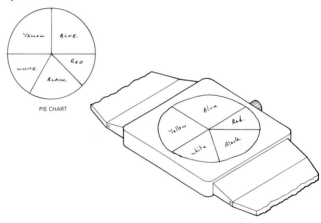

Pictographs (page 112)

5(a) This requires a drawing of half the existing symbol split vertically. One mark would be awarded for this correct interpretation and up to 2 marks for how well the drawing was produced.

(b) The correct name is pictograph.

(c) You would need to make reference to it being difficult to draw and/or understand a symbol representing anything less than 500 people.

(d) Appropriate reasons why it is quicker to produce this type of chart using a computer would be that the image can be scanned/drawn or selected using clip art/text could be added/coloured/sized/copied/printed out in multiple copies/changed or updated. Any two statements would each gain 1 mark each, or both marks could be gained by using one statement with a justification.

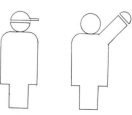

UNIT 6: MODEL MAKING AND PRODUCT MANUFACTURE

Nets: cubes and prisms (page 114)

1(a) Two marks would be gained for showing the three folding flaps required to complete the top of the box. One mark would be given for a flap to join the four sides of the box together. The bottom could be completed by adding three glue tabs or using the same closing method as the top. Either method could gain 2 marks.

(b) One mark would be given for both letters being in the correct place. Each letter, well drawn, would gain 1 mark.

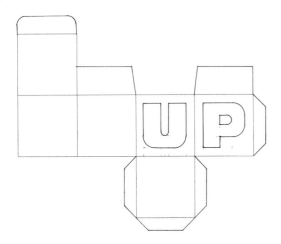

Nets: cylinders, pyramids, cones and truncated shapes (page 117)

2 This is a complex question targeted at A grade.

(a) A circle drawn to the correct size gained 1 mark, as did the three slots drawn to the correct size and in the correct position. Correctly constructing the quarter ellipse could gain you up to 2 marks, and if the template were the correct size the third mark would be given. If the development was the correct shape – i.e. a sector of a circle – 1 mark would be given and a second mark if it was the correct size.

(b) (i) If the pieces were arranged with a degree of economy, 1 mark would be given. The full 2 marks would be awarded for the pieces arranged in the most economical way.

(ii) If both dimensions were correct to the answer you produced in part (i), then the mark would be given.

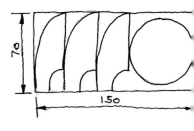

3(a) One mark would be allocated to each of the following points:
- The box is made from one piece of card.
- There is a separate lid made from one piece of card.
- There is an easy way of removing the plastic case (e.g. 'There are finger cut-outs' or 'The box is not as high as the case').

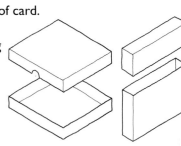

(b) Drawing an appropriate net for the box would gain up to 2 marks. If it was the correct size the next mark would be awarded, and if the correct number of glue tabs were added the fourth mark would be given. Drawing an appropriate net for the lid would gain a mark and if the size was a little bigger than the box the second mark was given. Appropriate glue flaps added to the lid gained 1 mark.

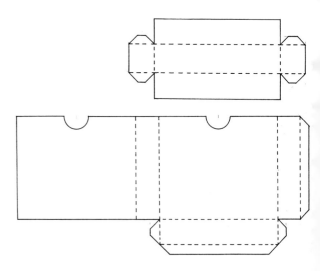

Nets: slot and tab fixings (page 122)

4(a) Up to 3 marks were available for a solution that **joined** the corner together, was **secure** (would not pull apart) and was of an **appropriate size** (one large or two small tabs). Clear communication using sketches **and** notes gained an additional mark.

(b) Up to 2 marks were available for a solution which both **joined** and **secured** the handle to the folder.

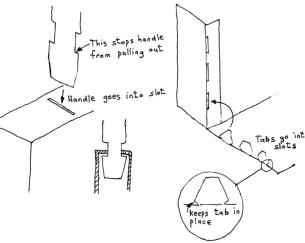

Fabrication (page 124)

5 If your answer showed an arrangement of strips to provide six spaces, 1 mark would be awarded. If the method showed pieces of foamboard joined but they did not slot together it would gain a further mark, but if they slotted together it would gain 2 further marks. One mark was available for the clarity of the sketching and notes.

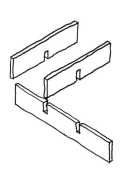

Forming (page 125)

6(a) Examples of suitable plastics for vacuum forming are Styrene/PVC/HIPS/HDPE and Polystyrene.

(b) A former showing sloping sides in both the front and side views would gain 2 marks. If the former has rounded corners then an additional mark is gained. If all three orthographic views were shown, 1 mark would be awarded and if they were in projection an additional mark would be added, giving a total of 5 marks for the question.

Typography and layout (page 128)

7 The three selections required are:
1 Select text size
2 Select text style
3 Select text position – left margin.
It would not matter which order these were listed in.

Colour (page 131)

8(a) The question asks you to develop a design. This means you would need to produce at least one design idea and improve or modify it in some way to gain the 2 available marks.

(b) There would be 1 mark available for drawing each letter and 1 mark for using appropriate sizes and proportions when drawing the word FAST.

Colour theory (page 132)

9(a) You could gain all 4 marks irrespective of which design you chose. Marks would be awarded for the quality of the reasons you gave for the choice and how well they related to shape, colour and the style of lettering used. You must apply your subject specific knowledge and not make very general statements such as 'People will remember it because it is a good design and uses a bright colour'.

(b) The three primary colours are red, blue and yellow. The three secondary colours are green, orange and purple.

(c) As with part (a), there is no one totally correct answer. Several different colours could be considered appropriate and your choice would have to be clearly justified by the reason you gave. For example: 'Green would be a good choice for an environmentally-friendly product because it is a colour which is symbolic of the natural word.'

UNIT 7: ICT APPLICATIONS

CAD/CAM (page 135)

1 Appropriate ways in which ICT has helped the designers to communicate with the printing company would be e-mail, the internet, video conferencing or using a CD Rom. It would not be sufficient to say 'Using a computer' or that 'it is a faster method of communication'.

Self-adhesive signs (page 137)

2 The CAM equipment could be identified as a vinyl cutter or by a trade name such as Roland CAMM machine, Lynx and Ultra cutters or a Stika.

Desktop publishing (page 140)

3(a) One mark would be gained for showing two tones of shading, light on the top and darker on the side. To gain the second mark there would need to be a graduation of tone or highlight used on the curved surface.

(b) Drawing an isometric view of the top surface of the letter L would gain 1 mark and adding the depth a second mark. A reasonable curve of the correct size drawn for the inside of the letter O gained 1 mark. If the correct depth were added to at least one of the curves, then a second mark would be awarded.

(c) Naming an appropriate piece of equipment such as a scanner or a digital camera would gain 1 mark, but there would need to be a brief outline of how the equipment is used in order to gain the second available mark.

(d) There are two parts to this process: how the font style and/or size would change and how the lettering would be correctly positioned. One mark would be awarded for showing some understanding about each of these two parts.

Paint and Draw programs (page 142)

4 Four different 'tools' are required to complete the drawings:
- Circle/ellipse
- Filled polygon
- Box and the text tool.

Identifying at least two of these correctly would gain 1 mark. By correctly choosing all four, 2 marks are gained.

Correctly completing two of the drawings gained 1 mark; correctly completing the four gained 2 marks.

One mark was gained for the process of drawing the wheel being correct (e.g. Move to centre, click and hold down, drag to edge of circle and release).

One mark was gained for the process of drawing the container (e.g. Move to one corner, click and hold down, drag to diagonally opposite corner and release).

One mark was gained for the process of drawing the filled window and having at least 2 co-ordinates correct. If the process and all the co-ordinates were correct then 2 marks were gained (e.g. Move to 2.5 click, move 3.7 click, move 4.7 click, move 4.5 click, move 2.5 click).

Mentioning the selection of a text style/shape gained a mark. If the process for producing the text was correct this gained a second mark (e.g. Move to starting position, click and enter text).

Researching and communicating information (page 144)

5 There were three additional stages required to complete the block diagram and 1 mark was allocated to each process. The first stage was to cut/save/copy or capture the image. Stage two was to load/open/import or paste the image into DTP. Stage three required the use of terms such as crop/drag/re-size frame or tool. Re-size on its own was not sufficient to gain the mark. One mark was then awarded if the stages were in the correct order and a box had been drawn round each stage.

Tables and spreadsheets (page 147)

6 Appropriate reasons why it is quicker to produce this type of chart using a computer would be that the image could be: scanned/drawn or selected using Clip Art/text could beadded/coloured/sized/copied/printed out in multiple copies/changed or updated. Any two statements would gain 1 mark each or both marks could be gained by giving one statement with a justification.

Remember: 2 marks require two aspects/points in your answer.

UNIT 8: INDUSTRIAL APPLICATIONS

Commercial production (page 155)

1 You should have circled 'batch'.

Packaging, marketing and advertising (page 159)

2 Two further specification points would be:
- that the shape of the box must allow for easy packing into outer cartons.
- that the box must not crush when stacked.

It is important to remember that the answers must relate to transportation and not be just general specification points.

3 An explanation of why the owl character would be used on packaging could include that it:
- has a link to children
- has a link with words such as wise and intelligence
- is an attractive character.

One mark would be awarded for each of two such points mentioned or 2 marks could be awarded if one point was qualified (e.g. 'It has a link with children **because** it looks like a cartoon character.').

Quality assurance (page 162)

4 The 'e-mark' indicates the minimum weight stated on a package. A barcode helps with stock control, product identification etc. For both designs, you would gain 1 mark for some understanding; an additional mark is available for showing full, clear understanding.

Commercial printing methods (page 164)

5(a) One mark for each correct colour: Cyan, Magenta, Yellow and Black.

(b) Correct answer: Offset Lithography – gains 2 marks.

Offset (1 mark); Lithography (1 mark)

(c) When building up the colour the darkest (black) is printed last.

(d) Correct positioning (Registration mark) gains 1 mark; correct strength of colours (Colour bar) gains 1 mark.

6(a) (i) The inscribed circle drawn with a reasonable degree of accuracy (but not freehand) would gain 1 mark. If the circle was drawn to within a tolerance of + or – 2mm then it would gain 2 marks. The third mark for this part of the question would be gained by correctly identifying the three magenta areas.

(ii) By drawing a circle consistent with that drawn in (i), even if was freehand, the first mark would be gained. The second mark was for drawing the letter T within the tolerance. The three cyan areas needed to be correctly identified to gain the third mark.

b) More common names:
Cyan – blue or turquoise (not green)
Magenta – red, pink or fuschia (not purple)

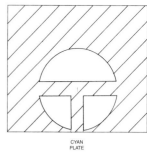

MAGENTA PLATE

CYAN PLATE

UNIT 9: GOOD WORKING PRACTICE

Process and block diagrams (page 170)

1(a) This question would be marked to a tolerance of + or – 2mm. The drawing shows how the marks would be awarded.

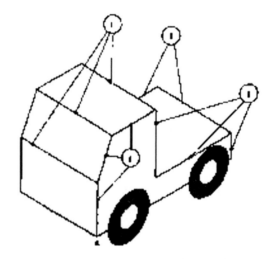

(b) There were 4 marks available for this part of the question. The examiner will be looking for mention of eight of the following in order to award full marks:
- Box A Coloured pencils, felt pens or paint
- Box B Cutting mat
  Make sure all lines are cut including line shown by arrow.
- Box C Score along dotted line with point of scissors and then fold.
  Make sure scoring does not cut through paper and that folds are made in the correct direction.
- Box D PVA, Pritt stick etc.
  Make sure glue is only placed on tabs and each is fixed in the correct position.

Flow charts (page 172)

2(a) FLOW CHART OF THE INSTRUCTIONS FOR THE PACKERS

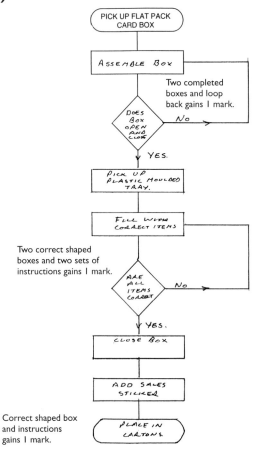

Two completed boxes and loop back gains 1 mark.

Two correct shaped boxes and two sets of instructions gains 1 mark.

Correct shaped box and instructions gains 1 mark.

An operation box and a stop box would be acceptable. One mark was available for the quality of the chart (i.e. symmetry) and the consistent size of the boxes.

(b) Protect the surface of the phone from being scratched/protect from dust/protect from moisture/aids security. One point qualified would gain the 2 marks, as would two points that were unqualified.

(c) (i) Suitable materials for vacuum forming include Styrene / PVC / HIPS / HDPE or Polystyrene. In the context of this question, Acrylic, Perspex, Nylon, Polythene or ABS would not be considered appropriate.

(ii) To allow the mould to be removed.

3(a) Six operations need to be listed:
- Market research starts
- Design approval given
- Materials ordered
- Printers' proofs approved or proofs prepared or both

- Batch production
- Dispatch to shops

Half a mark is given to each correct operation with the mark rounded up at the end of this part of the question.

(b) Market research. Start week 2, finish week 5 – both needed for 1 mark.

Approval begins at end of market research 1 mark.

Artwork produced, materials ordered in line for 1 week – both needed for 1 mark.

Printers proofs 2 weeks long – 1 mark.

Batch production begins after 1 week; 5 batches shown – both needed for 1 mark.

Dispatch/cards on sale both needed for mark.

In a question of this type, errors are not compounded.

(c) The correct number of weeks is 10.

UNIT 10: MATERIALS

Thin sheet plastics (page 181)

1(a) A die cutter would be used to cut out the profile of the shape and/or the hole in the shape.

(b) The reasons why corrugated card is not an appropriate material include:
- Difficult to cut/fold.
- Product is too small to make from this material
- Problems related to ridges or corrugating.

(c) Reasons why the packaging might be considered 'environmentally poor' include:
- Too much material is used.
- Too much waste materials.
- Too many parts.

2 Suitable flexible waterproof material identified would gain 1 mark (e.g. plastic/acrylic/perspex/styrene vinyl or acetate). Reference to self-adhesive or sticky back gains the second marks.

This question was targeted at grade G hence the reason for the wide range of acceptable answers. The best material for this purpose would be self-adhesive vinyl.

3 This question is targeted at A* grade. It asks you to develop a design. In order to gain full marks you would need to produce at least one idea which then has some improvements or modifications made to it.

When marking your work the examiner would award I mark for each of the following points that have been addressed in your design work. Remember: both sketches **and** notes must be used.

- Method to show how much money has been collected (e.g. a window, a dial or some form of moving scale).
- The product is free-standing and stable.
- There is an appropriate assembly method e.g. glue or slots and tabs.
- Size relates to a standard protective postal bag or to 50 coins.
- There is an opening for removal of coins.
- Details are given about materials and components.

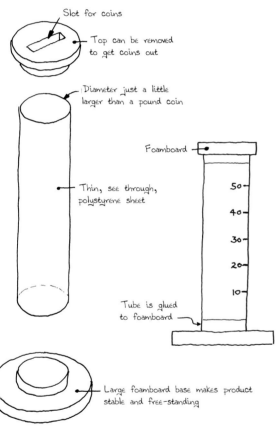

Slot for coins

Top can be removed to get coins out

Diameter just a little larger than a pound coin

Foamboard

Thin, see through, polystyrene sheet

50
40
30
20
10

Tube is glued to foamboard

Large foamboard base makes product stable and free-standing

Smart' and modern materials (page 184)

Your answer should identify that the colour changes (I mark) due to changes in temperature (I mark).

Joining materials (page 187)

The most suitable adhesives would be:

Glue stick or spray mount   Spray mount
Glue gun

Finishing materials (page 191)

6(a) Two printing effects that give a gloss finish are Laminating and Varnishing.

(b) You are asked to explain your reasons so the examiner will be looking for two aspects in each of your two answers to this question. Your explanations will need to make reference to factors such as high-quality finish, visual impact and improved durability. For example, you might explain that a gloss finish is required in order to increase the durability of a product such as a menu because it is going to be handled by a lot of people. An answer such as this would gain both of the available marks. Make sure that the two reasons and explanations that you give are distinctly different.

7 Three marks were available for this question – I for naming the printing effect and 2 for its description. In the description the examiner will want to see two pieces of information about the process you have chosen. Suitable effects would include:

- **Laminating** which gives paper a high gloss look/it strengthens and protects the printed surface.
- **Varnishing** enables selected areas of text or images to be highlighted for high visual impact and protection.
- **Die cutting** – complex and special shapes can be cut out to give high visual impact.
- **Embossing** is where a portion of the surface is raised to give high visual impact.

8 The industrial machine is called a guillotine. A 'rotary paper trimmer' is acceptable as an answer, particularly as they are preferred in schools for safety reasons.

9 One mark would be awarded for each of two appropriate uses for any of the items listed. For example:

- Black labels could be cut out and used for the windows.
- Dry transfer lettering could be used to add EUROSTAR.
- CAD could be used to add the stylised letter E.

10 One mark would be awarded for showing an appropriate method of fixing (such as a paper fastener or an eyelet) and I mark for identifying the component used.

UNIT 11: SYSTEMS AND CONTROL

Levers and linkages (page 200)

1(a) Since you have been asked to develop a design you must show at least one idea which you have then improved or modified in some way. Using arrows to show how the mechanism moves and adding notes to explain how it works will gain you more marks. Questions of this type always try to apply your knowledge of existing mechanisms rather than design something which is totally new. Even at this stage you should be giving some details about pivots.

(b) The position of the push–pull lever is given to you and you must make sure that you use it in its given position. The mechanism does not need to be very complex – as can be see from this exemplar answer below. The things which are crucial in terms of whether the mechanism will work are the position of, and the type of, pivot used and the location of the slot. You could gain at least some marks even if your design would not work. For example marks would be awarded for labelling the pivot points.

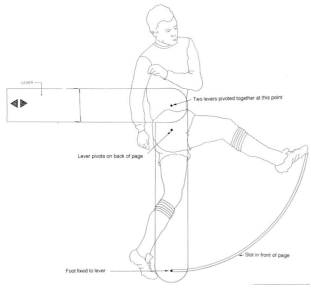

LEVER

Two levers pivoted together at this point

Lever pivots on back of page

Slot in front of page

Foot fixed to lever

2 (i) A horizontal arrow drawn in the same style as the given arrow would gain the mark.

(ii) Wheels on the bicycle move **round and round**.

(iii) Correct name: **reciprocating**.

(iv) Correct name of the type of motion is **oscillating**.

Gears and cams (page 204)

3(a) This question was targeted at A* level. In order to gain the 4 marks available you would need to use sketches and notes to produce a well-explained design which translates rotary into reciprocating motion with a distance of 20 mm. In your design you would need to show:
- a linkage (or cam) joining the ball and disc
- how the mechanism works
- that you have given consideration to the required 20 mm movement
- that you have identified appropriate materials, such as stiff or thick card and paper fasteners.

(b) (i) In order to gain the full 4 marks your answer would need to show:
- the ball in both views
- the disc in its correct position in both views
- the mechanism on at least the front view
- a slot or other method of attaching the mechanism to the ball.

(ii) Words and/or arrows could be used to show the input – **rotary** – and the output – **reciprocation** motions.

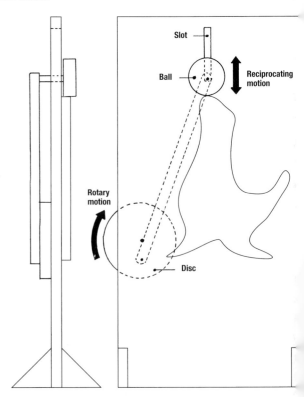

Slot

Ball

Reciprocating motion

Rotary motion

Disc

Loci (page 207)

4(a) (i) This requires two rectangles to be drawn, one 60 mm x 20 mm and one 40 mm x 40 mm. One mark would be awarded for each correct rectangle.

(ii) As the card closes, the rectangles become parallelograms. One mark would be awarded for each correct parallelogram.

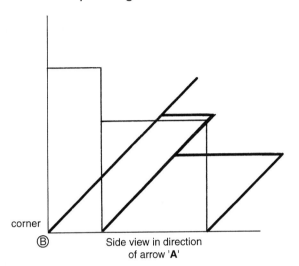

corner
Ⓑ Side view in direction of arrow 'A'

(b) The main design fault of the mechanism is that it sticks out 20 mm at the front of the card when it is closed.

(c) Appropriate properties would be: does not tear easily; is fairly rigid; is easy to cut/fold/crease/glue.

(d) The card could be cut by die cutting/stamping or by a guillotine.

(e) The input motion is achieved by hand, by opening the card.

(f) The answer should make reference to aspects such as:
- would allow simulation
- easy to see if it works
- potential problems can be seen.

Remember: an explanation requires two aspects (e.g. computer modelling would allow simulation [1 mark] to see if the card works [1 mark]).

5(a) Start by drawing FG in its horizontal position. Using the new position for G as the centre, draw an arc radius GH. With centre J, draw an arc radius JH. Where the two arcs cross gives you the position of H when the undercarriage is closed.

(b) The required slot will be an arc that extends between the two extreme positions for point H.

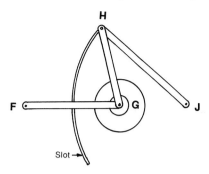

Slot →

Pop-up systems (page 210)

6 This question was targeted at around the A–B grade level. The question has two aspects. It asks you to show how the design could have been developed and how it works. The exemplar answer given below shows how both the design was developed using a V-fold mechanism. By making effective use of arrows and notes it clearly shows how the parts join together and how the mechanism works. Your answer would need to communicate this level of information in order to gain full marks. This is an example of where you need to apply your knowledge and understanding of existing mechanisms in order to establish the way in which a given product functions.

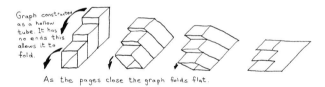

Graph constructed as a hollow tube. It has no ends this allows it to fold.

As the pages close the graph folds flat.

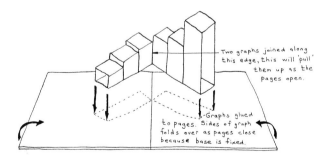

Two graphs joined along this edge, this will 'pull' them up as the pages open.

Graphs glued to pages. Sides of graph folds over as pages close because base is fixed.

The two parts of the graph are based on a V fold mechanism which is a very effective way of producing a pop-up effect.

Multiple layers (page 212)

7(a) (i) Stage 3 needs to explain that 20 mm is cut off each end of the strip of card.

Stage 5 needs to explain that glue is added to each end of the strip of card.

(ii) Stage 2   Stage 5   Stage 8

(b) Giving the correct size 230 mm x 180 mm would gain you 1 mark and clearly showing how you calculated the size would gain the second mark.

(c) Identifying an appropriate hazard gained 1 mark, e.g. using sharp pointed scissors or the fact that glue could be messy. Suggesting an appropriate solution gained 1 mark, e.g. replace with round ended scissors or plastic ones, or replace with a glue stick.

Electrical system (page 214)

8(a) The key word is **exploded**. If this was mentioned you would gain the mark.

(b) Appropriate purposes for producing this type of leaflet would include helping to identify parts/buy spare parts/assemble the lawnmower.

(c) In order to gain full marks your solution would need to show graphically varying heights (1 mark) in proportion to 20 mm–60 mm (1 mark) and have a clear link to grass (1 mark).

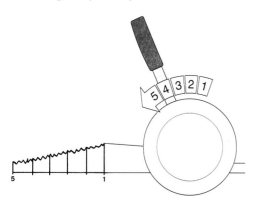

(d) Remember a schematic drawing means that your answer needs to be in a simple, stylised form. To gain the 4 marks your answer would need to show a 2D outline of the mower and handle (1 mark), the switch, battery and motor – these could be represented as symbols (1 mark). If these were in their correct

position on the mower an additional mark would be awarded. Finally, the wiring connections between the three parts needed to be clearly shown to gain the final mark.

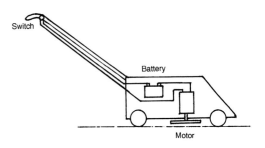

UNIT 12: QUALITY

What is meant by 'quality'? (page 218)

1 One mark would be awarded if the design for a template has been clearly communicated and explained using at least one sketch and notes. The template would need to be the same shape as the given net (1 mark) and have a method for easily marking out the fold lines (1 mark).

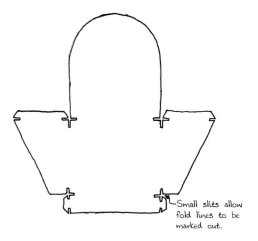

Small slits allow fold lines to be marked out.

Product function (page 220)

2(a) There are 2 marks for the question and an explanation is required. Always try to use a word such as 'because' in your answer to this type of question. It will help you to make sure that you cover both of the points required to gain both marks (e.g. 'The fingergrip cutouts are needed because an end has been put on the sleeve and this makes it difficult to get the tape out.').

(b) Reasons why this would increase the cost:
  • it uses more card
  • it is more difficult to assemble
  • takes more time to make.

Ergonomics (page 221)

3 Your answer would need to show an appropriate use of the data to establish the distance between the slots based on G (width of hand). The height of the handle from the folder needs to be based on E (depth of fingers). Either sketches and notes or a written answer would be acceptable methods of presenting your solution.

Various issues (page 223)

4 The reason why it is important to check if the name of a product exists elsewhere is because it could be offensive or insulting in another language or culture.

Further issues (page 226)

5 Recycled cardboard is not a suitable material for a chocolate box because there is a risk of contamination from previous use. One mark would be allocated for showing some understanding, e.g. 'poor quality'; 2 marks would be given for a full understanding of the risk of contamination.

6 Aspects of the bag which make it environmentally friendly include the fact that it can be recycled, as shown by the symbol, and that it is made from a material which is easily biodegradable.

Environmental symbols (page 229)

7 The sign indicates the percentage of recycled matter within the product or material. If your answer shows some understanding but is slightly confused, you would gain 1 mark; a good understanding of the difference would be granted 2 marks.

UNIT 13: HEALTH AND SAFETY

Product safety (page 232)

1 In order to gain both marks you would need to make reference to a specific matter, such as recycled card (1 mark) which could contaminate the chocolates or reduce their shelf life (1 mark).

2 Appropriate changes to the flag to make it safer include:
- making it from a softer material
- rounding the corners
- changing the shape to something like a circle.

A safe working environment (page 234)

3 Appropriate safety precautions when using a glue gun include:
- using a gluing surface to protect the desk top or bench
- keep fingers away from hot surfaces and hot glue
- avoid misuse such as squeezing too much glue out which can cause burns
- use a stand rather than laying the glue gun on its side
- make sure the equipment has been checked for electric safety.

Risk assessment (page 235)

4 A simple statement of consequence would gain you 1 mark; any reasoned consequence would gain you 2 marks.
- Wood-based products: e.g. deforestation, effects on wildlife, erosion.
- Plastics: e.g. non-renewable material, disposal of waste.

UNIT 14: PRODUCT EVALUATION AND ANALYSIS

Evaluating your own work (page 237)

1(a) This could be a physical test such as filling it with pens etc. or a consumer test.

(b) This should relate to your answer to part (a), for example 'See if it falls over or the bottom falls out' or 'To see if potential users of the desk tidy think that it is a good design'.

Products and applications (page 239)

2 Appropriate reasons why companies spend money on producing point-of-sale displays include:
- They inform customers.
- They promote products and influence customers.
- They can help increase market share.
- They can hold and display the product.
- They can encourage the retailer to stock the product.
- They can be used for a specific promotion or special offer.
- They can be used to launch a new product.
- They can focus attention on a product.

You would need to give two distinctly different reasons to gain both marks.

3(a) Appropriate reasons include:
- easier to transport
- easier to store
- take up less space
- less likely to get damaged.

(b) One mark would be given for an appropriate reason (e.g. 'It is quicker for the manufacturer to assemble ...') and 1 mark for an appropriate explanation or justification (e.g. '....... because they do not need any additional materials to join the corners').

(c) For completing the bottom section of the box you would gain 1 mark. Showing the top in a vertical position and correctly folded would gain you up to 2 additional marks.

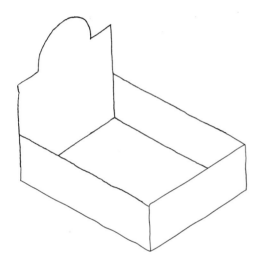

(d) To gain the 3 available marks you would need to communicate clearly, using at least one sketch and notes (1 mark), a fixing method that both slotted (1 mark) and locked in place (1 mark).

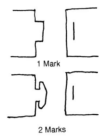

1 Mark

2 Marks

INDEX

Published by HarperCollins*Publishers* Ltd
77-85 Fulham Palace Road
London W6 8JB

www.collinseducation.com
On-line support for schools and colleges

© HarperCollins*Publishers* Ltd 2004

First published 2004
10 9 8 7 6 5 4 3 2
ISBN-13 978 0 00 720900 2
ISBN-10 0 00 720900 2

John Rolfe and Ray Blockley assert the moral right to be
identified as the authors of this work.

British Library Cataloguing in Publication Data
A catalogue record for this book is available from the
British Library.

Edited by Steve Attmore
Managing Editor Sue Chapple
Series and book design by Sally Boothroyd
Artwork by Jerry Fowler
Index compiled by Julie Rimington
Production by Katie Butler
Printed and bound by Printing Express, Hong Kong

**The Authors and Publishers are grateful to the following
schools and students for permission to reproduce items
of coursework:**
- Meden School and Technology College, Warsop,
  Mansfield, Nottinghamshire: Nicola Heaton; Natasha
  Medlam; Laura Morris; Martin Heaton; Lydia Parfrement;
  Zoe Houston; Kirsty Steward; Zoe Gardiner.
- Joseph Whitaker School, Rainworth, Mansfield,
  Nottinghamshire: Janine Fearick; Emma Price; Nicola
  Bowker; Charlotte Guy; Ryan Winfield; Rachel Pearson.
- Sharnbrook Upper School, Sharnbrook, Bedfordshire:
  Ilana Barnes; Midori Takagi; Sarah Archer.

The Authors and Publishers are grateful to the following for
permission to reproduce copyright material:
Photographs
Ace Photo Library: p. 165
Banana Stock: p. 155
Corbis: p. 164
Steve Attmore: pp. 77, 156, 179, 180, 221, 223, 232, 240
Fotosearch: p. 136
Paul Philpott: pp. 75, 104 (silkscreen printing photos
courtesy of the Art Department of The City of Ely
Community College, Cambridgeshire)
Hewlett Packard: pp. 74, 141
Russell Hobbs: p. 184
Simon Young: pp. 137, 138, 160 bottom, 161, 166
Science Photo Library: p. 135
Mike Watson: pp. 159, 160 top (courtesy of Harbourne
Products), 166, 182, 224 (left: courtesy of Little Chef;
right: courtesy of Hamble Estate Agency)
Roy Garner/REX FEATURES: p. 226
Sipa Press/REX FEATURES: p. 158
Smithsonian Institute/Science Photo Library: p. 151
The Design and Technology Department of Newmarket
Upper School, Suffolk: p. 106
Exam questions
AQA: pp. 77, 156, 163, 169(Q5), 192(Q8), 225, 228(Q1),
230, 236
Edexcel: pp. 95 (Q2), 99(Q4), 101, 110, 190, 192(Q6/7), 202,
211, 234
OCR: pp. 68, 71, 73, 76, 80, 84, 89, 93, 95(Q1), 99(Q3), 103,
107, 108, 109, 111, 112, 116, 121, 123, 124, 127, 130, 131,
136, 139, 141, 143, 146, 150, 161, 169(Q6), 171, 173, 175,
183, 185, 196, 203, 206, 208, 213, 216, 219, 220, 222,
228(Q6), 233, 238, 241

Every effort has been made to contact the holders of
copyright material, but if any have been inadvertently
overlooked, the Publishers will be pleased to make the
necessary arrangements at the first opportunity.